IT'S NOT FREE SPEECH

RACE, DEMOCRACY, AND THE
FUTURE OF ACADEMIC FREEDOM

IT'S NOT
FREE
SPEECH

MICHAEL BÉRUBÉ AND JENNIFER RUTH

Johns Hopkins University Press

BALTIMORE

Johns Hopkins University Press

2715 North Charles Street

Baltimore, Maryland 21218-4363

www.press.jhu.edu

Library of Congress Cataloging-in-Publication Data

Names: Bérubé, Michael, 1961– author. | Ruth, Jennifer, author.
Title: It's not free speech : race, democracy, and the future
    of academic freedom / Michael Bérubé and Jennifer Ruth.
Description: Baltimore : Johns Hopkins University Press, [2022] |
    Includes bibliographical references and index.
Identifiers: LCCN 2021036039 | ISBN 9781421443874
    (hardcover) | ISBN 9781421443881 (ebook)
Subjects: LCSH: Academic freedom. | Teaching, Freedom of. |
    Freedom of speech. | Universities and colleges—Social aspects. |
    Discrimination in higher education. | Critical race theory.
Classification: LCC LC72 .B47 2022 | DDC 378.1/213—dc23
LC record available at https://lccn.loc.gov/2021036039

A catalog record for this book is available from the British Library.

*Special discounts are available for bulk purchases of this book. For more
information, please contact Special Sales at specialsales@jh.edu.*

TO UNDERSTAND HOW EXPLICITLY

anti-democratic desires can be

framed as defending freedom,

as well as how moderate and left

responses to this political

violence seem to underestimate

its continuity from the past and

its threat to our future, we have

to grapple with the foundational

role of white supremacy in our

republic.

—KIMBERLÉ CRENSHAW
"The Capitol Riots and the Eternal Fantasy
of a Racially Virtuous America"
(2021)

CONTENTS

ACKNOWLEDGMENTS

Michael:

I want to thank Sonia DeLuca Fernández, senior vice chancellor for diversity, equity and inclusion at the University of Colorado–Boulder (and my former colleague at Penn State), for her whip-smart reading of the manuscript, and her generous and forthright response to it. Amanda Anderson read it and talked about Charles Mills's work with me—as I hoped she would. I need also to thank Zoom audiences at the University of Michigan and the Northeast Modern Language Association (NeMLA), who heard excerpts from the book and asked me great questions. (I hope I had some good answers.) And I thank my family—Janet, Nicholas, Jamie, and my daughter-in-law Rachel—for debating the arguments of this book with me over many dinners, huddled together as we were in the midst of a pandemic. (Nick and Rachel's baby Finn, my grandson, did not participate in those discussions but was remarkably patient with us.)

Most of all, however, I want to thank my coauthor, Jennifer Ruth, for thinking up this book in the first place and then convincing me that maybe, just maybe, academic freedom shouldn't cover advocates of white supremacy any more than it covers flat-earthers in the geology department or astrologers in the astronomy department. For most of my life, I had believed that tolerance of crackpot racist professors on campus was one of the regrettable corollaries of academic freedom. I now think that's suspiciously easy for a white guy to say, and that it underestimates the amount of damage that academic crackpottery of all kinds, but especially racist crackpottery, has done and can do. Jennifer and I had some disagreements in the course of writing this book, sometimes about whole chapters, sometimes about individual words, but we always worked them out, and the arguments here have been shaped, strengthened, and enriched by her wisdom. I am deeply grateful for that.

A shorter version of chapter 2 was published in the Modern Language Association journal, *Profession*, in winter 2019.

Jennifer:
First, let me thank my indefatigable and always brilliant coauthor, Michael Bérubé. I am extraordinarily lucky now to have written two books with someone who takes ideas and makes them things that do real work in the world. This book wouldn't exist without him. Michael, if you're ever up for a third book with me, I'll jump at the chance.

The book also wouldn't exist without my PSU-AAUP union friends who encouraged me to take on battles at PSU that I wouldn't have otherwise and who got me thinking in the first place about what academic freedom protects and what it doesn't. Special thanks to Aaron Roussell. Warm thanks also to Courtney Bailey, Tina Burdsall, Emily Ford, Andres Guzman, Megan Horst, Jennifer Kerns, David Kinsella, and José Padin. Thanks also to my AAUP Committee A comrades Emily Houh, Hank Reichman, and most especially Mark James, who talked through the vision of the book with me on multiple occasions and improved it considerably. Love and thanks to my dear friend Eliza Greenstadt and to my family, my incredibly supportive and charming husband, Scott, and my children, Charlotte and Tian, who are wonderful exemplars of a generation that is pushing its predecessors to be and do better.

INTRODUCTION

Does academic freedom extend to white supremacist professors?

The question became inescapable in the summer of 2020. In July of that year, in the *Daily Princetonian*, literary scholar Andrew Cole wrote, "When white supremacy masquerades as research and scholarship, it looks like eugenics, like phrenology, like the Tuskegee Study, like intelligence tests, like the Bell Curve, like the Troublesome Inheritance, like any number of white-washing histories of civilization, philosophy, religion, and literature that falsify arguments to the detriment of nonwhites. . . . Yet whenever white supremacy is challenged, or whenever white privilege (which is a subtler form of white supremacy) is questioned, people suddenly start talking about academic freedom" ("What Is Academic?"). Many universities began, however belatedly, to reexamine their entanglements with slavery, with Jim Crow, with the legacy of white supremacy in the United States. But few have been willing to extend the reexamination to the principle of academic freedom itself, and to ask: is academic freedom being used as a refuge for white supremacists?

The answer so far is yes, which is why, for example, Amy Wax still teaches law at the University of Pennsylvania. There is nothing ambiguous about Wax's racism: she expressly says that "Anglo-Protestant culture" is superior to other cultures and is not above lying about the academic records of students of color in her own law school (see Patrice). If "cancel culture" were as powerful and as pervasive as some alleged victims of it have claimed, Wax would have been out of a job years ago. As it is, she is free to promote white supremacy and to do so with the imprimatur of the University of Pennsylvania. That university ritually distances itself from her remarks and has removed her from required first-year courses but has not gone so far as to consider whether her beliefs and statements render her unfit for her position.

The same holds true for Bruce Gilley, a colleague of Jennifer's at Portland State University. Gilley made a name for himself as the author of the article, "The Case for Colonialism," whose publication by the journal *Third World Quarterly* in 2017 led to considerable controversy.[1] He has doubled down since, giving talks to the German far-

1. Taylor and Francis, the publisher of *Third World Quarterly*, claim that their "thorough investigation . . . clearly demonstrated the essay had undergone double-blind peer review" ("Withdrawal Notice"). In September 2017, the *Chronicle of Higher Education* reported on the internal debate at the journal:

[Editor Shahid] Qadir, who did not respond to messages seeking comment, said in a written statement last week that the paper had gone through the standard double-blind peer-review process. He did not, however, indicate what the reviews had concluded, which the board members who resigned say is misleading. Their resignation letter states that the board members asked to see the reviews, but that Mr. Qadir would not provide them . . .

According to their resignation letter, the 15 editorial-board members learned through backchannels that a pair of guest editors,

right Afd party about the glories of their colonial past and proclaiming King Leopold II a hero.[2] In a 2019 article published on the website of the National Association of Scholars (basically, a blog post rather than a refereed essay), he asks, "Was It Good Fortune to Be Enslaved by the British Empire?" His answer is yes: "To be black in America is, historically speaking, to have hit the jackpot." "For those who came ashore at Jamestown and in the centuries that followed," Gilley concludes, "being enslaved under the British empire was about as good as it got."[3]

———————

who had been offered Mr. Gilley's piece to edit, expressed their unease with the paper and rejected even considering it for peer review. It was then peer-reviewed and rejected by at least one reviewer, according to the letter, before being 'repackaged' as an opinion piece.

At *Third World Quarterly*, opinion pieces also go through peer review, and the same peer reviewer who had rejected it earlier also rejected it as an opinion piece, according to the resigning board members. 'Thus, the fact is established that this did not pass the peer review when we have documentation that it was rejected by three peer reviewers,' their letter concludes. (Patel, "Revolt.")

The paper was subsequently withdrawn, with Gilley's agreement. See also Flaherty, "Resignations."

2. In a June 30, 2020, tweet that is characteristic of his Twitter feed, Gilley admits that the Belgians should apologize to Congo, not for the murder of ten million Congolese but for

*not colonizing the King's estates sooner

*ending colonial rule despite mainstream Congolese opposition to independence

*not arresting or killing Patrice Lumumba sooner

And nothing else.

3. Gilley's approaches to imperialism and slavery are extreme examples of what Fara Dabhoiwala has called "balance-sheet historical apologetics" in

Gilley did not place his proslavery article in a peer-reviewed journal, and we doubt whether he could have. So, should we consider the essay extramural speech—that is, the speech exercised by professors when they speak as public citizens? The essay is of course protected by the First Amendment, but what we are asking here is whether it is protected by academic freedom. As we'll argue throughout this book, many people don't understand the difference. The American Association of University Professors (AAUP), the organization that created and continues to define the concept of academic freedom in the United States, has long held that extramural speech is protected by academic freedom unless it indicates a faculty member's unfitness to serve. The AAUP position grounds academic freedom in scholarly expertise, as well it should, but entails the corollary that professors enjoy *greater* protection for extramural speech when they have no idea what they're talking about than for speech within the areas of their research and teaching. The idea is that a historian who is a Holocaust denier is obviously unfit, whereas an electrical engineer who is a Holocaust denier is just a crank. But how does this principle guide us when dealing with white supremacists and apologists for colonialism and slavery? More to the point, how does it guide us when dealing with white supremacists and apologists for colonialism and slavery who claim to be speaking and writing on the basis of their scholarly expertise?

which the history of imperialism is reduced to "the inane question of whether, all things considered, the empire was 'good' or 'bad.' Did Britain's abolition of slavery not cancel out the sin of its previous participation in the slave trade? Shouldn't the introduction of railways to India count against the horrendous death toll of the many famines aggravated by British economic policies?"

The problem is compounded when we realize that most extramural speech now takes place in social media (rather than, say, in letters to the editor). The context-collapsing and democracy-destabilizing nature of social media makes it extremely difficult to cling to the traditional liberal belief that the best remedy for hate speech is more speech. Social media do not facilitate the resolution of disagreements or consensus-building but rather encourage the simplifying and intensifying of views to their (il)logical extremes, devoid of reality checks. On Twitter, Gilley likes to compare Black Lives Matter "terrorists" to the Mau Mau or the Maoists, whichever suits his taste for false historical equivalence at the moment. His First Amendment rights protect him on Twitter. But what about the fact that he is not platforming as an ordinary citizen? When Gilley tweets data showing that Western financial aid to impoverished countries has not led to significant progress on the ground, he is marshalling evidence in support for the return of colonial power—or at least for his case that colonialism came to a premature end. When he claims that Black Lives Matter "fanatics" are a frenzied mob akin to the Red Guards of the Chinese Cultural Revolution, he's doing it, as he says in a tweet on June 16, 2020, "based on my knowledge of Mao's politics." This is critical. For here he is saying that his extramural commentary is manifestly an extension of what he considers his area of expertise— the history and politics of various regimes. He's not staking his rights on his free speech as an American citizen but on his claim to expertise as a scholar of political science. The problem is that the overwhelming majority of experts in these fields—history of colonialism and post-colonialism, history of slavery and its aftermath—do not find his claims in these areas remotely credible. He's making claims that the academic world, the cultural capital of which he borrows, would reject on *both* ethical and scholarly grounds.

Tenure protects "controversial" ideas, to be sure. But does that mean it necessarily protects misinformation, discriminatory distortions of the historical record, and claims made with complete disregard for, or reflexive dismissal of, a settled body of knowledge built on well-documented scholarship and research? It is certainly a "controversial" idea that COVID-19 was deliberately engineered and spread by 5G networks so that vaccines could be developed that would install microchips in people. But that is not an idea that any reasonable person should hold, let alone promote at a university.[4]

Ordinarily, tenured faculty members who are found to be bullies, bigots, or harassers find themselves on extended paid leaves—a "punishment" that looks to many people, including faculty off the tenure track, like a reward. Or they are offered lucrative early retirement packages that, by the calculations of the general counsel's office, are less financially damaging to the university than a protracted lawsuit. Recently, though, one administrator attempted something more ambitious than throwing money at the problem to make it go away. Calling a faculty member's racist, misogynist, and homophobic remarks "stunningly ignorant," "vile and stupid," and "loathsome" but still defending his academic freedom, the administrator proclaimed that no student could be required to take his courses and mandated that he engage in double-blind grading of students' work. The professor was Eric Rasmusen of Indiana University, long known in the blogosphere for his (truly) vile and stupid views; the administrator was Indiana's provost, Lauren Robel, and her emphatic repudiation of Rasmusen made national news (see Straus). Public shaming is plausible and defensible here, certainly, but it's important to note the

4. This is a (very slight) parody of an actual position we will discuss in chapter 3, when we turn to the curious case of Professor Mark Crispin Miller.

refusal to question Rasmusen's academic freedom to promote discredited and repugnant views. The reasoning seems to be that it is better to keep a tenured professor on payroll, teaching an ever-shrinking number of students, than to ask whether his speech calls into question his fitness to serve as a professor. And the unseemly result is that we wind up defending academic freedom by refusing to question it.

In 2016, Columbia University Press published *Who's Afraid of Academic Freedom?*, a volume looking at attacks on faculty autonomy in research and teaching. From the proposed state bans on critical race theory to the University of North Carolina board of trustees' refusal to grant tenure to Nikole Hannah-Jones, attacks on academic freedom coming from outside the faculty are more serious than ever. But the fear of academic freedom comes from within as well—and not because some among us are reluctant to champion academic freedom, but because some among us are afraid that scrutinizing any aspect of academic freedom will effectively destroy it.

We believe, rather, that the bigger threat to the future of academic freedom follows from the refusal to think more deeply about the way academic freedom can be and has been weaponized in ways that undermine democracy. We cannot be afraid of talking honestly about whether academic freedom in a democratic society with the promise of equality before the law protects a defense of colonialism. We cannot be afraid of asking whether an adjunct professor can reasonably be considered to have academic freedom when the AAUP claims they do but their department chairs can refuse to rehire them on any pretext. We cannot be afraid to ask why it is that, if we believe academic freedom to be such an expansively protective concept, we don't confront the fact that faculty members' academic freedom (particularly as the concept is currently understood in many quarters) can be curtailed by offices of diversity, equity, and inclusion (DEI). (We'll say more about that in chapter 6.) These offices do not exist to protect faculty research and teaching but to protect the university community from discrimination and harm. Two moral goods are potentially in conflict, or at least can be viewed as in conflict: freedom of thought and freedom from discrimination. But for the most part, any such conflicts have taken place behind the scenes, largely out of faculty sight and usually framed as individual incidents and embarrassments.

When, in the summer of 2020, around four hundred faculty, students, and staff at Princeton University signed a statement ("Faculty Letter") that proposed, among other things, a faculty-led "racism committee" to investigate racist research and/or behavior, the widespread response was outrage at the very idea of such a "tribunal." Here's what got left out of all the outraged commentary: every campus *already has* people who investigate charges of racism. But they are typically diversity officers or human resources personnel, some of whom have never run a classroom or published a peer-reviewed essay or book. For libertarians and conservatives, this disconnection from faculty labor is an argument for the abolition of those offices; but antidiscrimination policies and personnel to enforce them are necessary. The question becomes: how can the policies be integrated into faculty governance? Faculty should participate in shaping policy and in adjudicating issues when an apparent conflict between academic freedom and equity arises.

We know that, to many, the thought of handing judgments involving questions of discrimination over to a group coming out of a still white-majority faculty is troubling at best and downright obtuse at worst. But we are not proposing that faculty participate on a kind of lottery basis; rather, we propose that faculty and professionals *with expertise in the relevant areas* be the primary drivers of any committee or review panel. The professionals hired by the university to DEI positions would retain significant influence, and any new burdens placed on faculty with such expertise would need to be negotiated and fairly compensated.

We discuss DEI investigations at greater length in chapter 6, but a few more words about the relationship between equity and academic freedom are important here. We postulate that the disconnect between what happens in faculty governance and what happens in DEI offices is primarily institutional—that is to say, while the two activities take place at most campuses on separate tracks with little or no intersection, their missions are not opposed in principle. When the justification for academic freedom is explicitly conceived as serving the common good—an academic freedom fit for a diverse democracy rather than an abstraction lending itself to the fetishization of a mythically neutral pursuit of truth—the gulf separating the spheres of university activity becomes bridgeable. Many BIPOC (Black, Indigenous, and Persons of Color) students and faculty have done the work, after all, to reorient the mission of universities to the "common good," a phrase the AAUP used early in the twentieth century to justify academic freedom but one diluted as other phrases (such as "free pursuit of knowledge") became as—or more—ubiquitous in AAUP documents.

Universities' understandings of themselves evolved in large part because of student activist groups like the Third World Liberation Front that established Black studies, ethnic studies, and Africana departments. Some might think of departments like these and women's/gender/sexuality or Indigenous studies as additive rather than transformative; but the reality is that their inclusion has had at least two cumulative effects over the years. First, the idea that a university community should reflect, include, and serve the diverse citizenry of the country has become widely internalized (though not realized in practice). Second, the scholarship produced in these departments over the last fifty years has influenced work in many other departments and has succeeded in at least planting the idea that all research in the human sciences is anchored (or "situated") in a necessarily partial perspective, and one purporting to be universal is likely to be centered on white or dominant culture. Indeed, even the allegedly neutral term "freedom," upon which the phrase "academic freedom" relies, has a racialized history, as numerous historians and philosophers have shown; the most recent study, as this book goes to press, is Tyler Stovall's *White Freedom: The Racial History of an Idea* (2021).

In *Agents of Change*, a documentary about the San Francisco State and Cornell University protests that led to the country's first Black studies departments, one woman says, "The basic question is can the white university expand its framework to accommodate Blacks in terms defined by Blacks?" It would be an act of repression and denial to say that the answer to this question then or now is "yes," but it also would be an act of repression and denial to claim that the work of Black scholars and scholars of color, many of whom began as student activists—such as Kimberlé Crenshaw and Mari Matsuda, discussed in chapter 4—has not influenced many white faculty members. Whether they ever read Joyce Ladner on the "death of white sociology" or bell hooks and Manthia Diawara on the oppositional gaze, white and nonwhite graduate students and junior faculty appear less likely to perceive the university's mission as the production of knowledge full stop and more likely to see it as the ethical production of knowledge in service of a diversely situated humanity.[5]

5. Joyce Ladner's book *The Death of White Sociology* (1973) opens with an epigraph taken from "The Challenge of Blackness" by Lerone Bennet that

We acknowledge that there are real dangers in attempting to rethink academic freedom. Since before the ascendancy of Donald J. Trump (the larger implications of which are far from disappearing after his one term as president) and accelerated by his rise, the alt-right in the United States has made no secret of its hostility to the norms and practices of liberal democratic society. Their long game with regard to ideals such as free speech and academic freedom is to exploit whatever erosion those ideals undergo at the hands of the left. Liberal defenders of academic freedom therefore wind up in the position of Thomas More in Robert Bolt's *A Man for All Seasons*, determined to give the Devil the benefit of the law for their own safety's sake. But the time has passed for crossing our fingers and hoping that received wisdom such as *free speech helps marginalized groups more than dominant ones* has withstood the last decades' worth of pressures. As Jill Lepore writes in the foreword to Jamal Greene's *How Rights Went Wrong* (2021), "Rights asserted by way of a remedy to rights for so long and so violently denied did not end the battle of rights but instead turned it into a war when, beginning in the 1970s, modern conservatives, adopting methods used by liberals, asserted not liberal claims to rights but *conservative* claims to rights" (xi). New thinking is necessary that grounds academic freedom's justification in its service to a democracy that works for all its citizens, not just a white, moneyed, cis-gendered subset of them.

---

reads: "It is necessary for us to develop a new frame of reference which transcends the limits of white concepts. It is necessary for us to develop and maintain a total offensive against the false universality of white concepts, whether they are expressed by William Styron or Daniel Patrick Moynihan. By and large, reality has been conceptualized in the narrow point of view of the small minority of white men who live in Europe and America."

In what may at first seem paradoxical on our part, we further argue that this responsibility can be shouldered only if faculty autonomy in academic decision-making (with the participation, where appropriate, of other actors in the university community, such as diversity officers) is fully respected within the public sphere—that is, *if the general public and its elected officials do not get a direct say over academic judgments.* The importance of a firewall between the university and the state, on the one hand, and the market, on the other, has long been the main pillar of academic freedom as articulated by the AAUP. Nonetheless, academic freedom is poorly understood in general (and, thus, often conflated with free speech), and because case law has historically played an oversized role in delimiting its parameters, times of political polarization regularly revive contests over who gets to control academic affairs.

Robert Post's work is indispensable in thinking through this particular knot. In his 2012 book, *Democracy, Expertise, and Academic Freedom: A First Amendment Jurisprudence for the Modern State*, Post walks readers through the difference between academic freedom and free speech, explaining why the maintenance of this difference is crucial for democracy to function. He argues that while *democratic legitimation* requires strong free speech rights so that the citizenry retains reasonable trust in the political process, *democratic competence* requires a high degree of academic freedom so that universities remain trustworthy sources of information and interpretation perceived to be largely free from manipulation by politics and special interests. Much of what we argue here relies on this distinction, which we regard as fundamental to any understanding of the difference between academic freedom and freedom of speech.

Any new practice will provoke paroxysms from culture warriors on the right, who will denounce it with every hyperbolic term they can think of—show trials, star chambers, reeducation camps. But that reaction will be patently disingenuous. We already have all kinds of practices and processes designed to safeguard the integrity of what goes on in, and in relation to, the university. Offices of research compliance, integrity, and fraud are one example. The intellectual and professional protocols of awarding tenure, widely perceived to be the guarantor of academic freedom, are another. The AAUP issued its 1940 statement on tenure and reshaped American higher education dramatically for the better. But that was eighty years ago. The realities of the twenty-first century—from the decline of tenure-track positions to the rise of social media—suggest to us that the gains of 1940 are now largely lost. Acknowledging this means acknowledging the need for new thinking. This is why we have written this book.

As for *how* we have written this book, we offer the following roadmap. We invite you to think of the book as having two parts, the first consisting of chapters 1 through 3 and the second of chapters 4 through 6. In the first part, we explore the current debates around academic freedom, free speech, and extramural speech in their contemporary context. In the second half, we propose some workable parameters for what academic freedom could be in a genuine democracy. We begin by remarking on the difficulty—and necessity—of establishing the relevant context for allegedly racist speech; and since we work in disciplines that have devoted a great deal of thought to what a "context" is and what "intention" means, we offer what we hope is a measured critique of the idea that in such matters, the impact of a statement must be prioritized over the intent of a speaker.

We then proceed, in chapter 2, to distinguish academic freedom and extramural speech from free speech, and to show how this distinction opens up new areas for faculty governance within the university. We also consider what happens when professors are "called out" or "cancelled" in ways that threaten to undermine faculty autonomy and the educational mission of the university. Though we are deeply skeptical of complaints about "cancel culture," we know that miscarriages of justice do occur on that front and that professors are sometimes criticized and disciplined without good reason and without due process. Robust faculty governance, we argue, will work to prevent antidiscrimination principles from prompting precipitous misinterpretations of defensible speech.

Chapter 3 then turns to the question of "fitness to teach." The bar for finding a professor unfit can't be so high that the idea of "unfitness" disappears altogether and academic freedom and free speech become indistinguishable from one another, but it must be high. Unless the bar for "unfitness" is set high and rigorous mechanisms are established for due process, academic freedom can be eroded by social-media outrage campaigns every time a professor offends someone's sensibilities—a student, a parent, a trustee, a legislator, a journalist, a passerby. Risk-averse university administrations can be amazingly spineless on such occasions, as when the University of Southern California suspended Greg Patton, a professor of business communication, for telling students that the "um" word in Chinese is "that," which is pronounced "ne ga"; or when Louisiana State University fired Teresa Buchanan for saying "fuck no" in class (see Goldberg); or when professors are disciplined or suspended for using the N-word in the course of teaching work by James Baldwin, as seems to happen about once every six weeks. The AAUP is rightly vigilant about such cases and is often joined by the American Civil Liberties Union (ACLU) and the Foundation for Individual Rights in Education (FIRE).

Furthermore, we are not, for the purposes of this book, considering as "racist" things like opposition to affirmative action or advocacy for restrictions on immigration (unless that advocacy is demonstrably grounded in white nationalism or western-civilization chauvinism, as it is for Wax). Affirmative action and immigration are subjects about which there can be legitimate political disagreement. But when it comes to the assertion that Black people are biologically or culturally less capable of self-government than others, for example, we are drawing a line in the sand. Such beliefs have poisoned so-called Western culture for over five hundred years and arguably reached an apex in the early twentieth century, when pseudoscientific racism laid the groundwork for eugenics and genocide. It is past time for them to go the way of beliefs in phlogiston, the philosopher's stone, and the efficacy of human sacrifice.

In chapter 4 we start to build the case for that argument, turning to the origins of critical race theory and its critique of systemic and institutional racism. That critique underlies our discussion of the limits of academic freedom in chapter 5 and our proposal for university academic freedom committees in chapter 6, but since American conservatives are undergoing (as we write) a paroxysm of spittle-flecked outrage over what they imagine "critical race theory" to mean, we need to establish here what we intend as the appropriate context for that chapter. To wit: we did not write it in order to combat the delusions of the Fox News Universe. We know that for people living in that world, "critical race theory" basically means "anything that deals with the history of racial inequity in the United States," and is the driving mechanism of the backlash to the activism inspired by the murder of George Floyd. We think it is worth remarking on that backlash and noting that the people who set it in motion have literally no idea what critical race theory is, because it is trying to rebrand antiracism as anti-American, and to set the parameters of what constitutes an acceptable discussion of racial injustice. And we know that in the long history of human hypocrisy, the right-wing moral panic about campus "cancel culture," followed by a nationwide attempt to ban an entire school of thought from classrooms from kindergarten to college, deserves a special place.

But our broader purpose in that chapter, and in the second half of the book more generally, is to bring the arguments of critical race theory to bear on the concept of academic freedom. We then turn in chapter 5 to Ulrich Baer's critique of free speech absolutism, but although we have a great deal of sympathy with that critique, we want to apply that critique not to free speech but to academic freedom—a more defensible undertaking, we think. Finally, in chapter 6, we lay out our case for the establishment of academic freedom committees on American campuses.

We imagine that this proposal for academic freedom committees will strike some readers as thin gruel. There is a joke in academe that goes something like this: *a fire broke out, engulfing the campus. Thinking quickly, the faculty convened and voted to create a Fire Committee to address the problem.* But people who work in higher education, and the more thoughtful observers of academe in the worlds of journalism and politics, know very well that academic freedom committees operating on the rationale we suggest here would constitute a significant change in business as usual. Quite apart from establishing the long-overdue expectation that pseudoscientific racism and white nationalism should not be considered legitimate academic pursuits, it would take adjudication of such matters out of the hands of attorneys and university administrators and place it where it belongs—with the faculty. Academic committees are often derided as the devices of bureaucracy and the source of tedious and trivial service work, and some academic committees deserve the derision. But the great virtue of committees, especially faculty-elected committees, is that they take decision-making power out of the hands of single persons (department heads, deans, provosts, presidents) and distribute the intellectual labor by means of lateral peer review. That is true of hiring decisions, of promotion and tenure, of proceedings that revoke tenure, and of sound academic determinations of how to handle serious accusations of misconduct. The best academic institutions and departments tend to be the ones with strong traditions of shared governance and collective deliberation, and the worst tend to be the places where individuals run private fiefdoms and are unanswerable for their capricious decisions. We believe that academic freedom committees would strengthen faculty governance everywhere by ensuring that academic freedom is protected in its own terms, not in terms of free speech—and help push back against the steady erosion of faculty governance over the past few decades.

IN 2014, Harvard undergraduate Sandra Y. L. Korn published an impassioned critique of academic freedom, arguing that it needs to be superseded by something called "academic justice." She asked:

> Does Government Professor Harvey Mansfield have the legal right to publish a book in which he claims that "to resist rape a woman needs . . . a certain ladylike modesty?" Probably. Do I think he should do that? No, and I would happily organize with other feminists on campus to stop him from publishing further sexist commentary under the authority of a Harvard faculty position. "Academic freedom" might permit such an offensive view of rape to be published; academic justice would not. ("Doctrine")

After #MeToo, many people asked why universities should continue to shelter tenured faculty members who are serial harassers. After the murder of George Floyd and the uprisings throughout the United States in protest against institutional racism, we should broaden the question: why should universities continue to hold that academic freedom covers unambiguously racist speech?

It is easy to forget now, but arguments like Sandra Korn's were being made *before* Darren Wilson killed Michael Brown in Ferguson, Missouri—before the ascendancy (though not before the creation) of Black Lives Matter and the wave of police murders of Black men and women that crested in (but certainly did not end with) the killing of George Floyd. So it would seem to be an urgent question: if we are renaming a college that honors John Calhoun (as Yale did in 2017) and taking Woodrow Wilson's name off a School of Public and International Affairs (as Princeton did in 2020), why are we not rethinking academic freedom for racists and considering academic equity for the people struggling against institutional racism of all kinds? If Princeton were to say, for example, "we are removing Woodrow Wilson's name from the School of Public and International Affairs but we will continue to employ and support faculty members who share Wilson's belief that the right to self-determination applies to peoples in Europe but not Africa and Asia," surely one would be right to dismiss the renaming as a purely symbolic, public relations gesture involving no substantial reckoning with the legacy of eugenics and white supremacy.

Academic freedom is not the only abstract liberal ideal under stress these days; *all* abstract liberal ideals are in bad odor, it seems, as the rise of Trump and the far right has rendered many activists impatient with laws that prohibit rich and poor alike from sleeping under bridges. Back in 2014, the brilliant progressive journalist Michelle Goldberg wrote in the *Nation* that Twitter trends like #Cancel-Colbert and "trigger warnings" on college campuses portended the return of an anti-liberal left, and she suggested that "the left can only afford to be contemptuous of liberal values when the right isn't in charge" ("#CancelColbert"). Goldberg turned out to be quite wrong about that: if anything, the antiliberal left's hostility to liberal values intensified during the Trump years, most likely because those liberal values seem to have offered little practical resistance to the return of an antiliberal fascism. And so, to many younger scholars as well as scholars of color at all stages of their academic careers, organizations like the AAUP look like dinosaurs, and ideals like academic freedom look like hazy, high-minded beliefs cherished by old white people oblivious to the ways in which right-wing provocateurs (in which we would include Wax and Gilley) have managed to weaponize the freedoms they enjoy. In fact, it looks like a dinosaur to *the majority of faculty*, since the majority of faculty teach off the tenure track, that track to which the AAUP has tethered its conception of academic freedom.

There are scholars who could write aspects of this book better than we can. We are not experts in the long entanglement of higher education with white supremacy, but the experts in this area are many. This history—whether it be the origins of political science in a logic equating whiteness with autonomy (see Smith and Lowery, Blatt), the influence of eugenics in the progressive era (see Leonard) and today (see Saini), or the rolling back of civil rights legislation in the 1980s (see Anderson)—has been written (though there is undoubtedly still more to write), has been vetted in the customary ways, and is now part of a more honest and more complete record. Our contribution is to think about what this record means for a reexamination of academic freedom, how the concept has been understood and misunderstood, and how it has been operationalized in practice. We are deeply committed to academic freedom, have long been involved with the AAUP, and hope to strengthen both the concept and the organization. Jennifer recently finished three years as her (unionized) AAUP chapter's vice president for grievances and academic freedom; she also serves on the national AAUP's Committee A on Academic Freedom and Tenure and was the editor of the *AAUP Journal of Academic Freedom* from 2015 to 2017. Michael served three terms on Committee A from 2009 to 2018, and another eight years in Penn State's University faculty senate, where he was elected senate chair for 2018–19. He guest-edited the *AAUP Journal of Academic Freedom* in 2014–15, devoting half the issue to the Steven Salaita case at the University of Illinois at Urbana–Champaign. In 2015, together we published *The Humanities, Higher Education, and Academic Freedom: Three Necessary Arguments*, arguing for a conversion-to-tenure track for contingent faculty. We made that argument in the belief that only tenure could afford contingent faculty the material protections of academic freedom; we are now following up with what we hope is a searching examination of what academic freedom itself should and should not protect.

It would be considerably easier, we know, to mount an impassioned defense of academic freedom as it has been traditionally understood and to issue warnings about how it is continually threatened by interference by forces external to the university. We could write a book about how professors' rights to teach, write, and speak freely are challenged by legislators, donors, trustees, and well-funded right-wing search-and-destroy organizations like Turning Point USA and Campus Reform, whose mission it is to harass and try to fire liberal and left-leaning professors. Because of their close ties to massive right-wing networks like Fox News, Breitbart, and the *Daily Caller*, those organizations have transformed campus life, leading some universities to develop protocols to ensure the safety of faculty who find themselves swarmed by trolls As one researcher found in a review of the Campus Reform website, "professors of color are disproportionately represented in its articles—and they often suffer the ugliest consequences" (see Gluckman). It is no consolation to realize that racist attacks on professors of color effectively prove the points that many of those professors are trying to make about institutional racism. (We will see a vivid example of this in chapter 2.) We know those attacks have escalated dramatically with the conservative backlash against the 1619 Project, the Trump Administration's proscription against the teaching of critical race theory, and state legislatures' bans that followed after Biden was elected—a perfect, and perfectly hideous, example of intellectual authoritarianism. Finally, of course we understand, having worked for years with the AAUP, why the AAUP would be defensive about the traditional understanding of academic freedom: the Association *literally exists to defend academic freedom*.

But we will argue that that traditional understanding is not serving the profession as well as it might, particularly with regard to scholars of color and to contingent faculty. So while it is right and necessary to defend professors from political attack, the harder task before us is to ask whether academic freedom in the United States, like the post-Enlightenment liberal ideals of which it is a part, needs to be reexamined for its relation to the nation's legacy of white supremacy. Please note that we never refer to the need to rethink academic freedom as our response to what is too often called "the crisis of academic freedom." The easiest way to attract eyeballs to a story about academia is to say that the sky is falling on academic freedom; but this is a lazy way to frame the current situation. It invariably leads to the construction of false equivalences, as in "Academic Freedom

Is on the Ropes," a *Chronicle of Higher Education* article in which Alexander C. Kafka writes:

> Academics are caught in a pincer grip from the political right and left. From the right, Arkansas, Florida, Georgia, and Iowa are among states meddling in colleges' curricula and speech policies. When a Georgia lawmaker asked the state university system to explain how it teaches "oppression" and "privilege," the system's leaders felt compelled to pull together a 102-page report. Boise State suspended 52 sections of a diversity and ethics course amid Republican attacks on the university's efforts to teach students about racism.
>
> From the left, some students declare views with which they disagree to be a form of violence, shouting down voices they don't want to hear.

In one case, we have specific, documented situations in which the state surveils how university professors teach within their classrooms, and in the other we have "some students" who vociferously disagree with . . . "views." What views? We are not told—and this is key, because if we did know more about what the students were objecting to: intentional misgendering? the "Lost Cause" version of the Civil War? procolonialism?—we might find that many of us loudly object as well.

After coming in hot with the rhetoric of crisis, and despite heavily relying on ideologues like Amy Wax and National Association of Scholars president Peter Wood crying that conservatives are "muzzled," Kafka's piece ends up revealing that a saner view of the contemporary tensions in higher education prevails just under the surface of what Kafka calls the "colorful culture-war controversies." "Freedom to teach a range of subject areas," Wesleyan president Michael Roth is quoted as saying, "is much greater than it was when I was a student or a young faculty member." According to Roth, a more expansive academic culture reflects "how we teach given the fact that whom we teach has changed." Kafka also consults Joerg Tiede, director of research at the AAUP, who points out that "there's a difference . . . between a left-of-center academic being fired for his or her views and a right-of-center academic feeling uncomfortable and ostracized." Kafka writes: "People on the right, when they talk about this," [Tiede] says, "seem to be more talking about being criticized or fearing being ostracized by their colleagues." The AAUP, he says, has historically focused more on administrative firings. "I would say there is a qualitative difference between the two."

The idea that academic freedom is under universal attack ends up mapping roughly onto the right-wing campaign that cancel culture has run amok. We're not saying that everyone who laments the state of academic freedom is consciously affirming a point of view that frames the political and cultural center-left and left as an ideological mob, but this Chicken Little approach to academic freedom has that effect nonetheless. A more accurate way of understanding what we're seeing requires that we observe the larger national dynamic. This dynamic consists of shifts in mainstream thinking about the nation's history of racism and about gay and trans rights *and* a simultaneous right-wing backlash to those shifts. A reckoning with historical and systemic racism has *already occurred* in the academy over the last few decades, as we mentioned above. It's just that the window for the mainstream to accept some of these facts seemed to open only in the last few years, particularly in the year after George Floyd's murder. As *New Yorker* writer Jelani Cobb rightly notes, "A growing body of progressive white scholars and scholars of color have spent the past several decades fighting for, and largely succeeding in creating, a more honest chronicle of the American past. But these battles and the changes they've achieved have, by and large, gone unnoticed by the lay public." Until now. But as some people learn for the first time of, say, the 1921 Tulsa Massacre or Juneteenth, and wonder why they never heard such things mentioned in school, others are actively fighting this growing awareness and painting it as unpatriotic. "The aversion to unflattering truths can be made into political currency," Cobb writes, and that's what we're seeing—with the political campaigns to ban critical race theory, with the political appointees' denial of tenure for Nikole Hannah-Jones and so on.

One body of work built up over the last few decades that has led to a more honest chronicle of the past is that conducted by political philosopher Charles Mills, whose critiques of traditional liberalism, which he redescribes as "racial liberalism," have changed our own minds about our relation to abstract liberal ideals (while convincing us that we took so long to rethink our relation to abstract liberal ideals because our whiteness got in the way). In *The Humanities, Higher Education, and Academic Freedom*, we took our distance from the poststructuralist/postcolonialist academic left's rejection of the Enlightenment, arguing, in the spirit of Thurgood Marshall's address on the bicentennial of the US Constitution, that Enlightenment egalitarianism was betrayed by its founders and never adequately realized in American politics (indeed, rendered all but impossible by American politics) but that the ideal of Enlightenment universalism leaves it open to any and all challengers who can argue that the universal is not yet universal *enough*. We thereby sought to agree with Jürgen Habermas that modernity—the project of Enlightenment—is an unfinished project, though without subscribing to the Habermasian belief that the purpose of communicative action is the achievement of consensus. We now think that our earlier argument does not do justice to the structural inequalities built into, and yet systemically downplayed or denied altogether by, the intellectual legacy of liberalism.

Mills's account mounts a searing critique of that legacy without giving up on its promise; in effect, Mills offers a more robust and explicitly race-conscious version of what we thought we were trying to argue. "The route taken by most philosophers," Mills writes in *Black Rights / White Wrongs*,

> purifies and Platonizes liberalism into an ideal Form of itself, and then—ignoring the exclusions that in fact deprive the majority of the population of entitlement to equal liberal status—produces a conceptual history in this elevated realm that never touches down to the hard ground of reality. Liberalism as it should have been is presented as liberalism as it actually was. This is not merely bad intellectual history, but is also a poor strategy for realizing the promise of liberalism. The real-life political struggles that were historically necessary to overcome liberalism's particularisms are erased by a myth of implicit potential inclusion. Better, in my opinion, to recognize these exclusions as theoretically central, admit their shaping of liberalism's array of rights and freedoms, and then confront the critics' case for discrediting liberalism altogether with the defense's arguments for how it can nonetheless be reclaimed and redeemed. (xiii)

The myth of implicit potential inclusion: this, we admit, is basically the myth in which we believed, as if liberalism simply always contained within itself the seeds of a more perfect union. In reality, one needs, following Mills, to conduct a thorough accounting of how the abstractions of liberal theory work to prevent liberalism from realizing its egalitarian promise. For Mills, racial liberalism

> is a liberalism in which key terms have been written by race and the discursive logic shaped accordingly. This position expresses my commitment to what has been called the "symbiotic" view of racism, which sees race as historically penetrating *into* liberalism's descriptive and normative apparatus so as to produce a more-or-less consistent racialized ideology, rather than seeing race as being externally and "anomalously" related to it. Unlike my post-structuralist and post-colonial colleagues, however, I see this penetration as contingent, not a matter of a pre-ordained logic of liberalism itself, but a consequence of the mandates for European liberal theorists of establishing and maintaining imperial and colonial rule abroad, and nonwhite racial subordination at home. Hence the hope of redeeming liberalism by self-consciously taking this history into account: recognizing the historic racialization of liberalism *so as better to deracialize it*—thereby producing a color-conscious, racially reflexive, anti-racist-liberalism on the alert for its own inherited racial distortions. (xv; emphasis in original)

Mills's primary target here is John Rawls's theory of justice. Though Mills divides contemporary liberalism into conservative/libertarian and left-liberal branches, represented by Robert Nozick and John Rawls, respectively, it is Rawls rather than Nozick that Mills seeks most energetically to revise, precisely because Rawls's putatively more egalitarian theory of justice presents a greater obstacle to the development of a critique of racial liberalism. The problem is not simply that "the person seen as the most important twentieth-century American political philosopher and theorist of social justice, and a fortiori the most important American contract theorist, had nothing to say about the remediation of racial justice, so central to American society and history" (35). The problem, rather, is that the kind of "ideal theory" proposed by Rawls, in which members of a society deliberate behind a "veil of ignorance" (which extends not only to their own position in that society but even to the knowledge of their own interests) in order to achieve "justice as fairness" and ensure a mutually beneficial polity for all, bears no relation whatsoever to the nonideal founding of the United States (or, indeed, any political entity) and cannot account for the persistence of brutal social hierarchies and injustices. Mills's critique of Rawlsian contractarianism is thus a critique of contractarianism as such.

We were already familiar with the disability studies critique of social contract theory, as first developed by Eva Feder Kittay and then adopted by Martha Nussbaum: since people with significant intellectual disabilities cannot be accounted for in any scheme that proposes a contract-making venture among "free, equal, and independent" parties (as per John Locke) organizing for their mutual benefit, the exclusion of people with intellectual disabilities from the contract is a feature rather than a bug of social contract theory. Mills's account of racial liberalism is similarly attentive to such exclusions, but it goes further in its insistence on the primacy of *non*-ideal theory. The importance of this move cannot be overstated, precisely because Rawls's theory is so ostensibly egalitarian: Rawls's "Difference Principle," after all, permits inequalities in the distribution of goods only if those inequalities benefit the least well-off. But for Mills, starting from the Rawlsian premise that society is a "cooperative venture for mutual advantage" renders unthinkable the possibility that societies might instead be constructed by people more interested in securing the supremacy of their own group and the subordination of others. Indeed, the social contract tradition renders unthinkable the possibility that not everyone at the contract-drawing table might be operating in good faith.

In place of the idea of the social contract, then, Mills offers "the domination contract," "the racial contract," which

> provides a way of translating into a mainstream liberal apparatus—social contract theory—the egalitarian agenda and concerns of political progressives. It offers a competing metaphor that more accurately represents the creation and maintenance of the sociopolitical order. The white privilege that is systemically obfuscated in the mainstream contract is here nakedly revealed. And the biasing of liberal abstractions by the concrete interests of the privileged (here, whites) then becomes transparent. It is immediately made unmysterious why liberal norms and ideals that seem so attractive in the abstract—freedom, equality, rights, justice—have proved unsatisfactory, refractory, in practice and failed to serve the interests of people of color. (39)

Again, this does not mean turning our backs on the very ideas of freedom, equality, rights, or justice; it means rethinking them because they have proved inadequate, incomplete, or skewed. "It should be clear by now," Dylan Rodriguez writes in *White Reconstruction*, "that whatever stubborn social-historical antagonisms the alleged postracial society was projected to displace or eliminate may have been inadequately conceptualized or improperly defined" (1). We will see, for example, that time and again, theorists of academic freedom have no problem excluding certain ideas from serious debate (phlogiston, the philosopher's stone, and the efficacy of human sacrifice) but keep making exceptions for theories of racial hierarchy based on or derived from the pseudoscientific theories that dominated Western intellectual life from roughly 1850 to 1950 and produced the widespread advocacy of eugenics. We will insist, therefore, that a robust theory of academic freedom must be premised on an equality that goes beyond formal equality, one that is not devoted to a false universality but rather *sees* color, gender, differing ability, etc. One problem with an unreflective invocation of "equality" is the belief that the solution to racism is colorblindness—and this colorblindness is then analogically extended to a general blindness to other differences. The favoring of abstractions over documented reality is the very trap Charles Mills exposes in the history of liberalism with regard to race and that Uday Singh Mehta has exposed for the history of liberalism and empire. It is precisely what critical race theorists confronted in the 1970s and 1980s: the reality that formal equality had not magically eliminated discrimination and injustice. If we do not internalize this critique of formal equality, we will inevitably create regimes of abstract "freedom" in which some people have to argue for their right to exist as equals as a precondition for arguing anything else. This, we submit, is freedom on a steeply tilted playing field. It is the field all of us have inhabited all our lives; those who benefit most from it are, predictably, the most susceptible to believing that the surface is level or needs only minor landscaping.

The field has long been tilted. But it's also been strewn with landmines, as the weaponizing of free speech has had knock-on effects for academia, creating what Johnny E. Williams calls "the academic freedom double standard." "When socially defined black faculty dare to speak and write truthfully about the collusion of self-identified 'whites' in sustaining systemic white racism," Williams writes, "we are attacked and maligned" ("Double Standard"). He continues:

> Such vile efforts of silencing by far-right and liberal white su-
> premacists are inverted to support the free speech and academic
> freedom of academicians espousing racism. Clearly, this is a
> profound double standard of academic freedom. The true goal
> of these new "free speech" campaigns is to silence faculty who
> seek to eliminate white supremacy and promote those who work
> to shore it up. (5)

The weaponization of academic freedom works like this: the far right legitimates itself and wins the support of centrists and liberals by converting what is unambiguously racist speech into grounds for a defense of the inviolability of academic freedom. *If you don't defend racist ideas*, the argument goes, *you won't be able to defend antiracist ones*. We will take on that argument in chapter 5. For the far more likely outcome is, as Williams's own story of faculty suspension makes clear, that antiracist voices are silenced while racist ones are hailed as courageous.

Also exploring the hypocritical dynamic that has underwritten academic freedom, Piya Chatterjee and Sunaina Maira argue in *The Imperial University: Academic Repression and Scholarly Dissent* that "the culture wars have worked to uphold a powerful mythology about American democracy and the American Dream and a potent fiction about freedom of expression that in actuality contains academic dissent" (22). They argue that the "exceptionalist mythology [that] has historically represented the U.S. nation as a beacon of individual liberty" fosters an environment of "academic containment" that inhibits some faculty members' speech while protecting others' in the name of (a libertarian) academic freedom (22). Writing before Trump's election, the height of the Black Lives Matter movement, and the murder of George Floyd, Chatterjee and Maira nonetheless speak to the issues raised by the resurgence and convergence of white nationalist and pro-colonialist voices in the last five years.

LAST BUT NOT LEAST, we want to conclude by revisiting the importance of the changing demographics of the university. For Mills, it is no coincidence that political philosophy has, until recently, been nearly oblivious to issues of race: philosophy is by far the humanities discipline most dominated by white men. Though, Mills noted in 2008, "the problem is not at all just demographic":

> Philosophers of color are absent not only from the halls of academe but from the texts also. Introductions to political philosophy standardly exclude any discussion of race, except, perhaps, for brief discussions of affirmative action. . . . The central debates in the field as presented—aristocracy versus democracy, absolutism versus liberalism, capitalism versus socialism, social democracy versus libertarianism, contractarianism versus communitarianism—exclude any reference to the modern global history of racism versus anti-racism, of abolitionist, anti-imperialist, anti-colonialist, anti-Jim Crow, anti-apartheid struggles. Quobna Cugoano, Frederick Douglass, W. E. B. Du Bois, Mahatma Gandhi, Aimé Cesaire, C. L. R. James, Frantz Fanon, Steve Biko, Edward Said are all missing. (33)

Mills adds that things have begun to change in the years since he published that essay in *PMLA* (the journal of the Modern Language

Association), but the point remains that philosophy remains an overwhelmingly white space. The humanities remain an overwhelmingly white space. The academy remains an overwhelmingly white space if we are looking at its faculty. That is surely part of the reason it has taken so long for theories of justice to foreground *racial justice*—even in a country whose history is defined by struggles for and against racial justice.

But while the demographics of the professoriate have changed only glacially in the past fifty years, the undergraduate population has undergone a transformation that too few commentators on higher education have acknowledged. In 2019, the American Council on Education issued a report, *Race and Ethnicity in Higher Education*, revealing that "in 2015–16, approximately 45 percent of all undergraduate students identified as being a race or ethnicity other than White, compared with 29.6 percent in 1995–96" (43). That passage is cited in the 2020 book, *From Equity Talk to Equity Walk: Leading Change in Higher Education*, by Tia Brown McNair, Estela Mara Bensimon, and Lindsey Malcom-Piqueux (a project supported by the Association of American Colleges and Universities and the Center for Urban Education at the University of Southern California). *From Equity Talk to Equity Walk* addresses a number of obstacles to equity on college campuses, among them the existence of faculty members who believe that racial inequalities are the result of cultural or genetic differences between white and non-white students. McNair, Bensimon, and Malcom-Piqueux thus define racial equity "as a project with three aims":

1. Correct the educational injustices perpetrated by policies and practices that resulted in the systematic marginalization of populations whose ties to the United States came about

involuntarily through enslavement, colonization, usurpation of territory, or genocide.

2. Elevate antiracism as an agenda that higher education must take on if we are ever to truly be the just and good society we imagine ourselves to be.

3. Make whiteness be seen as the problem that undermines higher education from serving as a societal model for racial justice. (109)

From Equity Talk to Equity Walk is a book about curricular and pedagogical practices that enhance or obstruct the establishment of a campus climate in which all students can participate equally, to the fullest extent of their desires and abilities; it is not a book about academic freedom. But we have come to realize that there is no way to answer the call for greater equity on campus without asking the questions about academic freedom we set out here. The tension between equality and liberty is the defining characteristic of the open society, informing the debate in which it cannot refuse to engage; and we believe that an excessively libertarian conception of academic freedom, underwritten by and often confused with an absolutist position on free speech, is inadequate to the challenges facing American higher education in the twenty-first century—if indeed we are going to continue to believe that American higher education should serve American democracy, and that academic freedom should serve the common good. In the pages that follow, we hope to persuade you that these beliefs are well founded.

CHAPTER 1

CONTEXT CULTURE

OR, A FEW CAUTIONARY WORDS CONCERNING THE POLITICS OF INTERPRETATION

A faculty member is accused of racism; the accusation goes viral. How can anyone determine the justice or injustice of the accusation? How can reasonable people gauge its severity? Let us begin with a cautionary tale about social media. For the next few pages, your narrator is Michael.

In the video, a middle-aged, white-haired white man is standing in a campus courtyard surrounded by angry students, the vast majority of them people of color. One woman of color tells the man she is sick just looking at him, that he is disgusting, that he is not listening. (He is clearly listening.) Another tells him he is racist, that he has created space for racist violence. (He denies this, calmly.) Yet another screams, "Who the fuck hired you? You should step down!" She is inches from him, yelling into his face. He is imperturbable. And at one point, he pleads for understanding: "I want you to own the fact," he tells the crowd, "all of you to own the fact that it's very easy to take something I say and misinterpret it" ("Yale Students").

When I first saw the video on YouTube—it did indeed go viral, and there are many other versions of it, since everyone now routinely carries a video recording device at all times—I was appalled at the students' behavior. What had this poor soul done to deserve such horrible treatment? He sent out an email? Really? Might this not happen to me some day? *Mon semblable, mon frère*, I thought: what if I were to offend the sensibilities of students of color somehow? Would I be as patient and as even-keeled with students surrounding me and screaming at me?

And yet I had some inkling that there might be more to the story, because I knew even on first viewing one version of the confrontation that it had been filmed by Greg Lukianoff, president and CEO of FIRE, the Foundation for Individual Rights in Education, and I do not always trust FIRE in such matters.[1] But the video is striking all the same, precisely for the contrast between the outrage of the students and the placidity of the man's demeanor. That was, of course, the point of releasing those videos in the first place: to give the impression that students of color were verbally and psychologically abusing an innocent, well-meaning faculty member who was only trying to engage in sincere and substantive dialogue with them. And *that* impression, in turn, would serve as concrete evidence that

1. We also do not always distrust FIRE. Over the years, they have done some good work and some tendentious work; especially when David French was at the helm in 2004–5, they were reliably on the conservative and libertarian side of the culture wars and all too willing to pretend that LGBTQ students were persecuting Christians. Still, they sometimes align with the AAUP and the ACLU, and are considerably stronger than the AAUP with regard to the rights of students, since the AAUP deals almost exclusively with faculty. For FIRE's videos of the Yale incident, see "Halloween Costume Controversy." For an instructive example of how FIRE and the AAUP can be at loggerheads (usually over the conflation of academic freedom and free speech), see Scott Jaschik, "AAUP vs. FIRE," regarding the two organizations' radically different accounts of an antiracist program at the University of Oklahoma.

"snowflake" students had become ideologically intolerant "social justice warriors" who bore out every criticism lodged against them in the book Lukianoff had recently written with Jonathan Haidt, *The Coddling of the American Mind.*

The episode is now well known, of course, so it will be no surprise if we identify the campus as Yale, the semester as fall 2015 (just after Halloween, which precipitated the confrontation), and the professor as Nicholas Christakis, then the master of Yale's Silliman College. In the weeks and months that followed, commentators tried to put the videos in context, to establish the chain of events that led to this ugly scene. Black students at Yale had allegedly been turned away from a Halloween party because of the color of their skin. Student activists at Yale and at the University of Missouri had been questioning those institutions' long history of racism, noting not only the difficulties attendant on being students of color but also the paucity of Black faculty—a paucity that has persisted, at those institutions and many others, for decades. But most of all, the immediate context involved a letter issued by Yale's Intercultural Affairs Committee, asking students to be mindful about Halloween costumes that might traffic in ethnic stereotypes or outright racism (as in the case of blackface and redface). The letter is boilerplate material for American college campuses, thanks to the fact that practically every year, some students somewhere decide that it would be edgy and funny to wear blackface or—to take a real example from Penn State in 2012—have an entire sorority dress up as "Mexicans" in serapes, sombreros, and mustaches, holding signs reading "WILL MOW LAWN FOR WEED + BEER" and "I DON'T CUT GRASS I SMOKE IT" (see Ponter).

And yet for some mysterious reason, Nicholas Christakis's wife, Erika, associate master of Silliman College, decided that this would be a good time to send Silliman students an email of almost nine hundred words, pushing back on the Intercultural Affairs Committee memo and suggesting that Yale was infantilizing its students: "this year," she wrote, "we seem afraid that college students are unable to decide how to dress themselves on Halloween." One wonders: was she somehow unaware that this has been an abiding concern for decades?

When I read Erika Christakis's email in full, the context of the confrontation between Nicholas Christakis and the students changed dramatically. The email opens in what is widely known, in internet culture, as "concern troll" mode: "Nicholas and I have heard from a number of students who were frustrated by the mass email sent to the student body about appropriate Halloween-wear." The hallmark of the concern troll is that the concern troll is speaking for many others; his or her concern is but a channel for *their* concerns. A number of students are frustrated: for all we know, this number could be two. But then things get worse.

The email proceeds into "yes, but" territory, characterizing the Intercultural Affairs Committee letter as well-meaning but subtly coercive:

> I know that many decent people have proposed guidelines on Halloween costumes from a spirit of avoiding hurt and offense. I laud those goals, in theory, as most of us do. But in practice, I wonder if we should reflect more transparently, as a community, on the consequences of an institutional (which is to say: bureaucratic and administrative) exercise of implied control over college students.

This passage resonated strongly with libertarians, for whom the idea of an institutional exercise of implied control conjures any number of horrors. But it is a very weird way to characterize a memo advising students not to wear blackface or engage in ethnic stereotyping— matters that many people (including many of our students!) consider matters of common courtesy. And it is all the weirder in the campus context, because of course universities are places that exercise all kinds of *explicit* control over college students, ranging from bans on open flames in public places to individual professors' class attendance policies. What kind of faculty member says, in effect, "I'm OK with the university having a code of student conduct and a policy on academic integrity, but I draw the line at issuing a memo about offensive Halloween costumes?"

Then there is a thoughtful and irrelevant argument:

> As a former preschool teacher, for example, it is hard for me to give credence to a claim that there is something objectionably "appropriative" about a blonde-haired child's wanting to be Mulan for a day. Pretend play is the foundation of most cognitive tasks, and it seems to me that we want to be in the business of encouraging the exercise of imagination, not constraining it. I suppose we could agree that there is a difference between fantasizing about an individual character vs. appropriating a culture, wholesale, the latter of which could be seen as (tacky)(offensive)(jejeune)(hurtful), take your pick.

If there is a difference between a child fantasizing about or play-acting as an individual character and appropriating a culture (and yes, there certainly is), then why bring up the Mulan example at all? Understandably, it is hard for Christakis to give credence to a claim that it is objectionable for a blonde-haired child to play at being Mulan for a day. But it is even harder to see why this is at issue, since the memo to which Christakis is replying made no such claim.

And then comes the payload. Note the surprise introduction of the "what about the sensitivities of religious conservatives?" argument, because apparently no one is thinking of them:

> Even if we could agree on how to avoid offense—and I'll note that no one around campus seems overly concerned about the offense taken by religiously conservative folks to skin-revealing costumes—I wonder, and I am not trying to be provocative: Is there no room anymore for a child or young person to be a little bit obnoxious . . . a little bit inappropriate or provocative or, yes, offensive? American universities were once a safe space not only for maturation but also for a certain regressive, or even transgressive, experience; increasingly, it seems, they have become places of censure and prohibition. And the censure and prohibition come from above, not from yourselves! Are we all okay with this transfer of power? Have we lost faith in young people's capacity—in your capacity—to exercise self-censure, through social norming, and also in your capacity to ignore or reject things that trouble you?

Those of you familiar with this genre will know that "and I am not trying to be provocative" is a version of "I know this isn't politically correct, but." Something nasty is sure to follow. *Is there no room anymore for a child or young person to be a little bit obnoxious?* Well, yes, there is. There are in fact lots of ways for a child or young person to be a little bit obnoxious. Wearing blackface (or redface, or dressing as "Mexican") is among the *least* imaginative of these. Again, I can draw on Penn State for an example. In 2003, a member of the campus College Republicans caused controversy by (wait for it, it will be a surprise) wearing blackface at a Halloween party (for a comprehensive retrospective account, see Dooling). The photos College Republican chair Brian

Battaglia posted to his private website also revealed, incidentally, that another student had gone to the party as Roy Horn of Siegfried and Roy, who had recently been horribly mauled and nearly killed by a white tiger. The costume involved lots of blood stains and a little white tiger strapped to the student's head. It was in supremely bad taste, it was more than a little bit obnoxious, and it offended precisely no one. See? It isn't that hard. It just takes a little imagination. And surely, as Christakis says, we all want to encourage the exercise of imagination.

Because, to return to the immediate context yet again, the occasion was an anodyne memo reminding students that some Halloween costumes can be stridently offensive and racist. This is not a difficult call.

Nicholas and Erika Christakis stepped down from their positions at Silliman College, though they still teach at Yale (indeed, in 2018 Nicholas was named a Sterling Professor, Yale's highest faculty rank). As well they should: nothing about this incident involves a firing offense, or even, arguably, a censure or reprimand. Over ninety faculty at Yale signed a statement of support for the Christakises (though four hundred signed a statement of support for the students), and the court of public opinion has generally decided in their favor: the students behaved shamefully, and the Christakises were the innocent targets of social justice warriors and cancel culture. Conor Friedersdorf was an early and vocal supporter ("New Intolerance"), and he was joined, in the ensuing years, not only by Bill Maher (predictably, perhaps; see "Martyrs") but by the writers for *The Simpsons*, who parodied the episode in April 2017 by having a character remark, "We also need to hire more deans to decide which Halloween costumes are appropriate" ("Caper Chase").

And yet there is one more contextual element that almost no one has mentioned. Even David Cole's long, thoughtful discussion of the incident in the *New York Review of Books*, setting *l'affaire Christakis* in the context of minority enrollment and hiring in American universities, does not glance at it ("Yale"). This was not the first trip to the racial-insensitivity rodeo for Nicholas and Erika Christakis. In December 2012, some student or students at Harvard University thought it would be a laugh riot to distribute flyers satirizing Harvard's notoriously exclusive student clubs. (No club admitted a Black student before 1965, for example.) The flyer announced the formation of "The Pigeon, Harvard's Newest Final Club"; at the top of the flyer were three asterisked words. Inclusion*, Diversity**, Love***. The bottom of the flyer read:

> *Jews need not apply.
> **Seriously, no fucking Jews. Coloreds OK.
> ***Rophynol [sic]

The final item is supposed to be Rohypnol, the date-rape drug commonly known as a "roofie."

It is doubtful that anyone at Harvard took the flyer as a serious announcement that a new, openly racist, anti-Semitic, pro-date-rape club was being established on campus. But one can nonetheless question the wisdom (or, for that matter, the humor) behind distributing such a flyer on a campus with such a sorry history of open racism and anti-Semitism. While it's clear that the flyer is satirical, it is also clear—at least to us—that it's not very good satire. Unsurprisingly, the Harvard administration issued a statement lamenting the flyer's "deeply disturbing" language and stating that it did not "demonstrate the level of thoughtfulness and respect we expect at Harvard when engaging difficult issues within our community" (see Robbins, "Campus Reacts").

And guess who took to the pages of *Time* magazine to defend the flyer and criticize the administration? Nicholas and Erika Christakis, citing Greg Lukianoff on the "stultifying atmosphere on campuses nationwide where unpopular ideas and offensive language are policed to an absurd extent," and decrying "the problem of living in a free-speech surveillance state." That problem, as they define it, is one whereby "otherwise sensible people tie themselves in knots trying to define which speech is acceptable and which is not" ("Whither"). Remarkably, they wrote this as if it were self-evidently a fool's errand to try to define unacceptable speech, as if there is no principle at stake in such matters other than free speech absolutism, and as if no one ever heard of outlandish, knot-tying things like common courtesy. At the time, the Christakises were masters of Pforzheimer House at Harvard.

That, finally, sets the relevant context for understanding what happened at Yale. The Yale incident, taken alone, might be a simple misjudgment, an inability on the part of the Christakises to imagine that an email criticizing an anti-blackface message from the Intercultural Affairs Committee might well be read as an endorsement of blackface. But when read in the light of the Harvard episode, in which a university administration says, in effect, "look, 'no fucking Jews. Coloreds OK' and a joke about drug-induced date rape is really not funny and potentially offensive," and the Christakises reply in a national magazine in a mode that suggests that some hapless students are being accused of thoughtcrime and sent to the campus Sensitivity Center for reeducation (that is, *policed to an absurd extent*), the Yale incident makes the Christakises look less like brave defenders of free speech (as their Wikipedia pages portray them) and more like provocateurs who make a point of being tone deaf to the concerns of students of color. Again, in no sense is that a firing offense. But it is certainly something worth taking into consideration when you're considering which faculty members might make good supervisors of undergraduates in residential colleges.

THE CHRISTAKIS EPISODE is old news. But it is useful as a Rorschach test, revealing who among us is likely to think of students as whiny, entitled, hypersensitive troublemakers—and who is likely to think that concerns about racism on campus are largely overblown. "The scene," writes Ulrich Baer, "became a flash point in the current culture wars, pitting what a national magazine [the *Atlantic*] labeled a 'coddled' generation of oversensitive students against reasonable adults" (144). And as we will acknowledge repeatedly in this book, there are often good reasons to be suspicious of administrative attempts to "manage" issues of diversity, inclusion, and equity on campus. (We just don't think there is good reason to be suspicious of a memo advising students not to wear blackface.) Moreover, there are almost always good reasons to resist "mobbing," especially when social media can generate instantaneous outrage over any perceived slight.

Social media can be insidious in any number of ways, but what we want to call attention to here is that they can often work as a kind of decontextualization apparatus. This is especially true with Twitter, but the difference between Twitter and other platforms in this respect is a difference of degree rather than of kind. Steven Salaita's 2014 tweetstorm offers a case in point, not least because it became the basis for his infamous "de-hiring" by the University of Illinois at Urbana-Champaign (and subsequent censure of UIUC by the AAUP). Responding to Israel's deadly incursion into Gaza that summer, which was widely condemned by human rights organizations, Salaita posted hundreds of tweets, some of which were notably incendiary. One of the most controversial tweets, dated June 19, 2014, read, "you may be too refined to say it, but I'm not: I wish all the fuck-ing West Bank settlers would go missing." The context here, un-doubtedly, is the murder of three Israeli teenagers, whose abduction on June 12 helped precipitate Israel's attack on Gaza.

Michael quoted that tweet in an essay for an issue of the *AAUP Journal of Academic Freedom* that was devoted in part to discussion of Salaita's de-hiring—and was told by a colleague that he had taken the tweet out of context. In his introduction to the issue, he wrote that Salaita's tweet was a challenge to the AAUP's 1940 Statement of Principles with regard to extramural utterances (an issue we will ex-plore further below, and again in the following chapter)—namely, the provision that faculty members should "exercise appropriate re-straint" and "show respect for the opinions of others":

> There is no clear way to show respect for the opinions of others in a medium that limits utterances to 140 characters. But more impor-tant is the admonition that professors should "exercise appropri-ate restraint." It is hard to argue that a tweet like "you may be too refined to say it, but I'm not: I wish all the fucking West Bank set-tlers would go missing" exercises "appropriate restraint"; on the contrary, it is deliberately crafted to flout appropriate restraint. That is what "you may be too refined to say it, but I'm not" is doing: it announces a standard of refinement (and civility) that the speaker is going to proceed to transgress. It may even be said the "you" *is* that standard, inasmuch as Salaita did not direct his tweet to any spe-cific individual. (I, for the record, am definitely too refined to say that I wish all the fucking West Bank settlers would go missing. I merely wish that the fucking West Bank settlers would go some-place other than the West Bank, preferably as part of a negotiated, peaceful, two-state settlement.) But then, what does "appropriate

restraint" mean in a medium such as Twitter? Salaita's tweet is by no means inappropriate or out of discursive bounds in a context where professors produce endless strings of colorful obscenities in all-caps mode, showing no respect whatsoever for the opinions (or the tweets) of others. ("Editor's Introduction")

Michael's colleague, however, did not object to this argument, or to the fact that he had not made it clear that Salaita was referring (brutally) to the abduction of those teenagers. Some readers of Salaita's tweet considered it a genocidal wish—but that wasn't the issue, either. No, his colleague insisted that taking *any single one* of Salaita's tweets, standing alone, did violence to the longer thread in which they were embedded—most of which, to be sure, looked nothing like that tweet. This seems to entail a problematic standard, as if a string of tweets should be considered a coherent body of work such that they could be printed, bound, and published as something in the genre of the *Meditations* of Marcus Aurelius, or perhaps a commonplace book. We are similarly skeptical of claims that tweets cannot be quoted alone because they take place in a dialogic medium, as Natalie Zemon Davis argued in her letter to the UIUC administration: "The lack of 'civility' in some of his tweets is linked to the genre itself: a tweet is often an answer to a tweet, and a tweet always anticipates a response. . . . Thus, in his public political life, Professor Salaita participates in a mode that always leaves space for an answer" (see Potter).

We will say more about social media in chapter 5, but for now, suffice it to say that the AAUP statement on "Academic Freedom and Electronic Communications," first published in 1997 and revised twice since (2004, 2013), does not adequately confront the challenges posed by social media, particularly with regard to determining the relevant context of an utterance. Nowhere is this clearer than when satire is at issue. Satire always, and by definition, raises questions of context because satire always has a referent: the creators of Harvard's "Pigeon Club," for example, were trying, however ham-fistedly, to critique Harvard's history of anti-Black and anti-Semitic discrimination. Absent that referent, it looks (and some commentators on the flyers helped to make it look) like the flyer itself was anti-Black and anti-Semitic.

Indeed, this is how "cancel culture" got its start: on Twitter, with satire. The "Cancel Colbert" campaign was launched in 2014 by Suey Park, who, at 23, had already established herself as an online presence by creating the #NotYourAsianSidekick hashtag; the *Guardian* named her one of the top 30 people in digital media. "Cancel Colbert" was a semiotic hall of mirrors, not because Park's work was satire but because she took aim at a piece of satire that (in Park's defense) did not name its referent. The tweet, posted by the Twitter account for The Colbert Report, read, "I am willing to show #Asian community I care by introducing the Ching-Chong Ding-Dong Foundation for Sensitivity to Orientals or Whatever." (The tweet has since been deleted; see Feldman.) This is seriously unfunny unless you know that it is aimed at a ludicrous decision by Daniel Snyder, owner of what is now known as the Washington Football Team, to create an outfit called the Washington Redskins Original Americans Foundation—a mind-bogglingly tone-deaf (or deliberately trollish?) attempt to respond to criticism of the name "Redskins" by . . . creating a foundation with the name "Redskins" in it.

As Jay Caspian Kang wrote in the *New Yorker*, the Colbert Report tweet "committed the comedic sin of delivering a punch line without a setup" ("Campaign"). But then, how much of a setup do you need to know that The Colbert Report *is* satire? Though the referent is unclear from the tweet itself, Colbert's entire schtick is a parody of Bill

O'Reilly—and associated troglodytes, including Dan Snyder when appropriate. Park, for her part, was well aware of this. But the #CancelColbert hashtag took on a life of its own (as hashtags are wont to do), and as it did, it became part of the decontextualization apparatus. As Park told Kang, she did not literally want The Colbert Report to be cancelled; she had a much more nuanced (and much more justified) complaint about the tweet, namely, that "well-intentioned racial humor doesn't actually do anything to end racism or the Redskins mascot. That sort of racial humor just makes people who hide under the title of progressivism more comfortable." Though it seems a rather stringent criterion by which to judge a tweet (one wonders what kind of tweet would end racism), one could say something similar about the misguided antiracist humor of Harvard's Pigeon Club flyer, and a few pages ago, we just did.

But let's take a context much closer to home—involving a non-tenure-track faculty member, an ill-advised, ironic comment on social media, and an instant outrage. The story is a horrible one, and it begins at Fort Hood, Texas on April 22, 2020, when Spc. Vanessa Guillen was murdered by fellow soldier Spc. Aaron David Robinson, who subsequently killed himself when he realized the investigation of Guillen's death was closing in on him. Guillen had reportedly endured sexual harassment at Fort Hood, and her family believed the harassment was related to her death; but Guillen herself never reported it, because, in the words of her sister Lupe, "no one would listen to her. They take sexual harassment, sexual assault, as a joke. They don't care." (See Schwartz, "FBI.")

The case resonated for one Dr. Betsy Schoeller, an instructor in the School of Information Studies at the University of Wisconsin–Milwaukee. Writing on a Facebook page titled "Veteran Humor," a private page for veterans of the US armed services, Schoeller wrote, in response to a post about Guillen's harassment and murder, "You guys are kidding, right? Sexual harassment is the price of admission for women in the good ole boys club. If you're gonna cry like a snowflake about it, you're gonna pay the price" (see Torres). As Schoeller made clear in a deeply apologetic followup statement, this statement was meant as an indictment of the sentiment it expressed; it was, Scholler explained, a critique of the military culture that tolerates and encourages sexual harassment, and punishes the women who come forward with reports of harassment. But it is not implausible to read it "straight": if all you know about Betsy Schoeller is that she herself is a veteran, a former colonel in the Wisconsin Air National Guard's 128th Air Refueling Wing, then you might imagine that she had, in the course of her military career, internalized the misogyny of her male peers to the extent that she would be willing to blame Guillen for her death. The phrase "good ole boys club" might be the tipoff that this isn't the case, that Schoeller was being bitterly ironic about the cost to women of joining the military's good ole boys club rather than endorsing the suck-it-up-buttercup ethos of that club. But then again, it might not. Absent a larger context for this utterance, it's hard to tell.

The UWM administration promptly took its distance from Schoeller's remarks, using the standard disclaimer formula and posting on Facebook and Twitter:

> The death of Army Private First Class Vanessa Guillen is horrifying. There can be no excuse or rationalization for the killing of Vanessa and the circumstances surrounding this tragedy. As the largest educator of veterans in the state of Wisconsin, UW-Milwaukee stands in solidarity with those opposed to violence against women, including those serving in the military. Under the First Amendment, the university cannot regulate the private speech

of its employees, but UWM does not condone the comments made by Betsy Schoeller in her Facebook posting. We are committed to a safe, welcoming, and inclusive campus. It is our expectation that all of our employees live up to the values of our university in the academic environment. (See Torres.)

That statement was posted on July 4, 2020. Schoeller's response followed the next day. In it, Scholler tried to re-create the context and explain the intention (two very different things, as we'll argue below) informing her seemingly callous, victim-blaming comment:

When I was on a private Facebook page for veterans, I saw the article about SPC Guillen's death and was shocked, horrified, and sickened by the tragic loss of this beautiful woman soldier. It was so brutal and so senseless. Senseless. We all try to make sense of these kinds of events. I continued reading, hoping to find some meaning in what others were writing about the article.

That's when I saw a posting written by Zach Bigger, who was clearly searching for meaning as well. He was asking questions about 'how' this could have happened, and 'why.' I knew immediately how and why. Because of the continued culture of sexual harassment in the military.

So, I posted a reply to Zach Bigger, "Sexual harassment is the price of admission for women into the good ole boy club. If you're gonna cry like a snowflake" (or any other demeaning term), "you're gonna pay the price." I did not mean to imply that this is how I feel. I was giving voice to the messaging that women hear in the culture of sexual harassment: The message we receive from the culture is not only will you suffer from sexual harassment, if you squawk about it, you will suffer even more. Because it isn't just the sexual harassment. That's just the beginning. Then comes the agonizing decision about reporting. Or not reporting. The pressure applied by friends who know about it and only want to help. Having to ultimately stand up to that culture of sexual harassment on your own. Adding suffering on top of suffering. Some endure continued harassment and assault, being forced to work with the perpetrator. Sometimes even death. The sexual harassment culture is still here. That's the 'why' I was looking for.

I am shocked and saddened that my original post was interpreted out of context. (Schoeller)

Unsurprisingly, Schoeller's clarification did not satisfy the people outraged by her original post; Emily Cruz, a student at UWM, launched a petition at Change.org calling for Schoeller to be fired, arguing that Schoeller's very presence on the faculty was threatening:

I speak on behalf of my fellow UWM students, staff, and community partners when I say that we want to see Professor Schoeller terminated from UW–Milwaukee staff. As a woman, and a student at UWM I feel unsafe knowing that we have professors who think the sexual assault of women serving in the military is justified.

The petition is still up at Change.org as we write and has garnered over 170,000 signatures (see Cruz).

But that's not the most worrisome thing about the Betsy Schoeller case. Professors get misunderstood on social media all the time, and university administrations sometimes respond foolishly; one especially notorious case is that of James Livingston, a history professor at Rutgers University, who in June 2018 posted a tongue-in-cheek Facebook rant about white people living in Harlem:

OK, officially, I now hate white people. I am a white people, for God's sake, but can we keep them—us—us [sic] out of my neighborhood? I just went to Harlem Shake on 124 and Lenox for a Classic burger to go, that would my dinner [sic], and the place is overrun with little Caucasian assholes who know their parents will approve of anything they do.

This is not satire, exactly, but it's not to be taken at face value, either; it is an attempt (the success of which can be debated) at a humorous version of what we might call the Gentrifier's Lament—the ambivalence any left-leaning white person might feel about having become swept up in a wave of white people moving into, and transforming, a historically Black neighborhood. (Let alone the most iconic of all Black neighborhoods in the United States.) Surely, the plea, "can we get us out of my neighborhood" is the tip-off that this complaint—however aggravated the complainant might be about young white people standing between him and his takeout dinner—cannot be taken seriously.

Nonetheless, Livingston quickly found himself in the crosshairs of right-wing media, and the post even qualified him for inclusion on the far-right Turning Point USA's "Professor Watch List": Livingston was now officially a racist. Facebook removed the post on the grounds that it violated community standards, whereupon Livingston doubled down with a follow-up post in the same vein. ("I just don't want little Caucasians overrunning my life, as they did last night.") (See Whitford, "White Professor Accused.") Death threats followed, along with complaints to Rutgers University. It should have been an open-and-shut case, both with regard to the First Amendment and with regard to AAUP policy on extramural speech. But it wasn't. Carolyn Dellatore, the associate director of Rutgers's Office of Employment Equity, determined that Livingston's second post had violated the university's discrimination and harassment policy:

> Professor Livingston clearly was on notice that his words were offensive, yet instead of clarifying that he meant to comment on gentrification, he chose to make another belligerent barb against whites. Given Professor Livingston's insistence on making disparaging racial comments, a reasonable student may have concerns that he or she would be stigmatized in his classes because of his or her race. As such, Professor Livingston's comments violated university policy. (Whitford)

That policy states, in relevant part, that "such conduct must be sufficiently severe or pervasive to alter an individual's employment conditions, or a student's educational opportunities which, in turn, creates an unreasonably intimidating, offensive, or hostile environment for employment, education, or participation in University activities" (Rutgers Policy 60.1.12). It is hard to see how a Facebook rant falls under the purview of this policy, but Dellatore's invocation of "a reasonable student" provided her with what she believed was sufficient cause for reprimand. Note that the Change.org petition calling for Betsy Scholler's firing at UW–Milwaukee makes the same move, as did UIUC Chancellor Phyllis Wise when she speculated that Salaita's tweetstorm might have a chilling and discriminatory effect on Jewish students (see Shibley); though Salaita had no record of discrimination against any students while teaching at Virginia Tech, the concern was for future, hypothetical students, as it was for Livingston and Scholler.

We believe that Dellatore's conclusion is ludicrous on its face. It met with swift opposition from the American Civil Liberties Union,

FIRE, and the AAUP, as it should have; and it was reversed later that year by Rutgers president Robert Barchi, who claimed that Dellatore's letter had been released to Livingston and to his dean, Peter March, before he was aware of its content (Barchi). But as we'll argue in chapter 6, we don't believe that Livingston's case is anomalous. Administrators like Dellatore are charged with making these decisions as a matter of course, and most of them fly under the radar of national media—just as they bypass faculty-driven forms of peer review and adjudication.

And yet we know there is no guarantee that faculty-driven forms of peer review and adjudication will not result in travesties of justice. That is the somber lesson of the Betsy Schoeller case, to which we can now return. For the truly alarming response to Schoeller's Facebook comment came not from university administration but from a member of the UW–Milwaukee chapter of the AAUP, who posted what purported to be the chapter's official statement on the matter:

> We are compelled by recent events to make a statement in support of our students and to demand accountability from the UWM administration on the role of Dr. Betsy Schoeller at our university. It became known in early July that Dr. Schoeller made comments on Facebook, regarding the murder of Ft. Hood Specialist Vanessa Guillen. A statement later issued by Dr. Schoeller attempts to clarify the intention of the post, but a commitment to inclusivity requires that impact is elevated over intent. And the harmful impact on the student body is clear. . . .
>
> The AAUP's Statement on Extramural Utterances protects the free speech rights of faculty. Social media posts are not grounds for dismissal. But the statement also recognizes the social and professional obligations of faculty. It "calls attention to the special

obligations of faculty members arising from their position in the community: to be accurate, to exercise appropriate restraint, to show respect for the opinions of others, and to make every effort to indicate that they are not speaking for the institution."

We believe Dr. Schoeller's statements appearing to castigate those seeking justice for Specialist Guillen's sexual assault and subsequent murder were careless. They did not exercise due restraint, nor did they exhibit respect for the opinions of others. What originally came across as her cavalier attitude toward the murder of this young woman is of particular concern because Dr. Schoeller is an educator charged with instructing students, many of whom are the age of the late Specialist Guillen, and many of whom are veterans themselves.

Again, as in the Salaita case, there is the invocation of "appropriate restraint" and "respect for the opinions of others," this time boosted by the axiom that "a commitment to inclusivity requires that impact is elevated over intent." We will return to this potentially dangerous principle below; first, however, we want to cite the extraordinary array of punishments proposed for Schoeller. They are bullet-pointed at the end of the statement:

- No student will be forced to take a class from Dr. Schoeller. UWM will provide timely and viable alternatives to her classes so that student progress in their academic programs is not impeded;
- We recommend a review of any past behaviors or complaints that may indicate problematic behaviors on the issues of gender, race, and/or sexual harassment, to be conducted with her department, and with an avenue for recourse for students who may have been adversely impacted by those past behaviors;

- Dr. Schoeller will use double-blind grading on assignments; if there are components of grading that cannot be subject to a double-blind procedure, UWM will have another faculty member ensure that the grades are not subject to her prejudices;
- Dr. Schoeller will undergo in-person training to ensure she is able to follow UW System and State of Wisconsin Mandated Reporter Training requirements without prejudice;
- We encourage Dr. Schoeller to reach out to the students who express their revulsion and hurt at her statements.

And for good measure, to make sure no stone is left unthrown, the statement adds, "If other steps are needed to protect our students or colleagues from bigoted actions, UWM should take them."

Indiana University instituted double-blind grading for Eric Rasmusen's classes, and the University of Pennsylvania removed Amy Wax from courses required for its law students; here, Schoeller is treated as if she has a comparable track record of discrimination, complete with a fishing expedition to determine whether, in fact, she has *any* record of discrimination. If this is what robust faculty involvement in shared governance with regard to allegations of discrimination and violations of university policy were to look like, we would want no part of it.

Thankfully, more level heads prevailed—almost immediately. The statement was quickly taken down, both from the UW–Milwaukee AAUP website and the blog of the AAUP's journal *Academe*; the executive committee of the UWM AAUP chapter announced that the statement had been issued without proper approval (see UWM AAUP Statement).

Still, the statement never referenced the due process provisions that constitute the core of AAUP policy with regard to the censure, punishment, or termination of faculty members. Schoeller's status as a non-tenure-track faculty member makes her especially vulnerable to outrage campaigns of this kind, and we suspect that statements like these might make non-tenure-track faculty members at UWM and elsewhere particularly skeptical of the ability or the willingness of the AAUP to defend their right to due process. We therefore want the Betsy Schoeller case to serve as a monitory example as we proceed: if our proposals for greater faculty involvement in the determination of "fitness" are to gain a hearing on American campuses, they must include safeguards against rushes to judgment, malicious or inadvertent decontextualizations of allegedly controversial utterances, and, not least, indiscriminate application of the interpretive principle that the impact of a statement or action should always take precedence over intent.

We understand why activists would want to elevate impact over intent as a matter of principle, especially when the issue is structural racism, which cannot be reduced to the intentions of individuals. Too often, people who give offense follow their initially offensive utterance with a non-apology apology, usually some version of *I'm sorry if my utterance gave offense to anyone* or *I'm sorry if my remarks were misunderstood*. The comedian Harry Shearer calls these "ifpologies," and their clear function is to dismiss the criticisms of the people who took offense, and to insist that the utterer of the offensive remark meant no harm. Sometimes, they are accompanied by protestations that the speaker simply didn't know that his or her actions might give offense, and it is notable how often this happens when white people are called out for racism. One of the more credulity-straining of these was Charles Murray's insistence that although he participated in a cross-burning as a teenager, he had no idea at the time that burning a cross might have any racist overtones or implications.[2] And as a general interpretive principle, the idea that a person's intention is determinative of the meaning of an utterance is something few reputable literary scholars can entertain seriously.[3] We know very well that the creation of "meaning" is an interactive process between texts and readers in literary studies and a process of negotiation among speakers and interlocutors in ordinary discourse. This shouldn't be controversial. On the contrary, the same principle about the limits of intention applies in every form of human interaction: you may not have intended to harm anyone by swinging a small tree branch around in your front yard, but if you inadvertently hit a passerby, you have undoubtedly done harm regardless of your intentions.

2. For Murray's insistence that "it never crossed our minds that this had any larger significance," see DeParle. More generally, the problem of "unconscious racism" puts intense pressure on the politics of interpretation, precisely because unconscious racism is (a) unconscious, and by definition unintended and (b) racist. One classic example, from Charles Lawrence III's essay, "The Id, the Ego, and Equal Protection: Reckoning with Unconscious Racism," is the now-unthinkable (we hope) "compliment," "I don't think of you as a Negro" (or I don't think of you as Black—i.e., I think of you as a regular white person like me) (236). Still, even the most dogged defenders of white privilege struggle to argue that the burning of crosses is insufficient evidence of an intention to express anti-Black sentiment. For that matter, any white American who does not know the "larger significance" of burning a cross is living in a bubble of ignorance that can only be understood as an artifact of white privilege—the "privilege," such as it is, of not knowing anything about the history of racism in the United States.

3. In 1982, Stephen Knapp and Walter Benn Michaels tried to do just that; in a notorious essay titled "Against Theory," they argued that meaning is identical to intention. They convinced precisely no one and have not pursued the argument since.

And yet precisely because we are trained in literary studies, we are unwilling to grant that the alleged impact of a statement or action should always and everywhere take precedence over a speaker's or actor's intentions. To do so would be to toss out many decades (if not centuries) of debates over the meaning of meaning. We are stressing the importance of context not only for the obvious reasons (so many of these controversies involve utterances taken out of context, or made in the decontextualizing apparatus of social media), but also because this was a widely influential argument in literary theory ranging from semiotics to deconstruction. *Meaning is context-bound, but context is boundless*: this was Jonathan Culler's one-sentence summary of the work of Jacques Derrida in his 1982 book *On Deconstruction*, and though deconstruction and semiotics are not the same thing, this pithy paraphrase grew out of Culler's earlier work on semiotics and structuralism.

But if "context is boundless," doesn't that mean that anything can be said to mean anything? Doesn't it open the door to relativism, in which everyone is entitled to their own opinion *and* their own context for interpretation (hence, their own facts)? No. It merely opens the door to the conflict of interpretations and the need to make explicit the grounds on which one reading of a sign or an utterance is more plausible or persuasive than another. To be sure, the utterances we've cited here from The Colbert Report, the authors of the "Pigeon Club" flyer, James Livingston, and Betsy Schoeller arguably did not make it clear, on the face of things, that they were not participating in the very kind of offensive speech they were satirizing and critiquing. But that is not a reason to elevate "impact" over "intent" as a matter of principle. It is a reason to say, in response, *you may have meant x, but you were widely and understandably taken to be saying y, so some form of apology and explanation is in order.*

To bring the discussion back to specifics, we will close with four examples of speech that seemed to some listeners to be racist. We will start with what we consider the most problematic (in theory and in practice): the professor who utters the N-word but insists that s/he is merely "mentioning" it rather than "using" it. (This is a distinction fundamental to speech act theory.) We distinguish this from cases in which a professor is reading a text that contains the word; that is another matter, involving the question of whether such passages really need to be read aloud in the first place. Rather, we are thinking of cases such as that of Gary Shank, who in October 2020 was fired by Duquesne University for using the N-word even though he insisted that he was not strictly "using" it himself. As reported by Bill Schackner of the *Pittsburgh Post-Gazette*:

> In one of two videos posted to Twitter, the professor—as he interacts with at least one student—brings up the N-word. In one video, Mr. Shank says, "I'm giving you permission to use the word, OK? Because we're using the word in a pedagogical sense. What's the one word about race that we're not allowed to use?"
>
> After being greeted with silence, he adds, "I'll give you a hint. It starts with 'N.' . . . It's even hard to say, OK? But, I'll tell you the word, and again, I'm not using it any way other than to demonstrate a point. Fair enough?" ("Duquesne Fires.")

In many ordinary circumstances, the distinction between mention and use is clear. If Michael says he lives in Pennsyltucky, he is *using* the word "Pennsyltucky," a tongue-in-cheek portmanteau denoting the conservative nature of the Appalachian center of the state of Pennsylvania. If he says "'Pennsyltucky' is a tongue-in-cheek portmanteau," then he is mentioning the word and remarking on its status as a word.

But (and this was another deconstructive argument that unsettled the tenets of speech act theory), is he not also, in some sense, using the cited utterance? As Culler asked, in the course of his defense of Derrida against speech act theorist John Searle, "If I write of a scholar, 'Some of my colleagues think his work "boring and incompetent" or "pointless,"' what have I done? Have I used the expressions 'boring and incompetent' and 'pointless' as well as mentioned them"? (119).

This is precisely the problem with Professor Shank's utterance of the N-word: his insistence that he is using it "in a pedagogical sense," and "not using it any way other than to demonstrate a point," ignores the fact that his mention of the word is also a use of it—and that his use of it to demonstrate a point involves an unstated (and deeply problematic) claim that he has the right to do so, and the right to give his students permission to say it as well. Perhaps a more attentive teacher might have noticed that his students pointedly did not take him up on the offer to say it and that this was very likely a sign that it would be a bad idea for him to proceed to do so, even if in a "pedagogical" sense. (If the point of the discussion was that some words are off limits, didn't the silence of the students indicate that they already understood this very well?) This is a principle that holds not only for the N-word but for any proscribed or off-limits term (including a word for a person with intellectual disabilities that somehow remains pervasive in popular culture, despite the fact that for over a decade, Best Buddies International and the Special Olympics have explicitly asked people not to use it): any mention of it is also a use of it, even (or especially) if you are mentioning it *as* an example of a proscribed word. Here we will offer our colleagues some advice: don't mention it.

We disagree strongly with Professor Shank's firing. We think this is the kind of thing that could be resolved by an apology (a real one, not an ifpology), a conversation with a dean or department head, and a promise not to make this particular boneheaded pedagogical decision again. But what of the professor who uses the word "niggardly"? In 1999, Amelia Rideau, an English major at the University of Wisconsin–Madison and the vice chairwoman of the Black Student Union, reported to the faculty senate that one of her professors had used the term in the course of teaching *The Canterbury Tales*, and in fact had explained Chaucer's use of it, noting that the word means "miserly" and has no etymological connection to the racial slur. "I was in tears, shaking," she told the faculty. "It's not up to the rest of the class to decide whether my feelings are valid" (see Kors).

Had impact been elevated over intent—or, for that matter, over the context of *The Canterbury Tales* and the history of the English language—perhaps that professor would have been disciplined in some way. As it happened, however, the complaint backfired badly, leading to the faculty's decision to rescind a policy that had been in place for ten years, forbidding "demeaning verbal and other expressive behavior." That policy, "Prohibited Harassment: Definitions and Rules Governing the Conduct of UW–Madison Faculty and Academic Staff," had been the target of libertarians and conservatives throughout the 1990s, and one of the chief exhibits of restrictive speech codes on American campuses. But the idea that it would cover the classroom use of the word *niggardly* in the work of Geoffrey Chaucer understandably drove many of the proponents of the policy into the camp of their opponents.

More recently, as we noted in the introduction, Greg Patton was suspended from a course in business communication at the University of Southern California for using the Chinese word *that* in the course of a lesson on "filler" words like "um." The Chinese is *ne ga*, and most of Patton's Black students were offended by his use/mention of it. As reported by Colleen Flaherty in *Inside Higher Ed*, the students wrote a letter to the dean of the Marshall School of Business, Geoffrey Garrett, among others, describing Patton as insensitive and incapable of teaching the three-week intensive communications course.

"The way we heard it in class was indicative of a much more hurtful word with tremendous implications for the Black community," wrote the students, who identified themselves as Black M.B.A. Candidates c/o 2022. "There are over 10,000 characters in the Chinese written language and to use this phrase, a clear synonym with this derogatory N-Word term, is hurtful and unacceptable to our USC Marshall community. The negligence and disregard displayed by our professor was very clear in today's class."

Dean Garrett, in response, declined to point out that the Chinese phrase is a homonym rather than a synonym and removed Patton from the course without so much as a hearing. "It is simply unacceptable for faculty to use words in class that can marginalize, hurt and harm the psychological safety of our students," Garrett wrote. Patton "repeated several times a Chinese word that sounds very similar to a vile racial slur in English. Understandably, this caused great pain and upset among students, and for that I am deeply sorry." ("Failure.")

In cases like those of Shank and Patton, the role of the AAUP (and the ACLU, and FIRE) is clear and necessary: protection of faculty from unwarranted punishment and/or termination, and opposition to serious miscarriages of justice and abrogation of the rights of faculty. But it remains the case that it is a supremely bad idea to utter the N-word in any context, "pedagogical" or otherwise; that one should probably try to avoid the word "niggardly" in contexts other than *The Canterbury Tales* (surely the synonym "miserly" will avoid any semantic confusion); and that it might make more sense to use the Chinese word "this" instead of "that" when demonstrating the ubiquity of filler words in all languages, given that "this" is just as much of a placeholder for many Mandarin speakers as "that" but it sounds like "zhe ge" rather than "ne ga."

Our final example involves another case of etymological misprision, though it never became national news (for reasons that will be clear). For decades, a rumor has circulated in Black communities that the word *picnic* has violent racist origins linked to lynching. In fact, the word has French origins (*pique-nique*) that predate the phenomenon of lynching in the United States and literally means "each pick a bit." A few years after Michael arrived at Penn State in 2001, a Black graduate student objected to the announcement of a departmental picnic to begin the school year. Michael was familiar with the basis for the complaint but decided at the time that this was not the proper occasion for a senior white professor to etymologysplain to this student that he was mistaken about the provenance of the word. Moreover, just as "miserly" suffices for "niggardly," "potluck" would do quite nicely for "picnic," and for Michael's department, it did. (It also made it clear that people were expected to bring side dishes to share, as "picnic" did not.) Around the same time, in January 2004, the Jim Crow Museum of Racist Memorabilia at Ferris State University received a question as to the origins of *picnic*. David Pilgrim, the curator of the museum, responded with a lengthy, thoughtful reply about the history and practice of lynching, noting that lynchings were, for white people, often festive, protracted events involving food, drink, photographs (some of which became commemorative postcards), and souvenirs of burnt human flesh. Pilgrim's reply opens by establishing the proper provenance of "picnic":

> The etymology of the word picnic does not suggest racist or racial overtones. Picnic was originally a 17th Century French word, picque-nique. Its meaning was similar to today's meaning: a social gathering where each attendee brings a share of the food.

But Pilgrim's conclusion adds an important layer of nuance:

> The claim that the word picnic derived from lynching parties has existed in Black American communities for many years. Although many contemporary etymologists smugly dismiss this claim, it should be noted that there is a kernel of truth in this month's question. The word picnic did not begin with the lynching of black Americans; however, the lynching of blacks often occurred in picnic-like settings. ("Blacks, Picnics, and Lynchings")

Again, on the off chance that someone might flinch at the word "picnic," however mistakenly, "potluck" will almost always suffice.

In more recent exchanges, Michael has asked a copyeditor to remove the word "scalawag" from one of his essays, because he did not want to use a term with which neo-Confederate partisans cast aspersions on advocates of Reconstruction (and had forgotten that it was such a term). He also asked a group not to decry Donald Trump's "denigration" of critical race theory on the grounds that using "denigrate" as a synonym for "demean" (which it certainly is) is especially awkward in the context of matters of race since its etymological origins in Latin go straight to *niger*, and that it is just bad optics to object to the "blackening" of critical race theory, where blackening is understood to be a *bad* thing. Was he being over-fastidious about the possibility of giving offense? It does not seem so to us. English is a rich language with lots of synonymic redundancy built into it. It is not difficult or onerous or bothersome or vexatious to think of words other than "scalawag" and "denigrate."

There are two conclusions we want to draw from these incidents and examples. One is that it is not all that difficult to imagine contexts in which seemingly innocuous terms might give offense and to decide whether it is better to correct someone's misunderstanding of *niggardly* or *picnic* or quietly move on to a synonym. The other—which we will develop in the following chapters—is that cases like those of Greg Patton and James Livingston, in which faculty members were disciplined for the flimsiest of reasons, and cases like that of Gary Shank, in which a faculty member was fired without due process and for questionable cause at best, ultimately trivialize the far more serious problems presented by a Bruce Gilley or an Amy Wax. And the punishment contemplated for Betsy Schoeller—both by those who wanted to fire her and by those who wanted to subject her to severe monitoring—demonstrates vividly the vulnerability of contingent faculty, who generally need much more political support from the AAUP (and often, from their own administrations) than they have received thus far.

For just as it is critical to put these cases in their proper contexts, even knowing that in theory context is boundless and "picnic" can be a controversial word, it is crucial to put Gilley's advocacy of colonialism and Wax's beliefs in white supremacy in *their* proper contexts—the five-hundred-year history of imperialism and genocide, in Gilley's case, and the sorry history of racist social science based on racist pseudoscience, in Wax's. Just as the Black Lives Matter protests have led so many cultural institutions, from the Sierra Club to the Second City comedy troupe to the worlds of art, museums, classical music, and civic-minded nonprofit organizations, to revisit and redress their legacy of complicity with and perpetuation of institutional racism, so too must we revisit the limits of academic freedom. The cultural context for our understanding of it has changed.

CHAPTER 2

TALKING OUT
OF SCHOOL

ACADEMIC FREEDOM AND EXTRAMURAL SPEECH

It will not have escaped your notice that our examples in the previous chapter, like the vast majority of controversies over academic freedom and professorial speech over the past decade, have involved extramural speech rather than research or teaching. Doubtless this is due to the fact that social media now pervade practically every aspect of human interaction, such that we are only belatedly realizing that Facebook and Twitter are exceptionally useful devices for stirring up primal antagonisms and generating spontaneous festivals of outrage. And as we have noted, recent years have seen renewed right-wing initiatives to harass and intimidate controversial left-leaning faculty members, usually with the object of pressuring university administrations to fire them. We believe that as a rule, such campaigns are illegitimate, insofar as the AAUP has long held that "a faculty member's expression of opinion as a citizen cannot constitute grounds for dismissal unless it clearly demonstrates the faculty member's unfitness to serve," and that "[e]xtramural utterances rarely bear upon the faculty member's fitness for continuing service" (*Statement on Extramural Utterances* 31). However, as we will argue in this chapter, it is urgently necessary to understand how the principles of academic freedom apply to extramural expression so as to disentangle academic freedom from First Amendment rights to freedom of expression in the United States.

The relationship between academic freedom and extramural speech leads to widespread misunderstanding of the relation between academic freedom and free speech, so we will start by trying to clear up some possible confusion. In May 2018, the *Chronicle of Higher Education* published an essay by Judith Butler, "The Criminalization of Knowledge: Why the Struggle for Academic Freedom is the Struggle for Democracy." It is an eloquent essay—it is excerpted from her keynote address at the 2018 Scholars at Risk Global Congress in Berlin, an ideal occasion for an argument such as hers—and its subtitle is exactly right. But it is also a curious essay, for its passionate defense of academic freedom and freedom of expression runs directly counter to American traditions of academic freedom as enunciated and elaborated by the AAUP. Since Butler was not purporting to speak on behalf of the AAUP, it is not as if she was misstating anything; she was simply offering her interpretation of the relation between academic freedom and extramural professorial speech, which is one interpretation among many in a crowded field (in short: there is no such relation). Her defenses of both are robust and necessary. But her absolute distinction between the two is problematic, as we will proceed to show.

Drawing on the work of Joan Scott, Butler distinguishes academic freedom from freedom of expression—an entirely necessary move, made more urgent by recent debates about the weaponization of free speech by the white nationalist right and its campus acolytes. "Academic freedom," writes Butler,

> belongs to faculty members within universities who have been appointed for the purpose of teaching and pursuing knowledge.

Political expression is the right of citizens to expound upon political viewpoints as they please. They converge when academics who speak "extramurally" suffer retaliation or punishment within the university or are threatened with the loss of their positions. Thus the rights of academic freedom and extramural political expression require institutional structures and support within the university, and they require an explicit and enduring commitment from universities. Indeed, the task of the university is undermined when either of those freedoms is imperiled.

So far, there is nothing to quibble with here. But later on, the rigidity of this distinction becomes troublesome, as Butler takes Scott's distinction and runs with it:

Academic freedom and freedom of expression are not the same. The professional activities pertaining to one's academic position should be protected by academic freedom. The extramural utterances any of us make about the world we inhabit, the institutions in which we work, or any matter of public concern should be protected by rights of free expression.

Thus, Butler derives from Scott's distinction between academic freedom and freedom of expression the conclusion that the former pertains only to activities pertaining to one's academic position (and, presumably, to one's academic expertise, though this is a thorny question that will take up much of this chapter), whereas the latter is properly protected by the state, as it is by the First Amendment.

This is a reasonable account of academic freedom, one that would be recognizable in many countries—including, notably, the countries that do not have strong protections for freedom of expression, the countries to which Butler is implicitly appealing in this address (and sometimes explicitly, as when she names Turkey, Brazil, and Iran). But it is at odds with the American elaboration of academic freedom, which since 1940 has included extramural speech as an aspect of *academic* freedom, quite apart from any First Amendment considerations:

> College and university teachers are citizens, members of a learned profession, and officers of an educational institution. When they speak or write as citizens, they should be free from institutional censorship or discipline, but their special position in the community imposes special obligations. As scholars and educational officers, they should remember that the public may judge their profession and their institution by their utterances. Hence they should at all times be accurate, should exercise appropriate restraint, should show respect for the opinions of others, and should make every effort to indicate that they are not speaking for the institution. ("1940")

There is some problematic language in these final two sentences; we saw it invoked in the Betsy Schoeller case, and we will return to it below. But the general point is clear: extramural speech is one of three aspects of academic freedom, the other two pertaining to research and to teaching. Like the Holy Spirit of the Christian trinity, it is the most mysterious and the most elusive of the three.

One reason it is worth trying to clear up any potential confusion on this question is that the AAUP did and does lay claim to academic freedom for utterances Butler would leave to protection by the state; another reason is that the AAUP definition of academic freedom has profound implications for what it means when one is or isn't speaking from a position of credentialed intellectual expertise. This will be critical to any determination of professional "fitness," including the question of whether a commitment to white supremacism should be seen as disqualifying.

Scott's distinction between academic freedom and freedom of expression rests on the claim that the former is tied to the development and demonstration of credentialed scholarly expertise. In this she is aligned with theorists of academic freedom such as Robert Post, who argues that academic freedom and tenure are based on a social contract whereby the legitimation of free scholarly inquiry by specialists in a discipline ultimately serves the common good in an open society. But Scott's reliance on the idea of disciplinary expertise is complex, for she takes a notably generous approach to scholars who challenge disciplinary norms: in her most recent book, *Knowledge, Power, and Academic Freedom*, she cites a 1986 Committee A statement that "in many instances a show of disrespect for a discipline is, at the very same time, an expression of dissent from the prevailing doctrines of that discipline" (52). Too reverent a conception of disciplinary expertise, according to this statement, "may end by barring those most likely to have remade the field" (52). The immediate context for this statement had to do with critical legal studies (some aspects of which provided intellectual inspiration for critical race theory, as we note in chapter 4), but anyone familiar with Joan Scott's career would know that such a principle would resonate for someone who had to argue forcefully for many years against disciplinary norms in which gender was generally not regarded as a useful category of historical analysis.[1]

1. Indeed, immediately before citing the Committee A statement, Scott writes, "Those of us historians who challenged prevailing views in the name of disciplinary redefinition remember well the kind of opposition we faced

We have close at hand another example of why it is problematic to predicate academic freedom on strict disciplinary norms: one of us (that would be Michael) has published and spoken widely on disability studies in the humanities, though he has no degree in disability studies. The reason for this is that when he was in graduate school in the 1980s, there was no such thing as a degree in disability studies. The field only began to emerge in English—where he received his degree and then was employed in an English department—in the mid-1990s, and his work was part of that emergence. So, to add to Scott's argument about how academic fields can change thanks to people who "disrespect" a discipline and persuasively dissent from its norms, we can add that academic fields can emerge *ab nihilo*, as so many have in the past fifty years. (This development is routinely decried by people who believe for some reason that the content of a university education should be identical to what they remember from their undergraduate days fifty years ago.) Finally, and perhaps most obviously, there is what we might call the Noam Chomsky phenomenon: though Chomsky is trained as a linguist, and is indeed so influential in that field as to have become adjectival, he is principally known to the general public as one of the most severe critics of American foreign policy, and though his work on that front is both renowned and reviled, there is no question that it is substantial, so substantial that no one could plausibly claim that he is not entitled to academic freedom for his work outside the field of linguistics.

The relation between disciplinary expertise and academic freedom is therefore unstable, and matters are rendered still more

---

when we asked who got to count as a historian, what got to count as history, and how those determinations were made. . . . Men's rejection of women's history was taken as a defense of the integrity of the field" (50–51).

complex by the fact that the meaning of extramural speech, and the AAUP's understanding of the relationship of extramural speech to disciplinary expertise, has changed over time. To simplify the issue somewhat, we might say that over the years, the AAUP has tended to deemphasize the notion that a professor should exercise "appropriate restraint" and "show respect for the opinions of others" in his or her public remarks, on the grounds that those norms come dangerously close to upholding a standard of "civility" that the AAUP otherwise rejects as a precondition for academic freedom. The 1964 Statement, which we have quoted above and which insists that the relevant criterion for dismissal of a faculty member is the criterion of "fitness," was incorporated into the original 1940 Statement of Principles by way of the "Interpretive Comments" of 1970. That is the gold standard, the standard which we will proceed to discuss: not the manner of speech—it can be coarse and crude and altogether disrespectful of everything—but the question of whether it suggests that a professor is unfit to be a professor at all.

The origin of the 1964 Statement requires some explanation. It involves a landmark case in the history of academic freedom in the United States, and we beg the indulgence of readers who are already familiar with it.

Leo Koch was an assistant professor of biology at the University of Illinois at Urbana-Champaign. In March of 1960, two conservative students wrote an article for the student newspaper, the *Daily Illini*, in which they argued that people should remain celibate until marriage. Koch decided to reply—indeed, at great length. Over the course of 2,500 words, he blasted the double standard "which accepts as respectable premarital sexual experience for men but not for women," inveighed against the prudery of religious authorities, and concluded that

[w]ith modern contraceptives and medical advice readily available at the nearest drugstore, or at least a family physician, there is no valid reason why sexual intercourse should not be condoned among those sufficiently mature to engage in it without social consequences and without violating their own codes of morality and ethics. A mutually satisfactory sexual experience would eliminate the need for many hours of frustrating petting and lead to much happier and longer lasting marriages among our younger men and women.

The outcry was immediate and widespread: an outraged public demanded that Koch be fired, and the UIUC faculty and administration promptly folded under pressure. The executive committee of the College of Liberal Arts and Sciences voted for Koch's dismissal, and within three weeks UIUC President David Dodds Henry—for whom the central administration building at UIUC is named today—fired Koch, writing that Koch's letter was "offensive, repugnant and contrary to commonly accepted standards of morality and his espousal of these views could be interpreted as an encouragement of immoral behavior and that for these reasons he should be relieved of his University duties." Sadly, the faculty body ostensibly devoted to academic freedom was little better; the six-member Senate Committee on Academic Freedom voted for a reprimand rather than a dismissal (eleven days after Koch's dismissal), but argued that "Koch did commit a breach of academic responsibility, not because he publicly expressed controversial views on sexual mores, but because of the way in which he expressed them." That committee also pointed out that Koch had signed his letter as an assistant professor of biology, and therefore "wrote the letter as a biologist." This was apparently damning evidence that Koch was irresponsibly bringing his disciplinary expertise to bear on the matter of premarital sex, but as John K. Wilson has pointed out in a trenchant discussion of the case, Koch's academic specialty was the study of moss. Moss. One wishes that Koch's faculty colleagues had taken the trouble to mention this in their reference to him as a biologist. (The quoted passages in this paragraph and the preceding one can be found in Wilson's essay, "Academic Freedom and Extramural Utterances.")

Many years later, the film critic Roger Ebert, an alumnus of Illinois (but not a student at the time Koch was fired—he arrived on campus the following year), wrote about the context in which Koch's letter appeared:

> Most universities took aggressive steps to prevent sex among undergraduates. Students weren't allowed to live in their own apartments. In women's dormitories, a strict curfew was enforced, and too many "late minutes" in a semester would get you hauled up before a Disciplinary Committee. It was assumed that by locking down the women, you would prevent sex; gay sex was off the radar.
>
> Police patrolled lovers' lanes and shone spotlights into suspicious cars. If actual sex was observed, arrests were made. University Police checked local motel parking lots for license plates registered to students. If a couple returned to a woman's dorm early, they could share a sofa in the lounge, a brightly-lighted room monitored by matrons who enforced the Three Foot Rule. This wasn't as bad as it sounds. It didn't mean boy and girl had to be separated by three feet, but it did mean that three of their four feet had to be on the floor, if you follow me. ("Making Out")

That was the context in which Koch's letter appeared—and Koch never taught again after being fired from Illinois. We cite this because we believe that one of the things that makes Koch's case so poignant today is that if he had only waited seven or eight years to make his case for sexual experimentation among undergraduates, no one would have complained, if indeed anyone would have so much as noticed. The incendiary utterance of 1960 would become the common sense of 1968.

Yet the Koch case represented a major episode in the AAUP's understanding of extramural speech, which eventually precipitated the 1964 Committee A statement that a faculty member's expression of opinion as a citizen cannot constitute grounds for dismissal unless it clearly demonstrates the faculty member's unfitness to serve. Along the way, however, there was considerable disagreement within the AAUP about the Koch case—indeed, even within the AAUP's Committee A on Academic Freedom and Tenure.[2] For our purposes, the important thing is that as a result of that debate, and no doubt partly as a result of the swiftly changing cultural context that would make Koch's sentiments seem entirely unobjectionable within a decade, the 1970 Interpretive Comments on the 1940 Statement of Principles incorporated the 1964 Statement on Extramural Utterances and rendered it all but irrelevant whether a professor is exercising appropriate restraint and showing respect for the opinions of others. The relevant criterion, *the only one*, is whether the speech is evidence of unfitness to serve. It is possible, theoretically, for an utterance to be so unrestrained and vicious as to suggest unfitness—but it is extremely difficult.

Still, the standard is that "extramural utterances *rarely* bear upon the faculty member's fitness for continuing service." What about the cases in which they arguably do? We mentioned the Steven Salaita case in the previous chapter, where the context was the difficulty of

2. For a detailed account of those disagreements, see Tiede, "Extramural Speech, Academic Freedom, and the AAUP: A Historical Account."

determining the relevant context of an utterance. Now we need to revisit it, because of a particularly pernicious argument that was made in favor of his de-hiring. The fact that it was made by Cary Nelson, a former president of the AAUP and the author of *No University is an Island: Saving Academic Freedom*, renders it something to which attention must be paid.

In the 2015 issue of the *AAUP Journal of Academic Freedom*, Nelson argued that Salaita's tweetstorm about Israel's incursion into Gaza in 2014 *did* demonstrate his unfitness to serve precisely because they were related to his area of scholarly expertise. Nelson's essay on Salaita opens with this statement from Matthew Finkin's and Robert Post's book *For the Common Good: Principles of Academic Freedom*:

> The most theoretically problematic aspect of academic freedom is extramural expression. This dimension of academic freedom does not concern communications that are connected to faculty expertise, for such expression is encompassed within freedom of research, a principle that includes both the freedom to inquire and the freedom to disseminate the results of inquiry. Nor does extramural expression concern communications made by faculty in their role as officers of institutions of higher education. Freedom of extramural expression refers instead to speech made by faculty in their capacity as citizens, speech that is typically about matters of public concern and that is unrelated to either scholarly expertise or institutional affiliation. (127)

Thus, for Nelson, Salaita's comments, though made on Twitter, did not properly constitute extramural speech and therefore had implications for the evaluation of his fitness to be a professor at all. Note that this is rather different from the claim that Salaita's tweets would have a chilling effect on any Jewish students who might enroll in his classes, a claim that was made in response to the argument that Salaita had had, to that point, nothing in his teaching record to suggest that he would be problematic in the classroom. Rather, Nelson's argument was that Salaita's tweets deserved less protection under principles of academic freedom than, say, a series of tweets suggesting that the Apollo moon landings never happened, because they concerned a subject about which Salaita had also written and taught as a disciplinary expert.

The potential application of this argument to the relation between academic freedom and extramural speech is troubling: it establishes an inverse relation between academic freedom and scholarly expertise, and redefines certain forms of extramural speech as intramural. As we remarked in the introduction, it is more damaging to one's intellectual and professional legitimacy for a historian to deny the Holocaust than for a professor of electrical engineering to do so (and here we are referring to Arthur Butz of Northwestern University), because one expects that the disciplinary protocols of history departments would militate far more strenuously against Holocaust denial than the disciplinary protocols of electrical engineering; Holocaust denial would seem to offer *prima facie* evidence that one is unfit to be a professional historian. By that token, a series of tweets from Steven Salaita about faked moon landings could not possibly be taken as evidence of professional unfitness; they would merely be evidence that Salaita subscribed to a belief associated with a fringe of conspiracy theorists. And yet the form of Salaita's statements was undeniably extramural precisely because they were tweets, and there are chilling consequences to the argument that the more well informed a professor's tweets may be, the more they involve his or her area of scholarly expertise, the less protection they deserve as a matter of academic freedom.

In order to address this argument, we need to go back to where it started, with Finkin and Post's chapter on extramural expression. It is a brilliant discussion, and we will walk through it carefully; in the course of doing so, we will revisit Judith Butler's argument as well. But first, we need to pause over their definition of extramural speech as "speech made by faculty in their capacity as citizens, *speech that is typically about matters of public concern and that is unrelated to either scholarly expertise or institutional affiliation.*" This is the move that then allows Nelson to argue that Salaita was justly fired. But as Joerg Tiede, AAUP senior program officer, notes, "although [Finkin and Post] cite AAUP policy statement throughout, this definition does not coincide with the AAUP's understanding of extramural speech, which can be documented by considering the AAUP reports of investigations involving dismissals of faculty members because of their extramural utterances" (109). On first blush, it makes sense to construe extramural speech as speech that is not related to scholarly expertise, because, as Finkin and Post note, scholarly expertise is ordinarily covered by freedom of research. But there is no language in the 1940 Statement or the 1970 Interpretive Comments that defines extramural speech as speech about matters of public concern unrelated to scholarly expertise; the principle says only that extramural speech occurs when faculty members "speak or write as citizens." Quite apart from the principle that no faculty member in the United States gives up a right of free speech upon taking an academic job, it should be obvious that faculty members might speak or write as citizens *either* on a matter close to their area of expertise (as when a Constitutional scholar argues that the Supreme Court case of *Shelby County v. Holder* was an evisceration of the Voting Rights Act) or on matters of general public concern (as when a Constitutional scholar argues that *Brokeback Mountain* should have won the Best Picture Oscar in 2006 over

Crash). Granted, it is more likely that an extramural utterance that draws on a professor's area of expertise will bear more heavily on the question of unfitness than an utterance that is unrelated to that area. But the AAUP definition of extramural speech does not specify *any* relationship between extramural speech and scholarly expertise.

However, when Finkin and Post address the rationales for why extramural speech should be considered an aspect of academic freedom rather than (per Butler) left to the protection of the state, they are convincing. On their account, there are three such rationales, and two of them are problematic. The first "rests on the premise that it is difficult and dangerous to set artificial limits on faculty expertise, so efforts to distinguish speech within a scholar's competence from speech outside that competence ought to be discouraged" (133). This approach, Finkin and Post argue, "is fraught with conceptual difficulties":

> It suggests that the very category of extramural expression is super-fluous because it is entirely indistinguishable from freedom of research. It also implies that professional standards of care and rigor ought to apply to extramural speech. . . . Most fundamentally, it seems implausible to claim that *all* extramural expression by faculty is connected to freedom of research and publication. It may be difficult to draw lines in particular cases, but surely we are not utterly incapable of distinguishing between speech that does and does not express scholarly expertise. (135–36)

Our closing example in this chapter will demonstrate that it is indeed difficult to draw lines in particular cases, but for now, let us grant that a Constitutional scholar who says that *Brokeback Mountain* should have won the Best Picture Oscar in 2006 over *Crash*, like an astronomer or a comparative literature scholar or a mechanical engineer who says the same thing, is doing so outside their scholarly expertise. (There is an argument that a film scholar who disagrees is manifestly unfit to teach film, but we will leave that to other commentators.)

The second line of argument involves something we will call the "risk management" approach to academic freedom, and it centers—as do so many of these controversies—on faculty members whose utterances provoke general outrage and demands for their firing. Pusillanimous university administrators can be cowed by arguments that their controversial faculty member is damaging the reputation of the institution (and, in the case of public universities, funding by the state legislature). Indeed, university administrators are too often cowed by such arguments, and matters can become especially intense if the faculty member has angered donors and trustees. As Finkin and Post write,

> Fundamental principles of academic freedom require institutions of higher education to resist public pressure to punish professors . . . whose research causes public outrage. But it is plain that universities and colleges would be placed in an extremely awkward position were they to refuse to discipline speech protected by freedom of research and publication, but seek to appease public indignation with regard to extramural expression that is unrelated to professional competence. (137)

Universities and colleges are placed in this extremely awkward position all the time, so, according to this line of thought, "institutions of higher education would thus strengthen their ability to protect freedom of research if they refused categorically to accept responsibility for the expression of their faculty, regardless of the precise connection between such expression and the academic expertise for which faculty have been hired or trained" (137–38). It is hard to see how this could work in practice. Though a professor might make every effort to indicate that they are not speaking for their institution, the purveyors of outrage will still insist that insofar as their university continues to employ them, the university is endorsing their statements, or, at a bare minimum, tolerating them. Finkin and Post therefore propose an analogy:

> Freedom of extramural expression can on these grounds be defended as a good strategy for minimizing the institutional vulnerability of institutions that must protect freedom of research. Just as universities and colleges disclaim responsibility for the many conflicting contentions of the millions of books that they collect in their libraries, so that no one can plausibly claim that a university supports a geocentric view of the solar system merely because its library contains a copy of Ptolemy, so universities and colleges can disclaim responsibility for the many conflicting political contentions of their faculty, so that no one can plausibly claim that a university supports the Palestinian cause because a computer scientist in its engineering department happens to take that position. (138–39)

The analogy nicely encapsulates what is wrong with this approach. No one would object to a university having Ptolemaic works in its library, because it is widely understood that university libraries, and libraries in general, are supposed to contain works of the past whose contents are not taught or promoted today but remain important because they are significant documents of intellectual history. But controversial statements or positions of living faculty members never receive the Ptolemaic exemption, and people generally understand that universities are paying faculty members and providing them with platforms whereas universities are not employing Ptolemy and allowing him to undermine heliocentrism. Indeed, advocacy of the Palestinian cause is routinely and sometimes viciously targeted by purveyors of outrage. The above passage is footnoted, and the footnote effectively unravels the argument: the pro-Palestinian computer scientist in the engineering department is Sami Al-Arian, the former University of South Florida professor whose post-9/11 interview on *The O'Reilly Factor* led to his firing. (He was initially placed on paid administrative leave and became a civil liberties *cause célèbre*, but was fired after he was indicted in 2003 on seventeen counts under the Patriot Act. A jury acquitted him on eight counts and deadlocked on another nine, but he was imprisoned for years, often in solitary confinement. The federal government did not drop its baseless charges against him until 2014, and even then only as part of an agreement that Al-Arian be deported.) The footnote references the AAUP's 2003 report on Al-Arian's case, but only with regard to the question of whether the University of South Florida successfully argued that Al-Arian failed to indicate that he was not speaking for his institution. (The AAUP found that USF did not do so.) If you want an example of a university failing to defend a professor's extramural speech, the case of Sami Al-Arian is arguably one of the most compelling.

But again, Finkin and Post are *not* endorsing this line of thought. We wish they had said more about its impracticality, but we agree with their critique of this risk-management approach: "viewed in this way, however, freedom of extramural expression ceases to constitute a distinct right of academic freedom, but instead finds its justification in counsels of institutional expedience and prudence" (139). In Al-Arian's case, of course, institutional expedience and prudence led USF President Judy Genshaft to fire Al-Arian the moment he was indicted by the federal government. Finkin and Post therefore close their discussion by outlining a far more robust and holistic model of academic freedom that offers decisive protection for extramural speech:

> Beginning with the premise that the experience of freedom is indivisible, this justification of freedom of extramural expression postulates that faculty can promote knowledge or model independent thought in the classroom only if they are *actively* and *imaginatively* engaged in their work. If faculty experience their institutions as repressive, they will be vulnerable to forms of self-censorship and self-restraint that are inconsistent with the confidence necessary for research and teaching. The harm would be enhanced if faculty were confused about which communications were protected by freedom of research and which communications would be exposed to punishment if freedom of extramural speech were not a recognized dimension of academic freedom. (139)

Finkin and Post point out that "such confusion would be inevitable" because of the blurriness of the line between statements based on scholarly expertise and statements unrelated to scholarly expertise; thus, "on this account, freedom of extramural expression is conceptualized as a prophylactic protection for freedom of research and freedom of teaching" (140).

This is key, and it is what Judith Butler's argument misses. To return to that argument: "The extramural utterances any of us make about the world we inhabit, the institutions in which we work, or any matter of public concern should be protected by rights of free expression." Indeed they should. As we have argued, there is no sense in which a professor in the United States should be understood to have forfeited any Constitutional freedoms upon taking a job at a college or university. But the First Amendment right to free speech concerns prior restraint of speech by the government; it does not cover speech that offends one's employer, as any number of fired ex-employees can tell you. Anyone can defend the right of faculty members to make controversial remarks while simultaneously insisting that they be fired by their universities. And this, in turn, takes us to matters that touch on "cancel culture" in general, so before we turn to our closing example (which will involve exactly this dynamic of acknowledging a professor's right to speak while demanding that he be fired), we need to take a brief detour into the controversy over cancel culture that followed the publication of the "Harper's Letter" in July 2020.

As is now well known, that letter, signed by 153 artists and writers, took the occasion of the nationwide protests over the murder of George Floyd to declare that

> this needed reckoning has also intensified a new set of moral attitudes and political commitments that tend to weaken our norms of open debate and toleration of differences in favor of ideological conformity. As we applaud the first development, we also raise our voices against the second.

This aspect of the letter—its status as a response to the police killings of unarmed Black citizens—was widely criticized, and that criticism, for some of letter's authors and signatories, bore out their complaint about the constriction of open debate. That complaint was this:

> The free exchange of information and ideas, the lifeblood of a liberal society, is daily becoming more constricted. While we have come to expect this on the radical right, censoriousness is also

spreading more widely in our culture: an intolerance of opposing views, a vogue for public shaming and ostracism, and the tendency to dissolve complex policy issues in a blinding moral certainty. We uphold the value of robust and even caustic counter-speech from all quarters. But it is now all too common to hear calls for swift and severe retribution in response to perceived transgressions of speech and thought. More troubling still, institutional leaders, in a spirit of panicked damage control, are delivering hasty and disproportionate punishments instead of considered reforms. Editors are fired for running controversial pieces; books are withdrawn for alleged inauthenticity; journalists are barred from writing on certain topics; professors are investigated for quoting works of literature in class; a researcher is fired for circulating a peer-reviewed academic study; and the heads of organizations are ousted for what are sometimes just clumsy mistakes. Whatever the arguments around each particular incident, the result has been to steadily narrow the boundaries of what can be said without the threat of reprisal. ("A Letter on Justice and Open Debate")

The first and last sentences of this passage are perhaps the most problematic, making empirical claims about the boundaries of debate that seem (to us and to many skeptical readers) ahistorical at best; and the waving away of details in the phrase "whatever the arguments around each particular incident" allows the letter to conflate manifest miscarriages of justice (David Shor being fired by Civis Analytics for circulating a study that showed that the 1968 riots helped Nixon) with utterly ordinary examples of people being criticized or fired for being really bad at their jobs.

We will mention, under this latter heading, two editors who ran "controversial pieces": James Bennet at the *New York Times* and Ian

Buruma at the *New York Review of Books*. Neither editor simply ran "controversial pieces." Bennet, after publishing an openly fascist op-ed by Senator Tom Cotton (R-AR) calling for military violence against peaceful protestors ("Send in the Troops"), acknowledged that he had not read the piece before running it. Buruma, after publishing an essay by Jian Ghomeshi, gave an interview to Isaac Chotiner in which he professed astonishing indifference to the question of whether Ghomeshi's essay was full of misrepresentations, also known as lies: "The exact nature of his behavior [i.e., Ghomeshi's sexual assaults]—how much consent was involved—I have no idea, nor is it really my concern" ("Why Did"). Ghomeshi's essay had portrayed him as the victim of a "contemporary mass shaming," and following suit, Buruma played from the same deck, telling Cara Buckley of the *New York Times*, "I made a themed issue about #MeToo perpetrators who were not convicted by the judiciary but by social media. And now I am on the pillory myself."

Lest these examples seem a bit far afield from a discussion of academic freedom and extramural speech, let us explain: the question at issue in the firings of Bennet and Buruma is one of *fitness*. Did they behave in such a fashion as to call into question their fitness as editors? We believe the answer to this question is a great deal less complicated than Bennet's and Buruma's supporters have made it out to be, and we further believe that their firing poses no threat whatsoever to the free exchange of information and ideas, the lifeblood of a liberal society. For it is a truth universally acknowledged that an editor should read things before publishing them and should care about whether the claims made in an essay are true or false. We have no animus toward Bennet, and we admire a great deal of Buruma's work. For that matter, we also admire the work of many of the signatories of the *Harper's* letter, if not their decision to sign it. But the letter conflates objectionable forms of mobbing and public shaming with incidents in which people were *rightly* criticized—and faced consequences. (Journalist Kara Swisher and others have begun referring to "consequences culture" in order to bring some perspective to the overuse of "cancel culture.") To argue that Bennet and Buruma were victims of social media cancel culture is to come uncomfortably close to the modus operandi of pundits who like to pretend that the principle of free speech forbids criticism of their work.

That's one important point of contact between the *Harper's* controversy and the question of extramural speech: when a professor does or says something that indicates their unfitness to be a professor, then, like an editor who has done an execrable job as an editor, that professor should be fired.

The other point of contact concerns the relation between the powerful and the powerless. It did not take long for critics of the *Harper's* letter to note that its signatories were luminaries, renowned artists and intellectuals whose work enjoys international platforms; as Hannah Giorgis wrote in the *Atlantic*, "That the signatories of a letter denouncing a perceived constriction of public speech are among their industries' highest-paid and most widely published figures is a large and obvious irony" ("Deeply Provincial"). In response, some of the signatories acknowledged their relatively prominent positions but argued that the letter's concerns addressed the very real worries of young and unestablished writers who are especially vulnerable to social media attack. Our own sense of this claim is that the letter would have been a lot more effective on this front if it had actually mentioned the plight of young and unestablished writers who are especially vulnerable to social media attack. But we share the concern voiced by Michelle Goldberg, one of the signatories whose work we admire most, when she wrote about the politics of firing people:

It's the involvement of human resources departments in compelling adherence with rapidly changing new norms of speech and debate that worries me the most.

In her scathing rejoinder to the Letter in *The Atlantic*, Hannah Giorgis wrote, "Facing widespread criticism on Twitter, undergoing an internal workplace review, or having one's book panned does not, in fact, erode one's constitutional rights or endanger a liberal society."

This sentence brought me up short; one of these things is not like the others. Anyone venturing ideas in public should be prepared to endure negative reviews and pushback on social media. Internal workplace reviews are something else. If people fear for their livelihoods for relatively minor ideological transgressions, it may not violate the Constitution—the workplace is not the state—but it does create a climate of self-censorship and grudging conformity. ("Do Progressives . . . ?")

Responses like Goldberg's moved the debate over the letter to new terrain, sparking a broader conversation, in social and in traditional media, about whether people in the knowledge-and-opinion industry deserve greater protection from mobs with pitchforks and torches. The real problem, suggested some commentators, is the at-will doctrine of employment itself, which allows an employer to fire an employee for any reason or for none at all.

And at that point, the relation between the *Harper's* letter controversy and the need to see extramural speech as a component of academic freedom became dazzlingly clear to us. We will say more about the involvement of human resources departments—and offices of diversity, equity, and inclusion—in chapter 6, where we will explain in more detail why we share Goldberg's concern. For now, however, we want to stress that if academic freedom were understood as Judith Butler describes it, as a matter of research and teaching, leaving extramural speech to the protection of the state, this is what would ensue: *people would fear for their livelihoods for relatively minor ideological transgressions.* As Goldberg says, this may not violate the Constitution, but it does create a climate of self-censorship and grudging conformity. This is what tenure and academic freedom were designed to guard against. This is why the third, most comprehensive rationale discussed by Finkin and Post is the right one: the experience of freedom is indivisible, and extramural speech must be protected as a prophylactic protection for freedom of research and teaching.

Now extend that argument to the 75 percent of faculty members in the United States who do not and will never enjoy the protections of tenure. If we, the authors of this book, are the rough equivalents of the *Harper's* signatories—far less renowned, to be sure, but still among academe's privileged members—non-tenure-track, contingent faculty are the vulnerable employees who fear for their livelihoods for any real or imagined transgression. That is why outrage-driven campaigns against untenured faculty are especially dangerous and often effective, and that is why we need to understand—or you need to understand, and we need to argue—that they too require academic freedom, as the AAUP defines it, in order to do their jobs. The academic freedom committee we propose in chapter 6 is intended to add a layer of protection that doesn't now exist for contingent faculty, even as it also offers the promise of holding tenured faculty accountable for misinformation.

WE RETURN TO the question of unfitness in the following chapter. We conclude this chapter with the example we promised earlier. We think it is especially resonant partly because it involved a junior faculty member (on the tenure track but not tenured), but mostly because it involved the generation of political outrage over an issue that has become ever more desperately urgent since the time of its occurrence.

In the spring semester of 2017, University of Wisconsin–Madison assistant professor Damon Sajnani offered a course called "The Problem of Whiteness," drawing the ire of Republican state legislators who demanded his firing—in December 2016, before the class began. The course itself should never have been controversial, and would not have been if not for the fact that for some very sensitive white people, along with some white people who understand that naming whiteness inevitably undermines white supremacist presumptions of universality and therefore protest its naming every time it happens, the very phrase "the problem of whiteness" is a problem. Professor Sajnani's webpage for the course (https://african.wisc.edu/content /problem-whiteness) clearly cites W. E. B. Du Bois's famous question from *The Souls of Black Folk*, "how does it feel to be a problem?", as well as Richard Wright's remark, "there is no Negro problem in the United States. There's only a white problem." According to the course description, "whiteness studies considers how race is experienced by white people. It explores how they consciously and unconsciously perpetuate institutional racism and how this not only devastates communities of color but also perpetuates the oppression of most white folks along the lines of class and gender. In this class, we will ask what an ethical white identity entails, what it means to be #woke, and consider the journal *Race Traitor*'s motto, 'treason to whiteness is loyalty to humanity.'" The University of Wisconsin defended the course, as well it should have, since it draws on a century and more of Black critical thought on whiteness and white supremacy, from Du Bois to Ta-Nehisi Coates; and one could argue, as did one intrepid (white) student writing for the student paper, the *Badger Herald*, that the backlash against the course demonstrates nicely why the course is necessary (Niehans):

> "The Problem with Whiteness" is not that every single white person is racist. "The Problem with Whiteness" is that in 2017, there are still people who are afraid that their white privilege will be taken away by a professor teaching a class on what it means to be white. . . . Sajnani has an opportunity this semester to engage in a meaningful dialogue with his students about the significance of whiteness in today's society, and frankly, it's a conversation we could all benefit from.

The legislator leading the campaign against Sajnani was Wisconsin state representative Dave Murphy, and for the most part his outrage followed the usual right-wing script with regard to public universities—that they are beholden to whatever the "taxpayers" are willing to pay for.[3] "UW-Madison must discontinue this class," Murphy declared. "If UW-Madison stands with this professor, I don't know how the University can expect the taxpayers to stand with UW-Madison." Helpfully, Murphy added in a statement emailed to the *Washington Post*,

> I support academic freedom and free speech. Free speech also means the public has the right to be critical of their public university. The university's handling of controversies like this appears to the public as a lack of balance in intellectual openness and diversity of political thought on campus.

3. This is especially galling at a place like Penn State, where state appropriations make up about four percent—yes, you read that right—of the university budget. The university's critics, in effect, are saying *we pay four percent of your salary, so we are entitled to monitor one hundred percent of your thoughts.*

Leaving aside the fact that the class had not yet been taught, and the more striking fact that even then-governor Scott Walker refused to back up Murphy's threat, it's notable here what the conflation of academic freedom and free speech can do. Opportunistically, that conflation erases any sense that academic freedom has something to do with the development of scholarly expertise, something not to be judged by a plebiscite, and replaces it with a free-for-all in which everybody gets to be "critical of their public university." The banner of "intellectual openness and diversity" Murphy waves is also useful for proponents of Intelligent Design and can in principle be extended to flat-earthers, anti-vaxxers, and people who believe the moon landings were faked.

But there was a complicating factor. Representative Murphy also cited a pair of Sajnani's tweets from July 2016, when five Dallas police officers were killed by a sniper. One consisted of a photo of CNN's coverage of the shootings, accompanied by the remark, "Is the uprising finally starting? Is this style of protest gonna go viral?" (see Wootson). The other read, "watching CNN, this is the song I am currently enjoying in my head" and linking to "Officer Down" by Uno the Prophet (see Savidge). (Sajnani is himself a hip-hop artist, stage name Professor D.us, lead singer for the Dope Poets Society.) Of course, it might be remarked that Black critical thought in popular culture has included many protests against police brutality, from Ice-T's "Cop Killer" and N.W.A.'s "Fuck tha Police" all the way back to that revolutionary West Indian figure who admitted he shot the sheriff (in self-defense) even though he did not shoot the deputy. And especially in 2020, after the murders of Breonna Taylor and George Floyd (among so many others), followed by dramatic video recordings of rampaging police officers in cities from coast to coast, it is not difficult to sympathize with the profound anger and frustration many people of color feel upon seeing their brothers and sisters killed by police officers who face legal consequences for their actions only in the most extraordinary of circumstances.

And yet there is arguably something discomfiting about the spectacle of a college professor apparently cheering on the murder of police officers, all the more so when the statements he makes have a nontrivial relation to his work as a scholar and teacher. The tweets do not openly express glee; in another context, they might even be read as apprehensive (*is this style of protest gonna go viral? oh no, if it does the police will mow us down by the hundreds*), except for the fact that Sajnani claimed to be "enjoying" rather than simply "thinking about" the song "Officer Down." Again, the course, "The Problem of Whiteness," is not a problem; the people who tried to make it a problem are a problem. But the tweets are problematic and might warrant the recommendation of a reprimand by an academic freedom committee—though certainly not firing or suspension.

We do not pretend to be able to adjudicate every such case in the country, and we see no need to cite the numerous other examples of faculty members who have come under fire for their extramural speech. But the Sajnani case strikes us as exemplary, not only because it continues to speak to political questions that remain on the nation's front burner but also because it demonstrates vividly how important it is to see extramural speech as an aspect of academic freedom that serves as prophylactic protection for freedom in research and teaching—even or especially when that speech cannot be clearly distinguished from a professor's research and teaching. Throughout this book, we are trying to strike a balance between individual hard cases and broad principles for rethinking the meaning of academic freedom. The necessity for this balance will become even clearer, we believe, in the following chapter, when we turn to the question of what constitutes "unfitness." For certainly, the question of unfitness has to be decided on a case-by-case basis. We will not attempt to address every case of alleged unfitness, but we hope the cases we do address provide some general guidance—and are compelling in their own right.

CHAPTER 3

WHAT IS A FIRING OFFENSE?

As we saw in the previous chapter, extramural utterances rarely bear upon a faculty member's fitness to serve. But of course that principle does not close the door completely: the AAUP does not say that extramural utterances *never* bear on fitness. What, you might ask, about cases in which they do? Again, we do not want to enumerate case after case, since we are ultimately concerned with the broader question of whether academic freedom extends to tenured white supremacists (and, less sensationally and from another direction entirely that we take up in chapter 6, to adjunct faculty as a whole who currently have very few, if any, protections). But a few recent examples help shine light on what kinds of beliefs and utterances can be deemed so outrageous as to be disqualifying across the board.

The first is that of James Tracy, the former associate professor in the School of Communication and Multimedia Studies at Florida Atlantic University who earned notoriety for promoting the theory that the Sandy Hook massacre of 2012, in which twenty young schoolchildren and six staff members were killed in Sandy Hook Elementary School, was in fact a "false flag" operation staged by proponents of gun control. In 2013, Florida Atlantic reprimanded

Tracy, saying that he had not done enough to make it clear on his personal blog that he was not speaking for the institution (notably, the university did not speak to the content of Tracy's work). By 2015, however, the stakes had risen considerably, as Tracy had become a go-to source for Sandy Hook "truthers" nationwide—and had begun harassing some of the grieving parents who had lost their children. Two of those parents, Veronique and Lenny Pozner, responded by writing an essay in the *South Florida Sun Sentinel* in which they noted that

> this professor achieved fame among the morbid and deranged precisely because his theories were attached to his academic credentials and his affiliation with FAU. Tracy has enjoyed tremendous success from this exposure and has since leveraged it into a popular Internet blog and radio program. Worse yet, it has elevated his status and fame among the degenerates that revel in the pleasure of sadistically torturing victims' families.
>
> It cannot be denied that Tracy has carved out a significant presence in the same Sandy Hook "hoax" conspiracy movement that has inspired a wave of harassment, intimidation and criminal activity against our family and others.
>
> In fact, Tracy is among those who have personally sought to cause our family pain and anguish by publicly demonizing our attempts to keep cherished photos of our slain son from falling into the hands of conspiracy theorists.
>
> Tracy even sent us a certified letter demanding proof that Noah once lived, that we were his parents, and that we were the rightful owner of his photographic image. We found this so outrageous and unsettling that we filed a police report for harassment. Once Tracy realized we would not respond, he subjected us to ridicule and con-

tempt on his blog, boasting to his readers that the "unfulfilled request" was "noteworthy" because we had used copyright claims to "thwart continued research of the Sandy Hook massacre event."

Florida Atlantic University fired Tracy in 2015. Tracy sued the university, charging that he had been fired for his views in violation of the First Amendment; in 2017, a federal jury rejected that claim. Florida Atlantic, in its defense, insisted that Tracy had been fired not for the content of his beliefs but because he flouted university regulations governing the reporting of outside activities and (again) failed to disassociate himself adequately from the university.

We strongly suspect that the First Amendment doctrine of viewpoint neutrality discouraged Florida Atlantic's attorneys from mounting the argument that Tracy's views were, in fact, disqualifying for a faculty member—as we believe they are. Let us not mince words about that. We strongly believe that anyone who claims that mass shootings such as Sandy Hook are staged events orchestrated by advocates of gun control is *prima facie* incompetent, unqualified to teach any relevant subject in any university in the United States. (Tracy also expressed a similar skepticism about the 2015 San Bernardino shooting that killed 14 and wounded 22.) The fact that Tracy was a tenured professor of media and communication studies is obviously relevant to his extramural utterances, according to the principles we set out in the previous chapter; his courses, listed on his faculty web page at FAU, were "Culture of Conspiracy," "American Media, Society, Tech," and "Public Opinion and Modernity." It is therefore difficult to discern any daylight between his areas of expertise and his utterances as a Sandy Hook denier. It does not seem hard to make the case that his utterances indicate an unfitness to teach. Last but not least, we know of no understanding of academic freedom, not even the most generously libertarian version, that would permit a tenured professor to harass and torment people like Veronique and Lenny Pozner.

Florida Atlantic played it safe, arguing that it was firing Tracy on grounds of insubordination, not on the grounds of unfitness. It need not have. Indeed, we believe it is a serious mistake to defend Tracy's academic freedom to promote vicious and easily disproven falsehoods while claiming to fire him only because of procedural regulations involving disclosure of outside activities and disclaimers. As the editorial board of the *Sun Sentinel* argued in its support for Tracy's removal, such a broad and flimsy conception of academic freedom threatens to delegitimate tenure entirely:

> Yes, freedom of thought and expression should flourish at universities, but so should high standards of research. If a professor wants to be famous for controversial theories, let him first offer some peer-reviewed proof.
>
> Tracy's behavior also should stoke the debate in Florida about whether tenure is a good thing, or whether its virtual "lifetime job" guarantee allows some professors to become lazy, incompetent or, in this case, a never-ending embarrassment to the university and its community. In September, the State College of Florida near Bradenton became the first state community college to drop tenure for new professors, in part so that the college could fire misbehaving professors more easily. Look for the trend to spread. ("Tenure Be Damned")

This too is one of the regrettable effects of the confusion of academic freedom with free speech: the loss of any sense that academic freedom relies on a rigorous system of peer review by which tenure is granted. It is a sad day when a newspaper editorial has to remind academics that academic freedom depends on academic rigor.

The case of Joy Karega at Oberlin College is a bit more complicated; it has more layers and went through more phases. The issue at bottom, however, is the same as with Tracy: whether some beliefs and utterances are evidence of unfitness to serve. Karega first came to national attention in 2016, when *Inside Higher Ed* framed her case as a question of whether academic freedom "extends to falsehoods." The context at Oberlin was that earlier in the academic year, "several hundred students and alumni at Oberlin College expressed their concerns about what they described as escalating anti-Semitic rhetoric on campus." Karega's vocal support for the Boycott, Divestment, and Sanctions (BDS) movement was singled out by the pro-Israel blog *The Tower*, which noted that Karega was promoting the theory that the 2015 Islamist attack on the Paris offices of *Charlie Hebdo* was in fact a false flag operation conducted by Mossad, the Israeli intelligence agency ("Unacademic Freedom?"). Leaving aside for a moment that point of overlap with James Tracy's conspiracy-mongering, Karega would seem easy enough to defend: we strongly affirm the right of our colleagues to support BDS, and we have no difficulty reaffirming the basic truth that criticism of the state of Israel is not identical with anti-Semitism.

But added to Karega's *Charlie Hebdo* theory, which takes us into a realm populated largely by anti-Semites and assorted crackpots, were Karega's statements that ISIS itself, the Islamist terrorist organization, is really Mossad and the American CIA in disguise: "I promise you, ISIS is not a jihadist, Islamic terrorist organization. It's a CIA and Mossad operation and there's too much information out there for the general public not to know this." This was but one of many unlikelihoods promulgated by Karega, along with the theory that Israel, and not pro-Russian separatists in Ukraine, had shot down Malaysia Airlines Flight 17 in 2014, and Louis Farrakhan's belief that Israel was responsible for the attacks of September 11, 2001.

Colleen Flaherty, writing in *Inside Higher Ed*, pointedly drew the connection to James Tracy, who by then had been fired by Florida Atlantic:

> Certainly there's more of a consensus around senseless gun violence involving children than there is around the Israel-Palestine debate. But the two different institutional responses suggest that there are different schools of thought as to whether patent falsehoods are protected by academic freedom.

The final section of Flaherty's article, bearing the lively subhead, "Covering the Crap? It Depends," turns to Joerg Tiede and John K. Wilson of the AAUP, British libertarian theorist of academic freedom Joanna Williams, and Stanley Fish, all of whom forge a rough consensus that Karega's remarks are not evidence of unfitness to teach unless they directly impinge on her teaching—a difficult call, it would seem, insofar as one of her areas of expertise was "social justice writing." Tiede, for his part, passes on the question of whether academic freedom protects rank falsehoods, as is standard AAUP practice:

> Tiede said AAUP doesn't make such "judgments of substance" but rather defers to a committee of the professor's peers. In any case where a professor's fitness is called into question by public statements, he said, the faculty member should be entitled to hearing before an elected faculty body that considers the professor's professional record as a whole.

We will return to this point, because, as it happened, Karega was eventually reviewed by a faculty body that recommended her dismissal, and she was fired in November 2016. For now, though, we want to call attention to Wilson's defense of Karega, which adduces the other famous University of Illinois case from the early 1960s (i.e., the one not involving Leo Koch)—that of the palindromic Revilo P. Oliver, the classics professor who promoted a conspiracy theory about the assassination of John F. Kennedy.

We have already remarked on the absurd injustice of the Koch case; at the time, the disparity between the university's response to Koch and to Oliver was striking and widely remarked on. The consensus of history, with which we concur, is that the University of Illinois at Urbana-Champaign did right by Oliver and not by Koch— and that Koch's statements seem, in retrospect, far more innocuous and well grounded than Oliver's. But the comparison between Oliver and Karega raises a thorny question too often unaddressed by free-speech absolutists like Wilson with regard to academic freedom. At what point does the promulgation of a falsehood, or of a demonstrably ungrounded belief, become so dangerous that the promulgation itself is disqualifying, so long as it has a plausible relation to a faculty member's area of expertise (be it "culture of conspiracy" or "social justice writing")? To get at that question, we have to be willing to do what cannot be done under the First Amendment but must be done with regard to academic freedom—make judgments about the content of the utterances in question.

Or, to return to the argument of chapter 1: we need to make judgments about the *contexts* of the utterances in question. To wit: Revilo P. Oliver's belief that Lee Harvey Oswald was part of a Communist conspiracy network that had infiltrated much of American media is highly idiosyncratic. To read his controversial essay, "Marxmanship in Dallas"—which induced William F. Buckley to sever ties between Oliver and the *National Review*, for which he had served as a book reviewer—is to go down a rabbit hole full of perfervid far-right fantasies not unlike those of QAnon today:

> It is quite true that the Communist Conspiracy, through the management of great broadcasting systems and news agencies, through the many criminals lodged in the radio and press, and through many indirect pressures (such as the allocation of advertising and harassment by bureaus of the federal government), have a control over our channels of communication that seems to us, in our moments of discouragement, virtually total. As was to be expected, a few moments after the shot was fired in Dallas, the vermin, probably in obedience to general or specific orders issued in advance of the event, began to screech out their diseased hatred of the American people, and, long after the facts were known to everyone, went on mechanically repeating, like defective phonograph records, the same vicious lies about the "radical right" until fresh orders reached them from headquarters.

The reference to journalists as "vermin" is a tad disconcerting, to be sure, but otherwise, the belief that Communists control much of American society—this despite the purges recently undertaken by McCarthyism—is bog-standard wackadoodlery for the American far right of the early 1960s. Later in his career—indeed, not long after this essay was published—Oliver moved still further right, breaking with the John Birch Society he had co-founded ("Marxmanship in Dallas" was originally published in the Bircher magazine *American Opinion*) and taking up with neo-Nazis and white supremacists such as Willis Carto, founder of the National Youth Alliance, NYA member William Luther Pierce, author of *The Turner Diaries*, and the Institute for Historical Review, perhaps the most prominent organization devoted to Holocaust denial. Under the standards we are advocating here, a professor who followed Oliver's trajectory today would not enjoy the protection of academic freedom for white supremacist and neo-Nazi activities. Elaborate paranoid theories about the Kennedy assassination, however, are as common as rain; Quincy Jones, in a 2018 interview with *New York* magazine, disclosed the surprising fact that the real assassin was Chicago mobster Sam Giancana, and he is not the only person who believes this (see Marchese). For a popular alternate theory, developed by New Orleans district attorney Jim Garrison, consult Oliver Stone's 1991 film *JFK*. Or make up your own.

Moreover, Oliver's theory about the Kennedy assassination bears no conceivable relation to his academic work as a classicist, whereas Tracy and Karega spouted conspiracy theories that are arguably closely related to their academic work. But the crucial point for us here is that the political context for Revilo's "Marxmanship in Dallas" essay is the fever swamp of postwar American ultraconservatism, à la Phyllis Schlafly and Barry Goldwater; he has not yet crossed over into the shadowy world of the neo-Nazis. And there is no way that Oliver could have operationalized his odd beliefs about JFK, just as, if Steven Salaita had been a Moon landing denialist, there would be no practical consequences for those beliefs. Whereas the beliefs of Karega and Tracy operate in very different contexts: Karega is reading from a global network of anti-Semitic beliefs, some of which eventuate in actual attacks on synagogues and the offices of *Charlie Hebdo*; Tracy is participating in a national network of radical gun-rights advocacy that provides the infrastructure (and the literal ammunition) for America's plague of mass-murder shooting incidents. It can be argued, therefore (and so we will argue), that the beliefs of people like Karega and Tracy are demonstrably more dangerous, more conducive to murderous political violence, than the beliefs of someone who has a highly developed fantasy life with regard to the Kennedy assassination. Admittedly, one wing of the Kennedy conspiracy-mongering enterprise wound up having direct ties to neo-Nazis, white supremacists, and Holocaust deniers. Oliver's subsequent career clearly demonstrates as much. But at the time of "Marxmanship in Dallas" he would have appeared to be a more harmless conspiracy theorist—too far out for the *National Review* but right at home in the John Birch Society.

In his 2019 book, *The Future of Academic Freedom*, former Committee A chair Henry Reichman (with whom both of us have worked closely) writes that "a strong case can be made that Karega did not deserve to be dismissed" (59). In support of that case, he adduces remarks by Steven Lubet, Williams Memorial Professor of Law at Northwestern University, who wrote,

> I am wary of disciplining any professor for extra-academic writing or social media posts, no matter how obnoxious, so long as they are not reflected in her teaching or interactions with students. I work at a university where Arthur Butz—one of the nation's premier Holocaust deniers—has been teaching electrical engineering for decades. As far as anyone can tell, he respects the line between his deeply offensive prejudices, which he does not express on campus, and his teaching assignments. Perhaps Karega could do the same (although perhaps not). ("The Mess at Oberlin," quoted in Reichman 59–60)

Lubet's last sentence, for us, undoes the analogy to Butz. Reichman then quotes at length Jonathan Marks, a professor of politics at Ursinus College and frequent contributor to *Commentary* magazine:

> I oppose firing academics over constitutionally protected hate speech, whether it is directed against blacks, Muslims, women,

homosexuals, or Jews. I share the view of old fashioned liberals that, at least at colleges and universities, we run little risk in giving wide latitude to rotten and even unhinged ideas. If we limit ourselves to firing only people whose terrible ideas undermine their ability to teach, conduct research, and serve on committees, we will probably be rid of most Karegas anyhow.

The excerpt quoted by Reichman goes on to conclude that "[d]isgusting and unhinged views will always be with us. Our dedication to the protection of speech and academic freedom cannot be contingent on the elimination of such views" ("Is Anti-Semitism," quoted by Reichman at 60). Again, we note here the unfortunate conflation of freedom of speech and academic freedom. And we are quite aware of the fact that we are effectively proposing a less liberal conception of academic freedom than that of someone writing in *Commentary* to defend a professor with manifestly anti-Semitic beliefs about the worldwide Jewish conspiracy. (After all, one of the reasons we have written this book is to question the views of "old fashioned liberals.") But we are struck by Marks's confidence that "we will probably be rid of most Karegas anyhow"—only if it is determined that her beliefs affect her teaching, research, or service. This seems too close to the position that extramural speech can *never* be relevant to fitness. It seems to us that Karega's statements, like Tracy's, present more of a problem for the determination of fitness than Marks (or Lubet, or Wilson, or even Reichman) is acknowledging—though notably, there is no evidence that Karega ever harassed anyone as Tracy did the Pozners.

Reichman goes on to explain that the AAUP did not open an investigation into Karega's dismissal because Karega, unlike Steven Salaita, was provided with every measure of due process including a review by a faculty body, and the AAUP, as a faculty body itself, is not in the business of swooping onto a campus and overturning the decisions of local faculty:

> It is not the AAUP's role to function as some sort of court of appeals to review the substance of faculty decisions, especially when the institutional processes pursued hew closely to AAUP guidelines. It is not up to the AAUP to decide which faculty members should be granted tenure, which should be dismissed, or which should be disciplined and how severely they should be punished. That is the responsibility of the faculty and administration at the institution concerned, acting within the parameters defined by the 1940 *Statement* and derivative AAUP policies. While there were faculty members who would not have recommended Karega's dismissal, the fact that a duly constituted faculty committee did in the end so recommend suggests that the AAUP's procedural standards were essentially followed. (61)

Reichman is right that AAUP precedent defers to the procedures of faculty review at individual institutions and that the AAUP does not operate (as many faculty unfortunately believe) as a supra-institutional device for overturning the results of such reviews. But we note that this deference to faculty governance at Oberlin puts a substantial dent in Reichman's framing remark that "a strong case can be made that Karega did not deserve to be dismissed." Perhaps. But a strong case was made by Karega's peers that she *did* deserve to be dismissed, and we find that case more persuasive—not merely on procedural grounds, but on substance.[1]

1. Reichman unfortunately follows this discussion with a caveat that damages his argument about deferral to the judgment of faculty review procedures: "To be sure, however, not all faculty committees are truly representa-

tive, and not all disciplinary proceedings are fair. The case of Ward Churchill in Colorado some years ago is one example of how a handpicked and biased 'faculty committee' can serve as a useful tool for the violation of genuine due process rights, as an exhaustive report prepared by the AAUP's Colorado Conference demonstrated" (61–62).

The "exhaustive report" of the Colorado Conference—a body of three UC faculty—is, in our opinion, terrible. Though the details of Churchill's case are complex, and reasonable people can disagree as to whether (a) Churchill's research fraud merited dismissal and (b) the investigation was colored by the controversy over Churchill's notorious "little Eichmanns" remark about the people killed on 9/11, the Colorado Conference report simply refuses to admit that there is anything wrong with writing scholarly articles, signing other people's names to them, and then citing that work in articles written under your own name. The Investigating Committee Report concluded, with good reason, that this constituted research fraud:

> We find that the publication of one's own scholarly work . . . under another name constitutes . . . [academic misconduct]. The failure is aggravated when the name used belongs to another actual person, especially one working in the same field, whether or not the other person consents to this use of his or her name. The failure is particularly egregious when a misattribution of one's own writings to another actual person is then exploited by the author by using the misattributed work as apparently independent authority for claims that he makes in his own later scholarship, as Professor Churchill has done. . . . Moreover, a reader of Professor Churchill's work . . . cannot help but encounter other instances of his citation to these works as authority. This sequence of events permits the author to create the false appearance that his claims are supported by other scholars when, in fact, he is the only source for such claim. (89–90; qtd. in Colorado Conference Report at 102)

The Colorado Conference Report responds by thoroughly misconstruing the issue at hand, citing UC professor of sociology Tom Mayer:

Tracy and Karega are examples of professors whose beliefs are so outrageous, so untethered to anything resembling reality, research, or reason, that they lost their jobs. But they are not utterly anomalous. On the contrary, they have counterparts in two faculty members who suddenly became controversial as we were writing this book. Those cases are perhaps more disturbing than those of Tracy and Karenga, not only because they involve people who remain in good standing as we write, but because they suggest that "controversial"

> Having dismissed the plagiarism charge, the investigating committee should have dropped the matter altogether. Instead, the committee resorted to an ad hoc reformulation of the misconduct charge, bringing up the issue of ghostwriting. According to its strained and adventitious interpretation of the standing rules, publishing one's own work under another name constitutes research misconduct. This interpretation effectively proscribes using a pseudonym or ghost writing of non-fiction papers and books. Yet not only is the practice of ghost writing relatively frequent, but during times of political repression (e.g. the McCarthy era and perhaps today) it enables vulnerable scholars to publish and participate in public discourse. The notion that ghost writing of non-fiction work is impermissible is not only pernicious but astonishing. Ghost writing is common in the fields of medical research, political commentary, and biography. . . . (103)

This is a jawdroppingly bad argument, suggesting that neither Mayer nor the Colorado Committee understood that ghostwriting does not entail using the names of actual people and then citing them as independent support for your own claims.

Reichman is of course correct that some faculty review committees can be handpicked surrogates for administration. But in the case of Ward Churchill, there is far more reason to be skeptical of the Colorado Conference Report than the report of the Investigating Committee that rightly found Churchill guilty of research fraud.

faculty members can spew nonsense for years without attracting the attention of anyone but their outraged students—whose complaints are not always pursued.

The first is the strange case of Mark Crispin Miller, an accomplished and influential media theorist. Miller apparently began going off the rails after 9/11, the official account of which he calls "preposterous on its face," and now is so far from any rail that he believes (among other things) that the Sandy Hook shootings were a false flag operation and that Black Lives Matter is funded by the CIA.[2] But he only came to attention for these things in the midst of the COVID-19 pandemic, since his brand of COVID trutherism placed him at the forefront of the cranks who claim not only that mask mandates are tyranny but that vaccines are poison—in Miller's words, "a rushed, inhuman witch's brew of nanoparticles, human DNA (from fetal cells), and toxic adjuvants." Cultural critic Mark Dery, writing in the *Chronicle of Higher Education*, asked the obvious but necessary question: *how did this happen?*

> How does a leading light in media studies, known for his trenchant critiques of the role played by advertising and the media in manipulating public opinion, and for sounding the alarm about the threat posed to democracy by the media monopoly—fewer and fewer corporations controlling more and more of our news and entertainment outlets—morph into a lapel-grabbing true believer who fervently believes, on top of everything else, that "the Great Reset"—the World Economic Forum's rebranding of the pandemic as a historic

2. See Mark Dery, "The Professor of Paranoia," *Chronicle of Higher Education*, May 12, 2021. https://www.chronicle.com/article/the-professor-of-paranoia. Michael is quoted twice in Dery's article.

opportunity to radically rethink society and the economy along more sustainable, equitable lines—is in fact a vast eugenicist conspiracy? Bill Gates, George Soros, the Rockefellers, the Windsors (!), Ted Turner (a "eugenicist" whose "huge herds of bison" will feed the globalist cabal), they're all in it together: a monstrous plot to eradicate the unfit so the puppet masters can have the planet all to themselves, while the rest of us subsist on lab-grown "human steak."

Dery provocatively answered his question by suggesting that Miller's decline could have its basis partly in the discipline of media studies itself, specifically the ostensibly "left" version dominant in most universities: "Was there always a conspiratorial undertow to media studies, a paranoid style of mind that might make the transition from 'media monopoly' to 'deep state' easier than it seems?" But Miller's beliefs are not common in his discipline, and they go all the way to full-blown delusion. Our sense is that if Miller is indeed teaching such material in his course on "Mass Persuasion and Propaganda," he should be treated as someone who tells students that the secret Apollo 18 mission discovered hostile life forms on the Moon, which killed both astronauts in the lunar module and ensured that we would never return to the Moon again (though NASA has covered this up for almost fifty years).[3] The only difference between Miller and the hypothetical believer in Apollo 18, we think, is that Miller's beliefs have the potential to do real

3. This shocking truth was finally revealed in the documentary film *Apollo 18* (2011), but the leaked footage recorded by the mission's astronauts was, perhaps predictably, spun by the film industry and the Deep State as "fictional." To this day no one has challenged the official NASA narrative or demanded a formal inquiry.

harm in the world, linked as they are to a network of profoundly un-hinged people sharing similar material on social media.

There is one aspect of Miller's case, however, that has interest-ing implications for the larger argument of this book: the letter of complaint authored by 25 of his colleagues in NYU's Department of Media, Culture, and Communication. The letter calls for an "expe-dited review" of Miller's "intimidation tactics, abuses of authority, aggressions and microaggressions, and explicit hate speech"; Miller responded by suing his colleagues for libel. Dery incisively asks, "Why did his colleagues, in the letter that provoked his lawsuit, fo-cus not on his seeming disregard for core academic values like intel-lectual rigor and objective fact, at a moment when the very notions are under assault, but rather his alleged 'hate speech,' 'microaggres-sions,' and transphobia?" The answer, we propose, is that NYU has an office and a procedure for dealing with hate speech, microaggres-sions, and transphobia. It does not have an office or a procedure for dealing with faculty whose teachings violate every standard of legiti-mate and responsible research. And so Mark Crispin Miller's case is adjudicated by means of a category error, as if the real problem is his allegedly nasty attitude and transphobia rather than his manifestly falsifiable claims about COVID-19. *That* is why universities need academic freedom committees.

The case of Gregory Christainsen at California State University–East Bay is more straightforward but also (as we will see in the remain-der of this chapter) more unsettling in its implications for the history of white supremacist research and teaching on American campuses.[4]

4. See Jason Fagone's admirably thorough account, "The 'Race Realist' on Campus," *San Francisco Chronicle*, June 24, 2021. https://www.sfchronicle .com/projects/2021/race-realist-cal-state-east-bay/

Christainsen is a "race realist" who teaches that there are measurable differences in the intelligence of various "races," that these differences are captured in IQ scores, and that they are attributable to genetics rather than to social variables. These beliefs have of course been central to pseudoscientific racism for over a century; but only in this century have they been rebranded as "race realism," a term that asks you to believe that the charlatans peddling long-debunked beliefs are in fact steely-eyed realists willing to confront the hard truths of life.

Christainsen does not have any expertise in biology, genetics, evolution, or the study of intelligence. He is an economist. He began teaching at Cal State–East Bay in 1983, moving quickly through the ranks to full professor by 1988, and apparently did not turn to "race realism" until the Obama years. He retired in 2016, and since then has enjoyed emeritus status that allows him to continue teaching.

In one sense Christainsen is out of place in a discussion of what constitutes a fireable offense, since he cannot be fired; the only question before his colleagues and his university, now that his work has come to light (thanks in part to the interview he gave to the white supremacist website American Renaissance in September 2020), is whether his emeritus status should be revoked. (We think it certainly should.) But in another sense he is central to our argument precisely because he was *not* fired—or rebuked, or censured, or disciplined in any way. On the contrary, he continued to be rewarded by his department, continued to serve on tenure and promotion committees, continued to earn a salary in the low six figures—even after a student filed a complaint about him 2014. That complaint involved Christainsen's course in public sector economics, and "the syllabus promised lessons in government finance and health insurance markets" (Fagone); what alarmed the student, Alex Bly, was that Christainsen spent most of the course promoting "race realism." As Jason Fagone reports:

Originally from Texas, Bly, now 35, said she found the experience "surreal." One day, she said, Christainsen gave students an article about how Jews run Hollywood. It struck her as a classic anti-Semitic trope, which "blew my mind," she recalled. But it also seemed irrelevant: What did Jews in Hollywood have to do with public sector economics?

About halfway through the semester, around March 2014, Bly drafted a complaint about the class. She addressed it to Jed DeVaro, chair of the economics department. To protect herself from possible retaliation, Bly created an anonymous email account.

She hit send, then waited for the university to do something.

For our purposes, there are three issues here. One is that Gregory Christainsen was effectively teaching students that phlogiston exists in all combustible substances and is released in combustion. The second is that he was teaching students about phlogiston in courses that purportedly address public sector economics—and that were requirements for economics majors at Cal State–East Bay. The last is that even though academic freedom does not cover the teaching of phlogiston or the teaching of phlogiston in courses about public sector economics, Alex Bly's complaint never received a response.

The student body at Cal State–East Bay is 86 percent nonwhite. The Gregory Christainsen case might well serve as Exhibit A of the disconnect between the changing demographics of American higher education and the entrenched, unshakeable beliefs of the white supremacist professoriate.

IF WE ARE going to maintain that the promotion of white supremacy is disqualifying for a college professor, we need first to establish a basis for determining whether a professor can be fired for his or her beliefs. Having done so, we can now try to address the white elephant in the room. For as the case of Gregory Christainsen suggests, the problem here is unfathomably larger than any one Bruce Gilley or Amy Wax.

In July 2020, Lawrence Mead, a professor of politics and public policy at NYU, published an essay in the journal *Society*, titled "Poverty and Culture." The article immediately sparked controversy and calls for its retraction, on the grounds that its argument was not only overtly racist but utterly unsupported by scholarship on poverty. (Mead assumes throughout, for example, that the poor are unemployed, thereby conveniently ignoring the vast numbers of working poor who have not seen an increase in the minimum wage since 2009.) There is no question, we think, that the argument is racist. The really challenging and daunting thing about it, however, is that is not an outlier and not unsupported by other scholarship. On the contrary, it draws on decades of white supremacist work in the social sciences, including much of Mead's prior work.

The thesis is simple, and probably familiar to you: poverty is not, by and large, caused by structural oppression, historical and compounded inequities, or racism. It is caused primarily by cultural differences, by which Mead means the enterprising individualist culture of "the West" and the collective, less-than-enterprising cultures of the "non-West": "Today, the seriously poor are mostly blacks and Hispanics, and the main reason is cultural difference. The great fact is that these groups did not come from Europe. . . . Their native stance toward life is much more passive than the American norm." Mead argues that the non-West is the source of "minorities": "the West has simply chosen a more ambitious way of life than the non-West, where minorities originate. An enterprising temperament, historians suggest, chiefly explains why the West has dominated the globe in recent centuries." You will not be surprised to learn that there is no footnote to indicate which "historians" have suggested this. Nor need there be one, apparently, because this belief is so entrenched in the Samuel Huntington "clash of civilizations" school of thought, the leading contemporary exponent of which is probably Niall Ferguson, that it almost literally goes without saying; it certainly, as here, can often go without citing. But you might be surprised to learn that Hispanics—who, last we checked, came to the Americas from Spain—are part of the "non-West" in which minorities originate. It is the clash-of-civilizations version of the Iberian Expulsion—not about the fifteenth-century expulsion of Jews from Spain, of course, but about the ideological expulsion of Spain from Europe.

If the relegation of Hispanics to the non-West were not bad enough, Mead treats his readers to some straight-up anti-Black racism, laced with a degree of ignorance that should embarrass anyone claiming the title of professor:

> Academics blame black social problems on white oppression. By that logic, the problems should have been worst prior to the civil rights reforms in the 1960s. But in fact the opposite occurred. The collapse of the black family occurred mostly *after* civil rights rather than before. Most blacks came from a highly collective society in Africa, then lived under slavery and Jim Crow in the South. Those structures kept disorder at a low level. In that era, black levels of crime and female-headedness were not much higher than among whites. But blacks lost that structure after many migrated to the Northern cities in the last century, and especially after Jim Crow was abolished in the 1960s. So black social problems escalated even as opportunities broadened.

One hardly knows where to begin. Should one point out that the black family was nonexistent under slavery, insofar as marriage was illegal and children were routinely sold away from their mothers? Natal alienation would seem relevant to any historical understanding of the "black family." Or should one point to the fact that the white pathologization of the black family continually moves the goalposts? Remember, for Daniel Patrick Moynihan, the "female-headedness" of the black family was a problem that subtended the entirety of American history prior to the post-civil rights era: *The Negro Family: The Case for National Action* was published in 1965. Mead, by contrast, agrees that female-headedness is a problem—but not before 1965, only afterwards. Or should one remark on the Gilley-esque implication that slavery and Jim Crow had benefits for black families, by keeping "disorder at a low level"? Or should one stop and marvel at length at the culturally illiterate claim—again, embarrassing for anyone with the title of professor—that "Africa" is a highly collective society? It is surely but a half-step from there to the belief that Africa is a backward country.

Not long after Mead's essay was published, Mohamad Bazzi, a professor of journalism at NYU, tweeted a series of screenshots of excerpts of what he called "this stunning article" (those screenshots are now all that remain of Mead's article on the internet; see Bazzi).[5] The tweets drew the attention of Timothy Burke, a historian and Africanist at Swarthmore who from 2002 to 2021 maintained a highly respected blog, "Easily Distracted" (he has since moved, like so many other bloggers, to Substack). Burke proceeded to compose a nearly 3,500-word blog post detailing the numerous inaccuracies and failures of scholarship in Mead's essay. We have

5. As we note in the Works Cited, Bazzi's Twitter thread was "unrolled" and preserved as a single document at https://threadreaderapp.com/thread /1286740934466719744.html.

enumerated a few of these above, because they were evident to us and should be familiar to any decently literate person; but what was especially striking about Burke's response was his breakdown of the claim that Africa is a highly collective society. We apologize for the length of this citation (for which we have Burke's permission), but we feel sure that the richness of detail will prove the point of the astonishing oversimplifications underwriting Mead's misinformation.

First off, we're not dealing with one generically "African" perspective across that vast geographical and chronological space, and we're not dealing with collective or individual perspectives that remained unchanged during that time. I'm going to be somewhat crudely comparative here (but what I'm calling crude is essentially about ten magnitudes of sophistication above Mead's crayon scrawling: in his 2018 essay "Cultural Difference", Mead says "most blacks came from Africa, the most collective of all cultures"). Consider then these differences, quickly sketched:

a. Igbo-speaking communities in the Niger Delta/Cross River area between 1600–1800 famously did not have chiefs, kings or centralized administrative structures but were woven together by intricate commercial and associational networks, and in these networks both men and women strove to ascend in status and reputation and in wealth (both for themselves and their kin). There was a strong inclination to something we might call individualism, a tremendous amount of emphasis on aspiration and success and something that resembled village-level democracy.

b. Mande-speaking societies associated with the formation of the empire of Mali in the upper Niger and the savannah just west of the Niger and subsequent "tributary" empires like Kaaba in upper Guinea were structured around formal hierarchies and around the maintenance of centralized states with an emperor at the top of the hierarchy. But they also invited Islamic scholars to pursue learning and teaching within their boundaries (and built institutions of learning to support them) and reached out to make strong new ties to trans-Saharan merchants. Moreover, the social hierarchies of these societies also had a major role for groups of artisans often called nyamakalaw: blacksmiths, potters, weavers, and griot[s] or "bards," who not only were a vibrant part of market exchange but who also had an important if contested share of imperial authority that involved a great deal of individual initiative and aspiration.

c. The Asante Empire, one of a number of Akan-speaking states in what is now Ghana, rose to pre-eminence in the 18th and 19th Century, and both its rulers and its merchant "middling classes" showed a tremendous amount of personal ambition and investment in individual aspiration, as did their antagonists in the Fante states to the south, who were heavily involved in Atlantic trade (including the slave trade) and who were very much part of Atlantic commercial and consumer culture. Cities like Anomabu and Cape Coast (and others to their east) were commercial entrepots that in many ways resembled other cosmopolitan Atlantic port cities in Western Europe and the Americas.

d. (I can keep going like this for a long while.) But let's throw in one more, just because it's illustrative, and that's the Kingdom of Dahomey. It was an authoritarian state—though so was most of "the West" in the 17th and 18th

Century, coming to that soon—but it was also deeply marked by religious dissent from those who profoundly disagreed with their ruler's participation in the Atlantic slave trade, as a number of scholars have documented, as well as very different kinds of personal ambitions on the part of its rulers.

e. The upshot is that you cannot possibly represent the societies from which Africans were taken in slavery to the Americas as conformist, as uniformly authoritarian, as fatalistic or uninterested in personal aspiration, or as unfamiliar with competitive social pressures. I think you can't represent any of them in those terms (I'm hard-pressed to think of any human society that matches the description) but none of the relevant West or Central African societies do. It's not merely that they don't match, but that they had substantially different ideas and structures regarding individual personhood, labor, aspiration, social norms, political authority, etc. from one another. ("Mucking Out Mead")

Burke's post is dated July 28, 2020; the following day, an "editor's note" appeared online at the head of the article, reading, "Concerns have been raised with this article and are being investigated. Further editorial action will be taken as appropriate once the investigation into the concerns is complete and all parties have been given an opportunity to respond in full." (We do not mean to imply that Burke's post alone was responsible for this note; the outcry sparked by Mead's article was immediate, loud, and widespread.) Two days later, the editor-in-chief of *Society*, Jonathan B. Imber, Jean Glasscock Professor of Sociology at Wellesley College, together with Springer

Nature, the publisher, retracted the article. Imber has since stepped down as editor-in-chief.

This regrettable sequence of events seems to us right and just, for as with Gilley's "The Case for Colonialism," the publication of "Poverty and Culture" appears to have rested on editorial judgment that is questionable at best, and certainly not in line with standard academic practice (see also, above, in the world of journalism, Ian Buruma and James Bennet). As Imber explained in a statement, his decision "was a mistake, and one I deeply regret. My intent was to have this commentary published alongside two critical reviews of his 2019 book, *Burdens of Freedom*, on which Mead's commentary is based, that identify flaws in Mead's arguments. The decision was entirely my responsibility and no other member of the editorial board of *Society* was consulted or participated in that decision" (Flaherty, "Journal Editor Regrets"). Mead, for his part, refused to agree to the retraction.

But the mention of Mead's book *Burdens of Freedom: Cultural Difference and American Power* raises the larger question at stake. *Burdens of Freedom* was published by the conservative press Encounter Books, not by an academic press, but it testifies to the fact that for Mead, "Poverty and Culture" was not a one-off. Quite the contrary, the ideas in that essay are the foundation of Mead's career; in fact, *Society* had recently published (in 2018) a substantially similar essay by Mead, "Cultural Difference." And Mead has been recycling this material for quite some time; as Burke notes in his blog post,

> It also takes some astonishing arrogance and laziness to say that arguments that racial bias, lack of access to education, or lack of access to child care play a role in causing structural poverty have been flatly and undebatedly disproven—with only a footnote to your own book written in 1992 as proof of that claim.

Furthermore, it is not as if Mead is an obscure academic, quietly ruminating on why people of color lack individual initiative while whittling on his front porch; he is, by all accounts, one of the most influential voices in American public policy on welfare, having provided the intellectual apparatus for welfare "reform" in the 1990s as enacted by Rudolph Giuliani in New York City and President Clinton at the federal level. (One of the blurbs for *Burdens of Freedom* reads, "Lawrence Mead's ideas have formed much of the political basis for the sweeping national reforms of the American welfare system since the 1990s." That blurb was provided by former New York Health and Welfare Commissioner Jason Turner.)

The problem with Mead, therefore, is not the narrow question of whether "Poverty and Culture" was properly peer reviewed. It is not even whether his account of poverty or his characterization of "African society" makes any sense. One last time, we will turn to Timothy Burke, whose conclusion is very much in line with our larger argument in this book:

> I've bothered to lay all this out because I want people to understand that many critiques that are dismissed breezily as ideological or "cancel culture" derive from detailed, knowledgeable, scholarly understandings of a given subject or concept—and that in many cases, if a scholar or intellectual is arguing that another scholar should not have a platform to publish and speak within it is because the work they are producing shows extraordinary shoddiness, because the work they are producing is demonstrably—not arguably, not contentiously, but unambiguously—untrue. And because it is so dramatically bad, that work has to raise the question of what that scholar's real motivation is for producing that work. Sometimes it's just laziness, just a case of recycling old work. That isn't anything that requires public dismissal or harsh critique.

But when the work is not only bad, but makes morally and politically repellant claims, it's right to not merely offer public criticism but to raise questions about why a respectable scholarly journal would offer a place to such work: it mocks the basic ideals of peer review. It's right to raise questions about why a prestigious university would regard the author of such work as a person who belongs on its faculty and tout him as an expert consultant in the making of public policy. That may be an accurate description of his role in setting policy on poverty in the past and his past work may possibly be not as awful as this recent work (though the contours of some of this thinking are visible, and reveal anew just how deeply flawed the public policy of the Clinton Administration really was). This is not about punishing someone for past sins, nor for their political affiliations. It is about what they have chosen to put to the page recently, and about the profound intellectual shoddiness of its content, in service to ideas that can only be called racist.

There is no question, we believe, that Mead's article makes morally and politically repellant claims, just as Gilley's "The Case for Colonialism" and "Was It Good Fortune to be Enslaved by the British Empire?" do. But as to the question of whether it is "bad" in a scholarly sense—well, yes, of course. It is very bad. But then that judgment is an indictment not merely of this essay but of the entire "clash of civilizations" school of which it is a part. And now the white-supremacist dominoes start to tumble.

Let us imagine an historian who decides to troll his field as Bruce Gilley has done with regard to colonialism: let us imagine an historian who publishes an article or a book arguing that after the Civil War, Reconstruction failed because newly freed Black people were incapable of exercising the franchise properly and ill equipped for self-government. Let us further imagine that this historian proposes that the withdrawal of Federal troops from the South after the corrupt election of 1876 was a good thing, and that his account of the following decades makes passing mention, or no mention at all, of the system of white terrorism that produced thousands upon thousands of lynchings and the so-called race riots that involved mass murders of Black people and the wholesale destruction of Black neighborhoods from Wilmington, North Carolina to Atlanta, Georgia to Springfield, Illinois to Tulsa, Oklahoma—to name just a few.

That historian would not have far to look for support for the argument. It was for many years the dominant strain of historiography in the United States, inaugurated by Columbia professor William Archibald Dunning and carried on by his legions of students for generations. The Dunning school was, in effect, the intellectual arm of the neo-Confederate, white supremacist movement that continued to prosecute the Civil War—with great success. The derogatory and heavily laden terms "carpetbagger" (for Northerners who came to the South for political or economic reasons) and "scalawag" (for Southerners who supported Reconstruction) made their way into countless American history textbooks, and there was an entire cottage industry devoted specifically to besmirching the record and the person of President Ulysses S. Grant. The archive of the Dunning school is impressively large and impressively influential. It was, in effect, the academic accomplice to Jim Crow.

Nor is the Dunning school itself anomalous in the history of American academe. Charles Mills argues, rightly, that white supremacism suffused much of what passed as history and social science in the first half of the twentieth century in American universities:

Consider, for example, an anthropology founded on the "obvious" truth of racial hierarchy. Or a sociology failing to confront the central social fact of structural white domination. Or a history

sanitizing the record of aboriginal conquest and black exploita-
tion. Or a political science representing racism as an anomaly to a
basically inclusive and egalitarian polity. Or, finally—in my own
discipline—a political philosophy thriving for forty-plus years
and supposedly dedicated to the elucidation of justice that makes
next to no mention of the central of racial *injustice* to the "basic
structure" of the United States and assumes instead that it will be
more theoretically appropriate to start from the "ideal theory" assumption that society is the product of a mutually agreed upon,
non-exploitative enterprise to divide benefits and burdens in an
equitable way—and that this is somehow going to illuminate the
distinctive problems of a society based on exploitative white settlement. In whatever discipline that is affected by race, the "testimony" of the black perspective and its distinctive conceptual and
theoretical insights will tend to be whited out. Whites will cite other
whites in a closed circuit of epistemic authority that reproduces
white delusions. (69)

The latter half of this passage is directed at social contract theory in the
tradition that runs from John Locke to John Rawls, and we addressed
it in the introduction; here, we simply affirm Mills's account of mainstream American history, anthropology, sociology, political science,
and philosophy. (As scholars of literature, we can attest that the field of
American literature, from its origins in the 1920s, was almost exclusively an all-white affair as well, and remained so until the 1980s.) It is
not only that American universities like Princeton and Yale had schools
and buildings named after Woodrow Wilson and John C. Calhoun. It
is that for much of the first half of the twentieth century, the work produced *in* those universities, in many fields, was either complicit with or
actively engaged in promoting the projects of white supremacy.

So for those of us living and working in academe today, what is to be done? Are we to retroactively cancel William Dunning and all his epigones, firing them posthumously and removing their books from the libraries? Of course not. Like D. W. Griffith's *Birth of a Nation* and Thomas Dixon's *The Klansman*, the novel on which the groundbreaking film was based, they are part of the legacy of American white supremacy just as surely as Black disenfranchisement, persecution, and lynching. We need to acknowledge that today, not cancel it. (Likewise, we are not saying that Lawrence Mead should be fired, though at 78 years of age and apparently out of fresh or plausible ideas, retirement does not seem out of order for him. We are saying that his line of argument should no longer be taken seriously in academe.) But we also need to say, after 250 years of slavery and another 150 of systemic racism in all areas of American life, from voting to finance to housing to K–12 schooling to higher education, that *enough is enough*. White supremacist scholarship is bad scholarship; it serves morally and politically repugnant ends; and though we can't wish its legacy away, we can and should say that it has long outlived its expiration date. The same holds true for the allied project of eugenics, which enjoyed the enthusiastic support of liberals and conservatives alike until the revelations uncovered by the Holocaust. Though eugenics—the pseudoscience of improving the human stock, like cattle breeding—was directed primarily at people with disabilities, especially those with intellectual disabilities, it was also a racist project through and through, a white supremacist enterprise that ranged from evolutionary theories of polygenesis (i.e., that different human "races" had different ancestors, a belief no serious scientist holds today) to the insistence that races could be ranked by intelligence as measured by IQ. Like the "clash of civilizations" school, the "bell curve" school that derives from the project of eugenics has never died out in American academe—a phenomenon that, we believe, casts grave doubt on the liberal belief that good ideas will always prevail in the free marketplace.

White supremacism is baked into the foundations of some academic fields in this country, and it remains a powerful obstacle to any attempt at honest and free intellectual exchange, let alone any attempt to forge a more perfect union. Tenure, as we have noted above, is part of a social compact that is meant to serve the common good; and we can see no sense in which the common good is served by groundless and pernicious beliefs in white supremacy. In chapters 5 and 6, we'll spell out what that means—first in theoretical and then in practical terms. First, however, we'll revisit the foundational works of critical race theory and their potential for reimagining academic freedom today.

CHAPTER 4

WHO'S AFRAID
OF CRITICAL RACE
THEORY TODAY?

Critical race theory (CRT) emerged in the late 1970s and flourished in the 1980s and 1990s with the work of scholars such as Derrick Bell, Kimberlé Crenshaw, Mari Matsuda, Richard Delgado, Patricia Williams, and Charles Lawrence III.[1] Growing out of the short-lived Critical Legal Studies movement (but eventually taking its distance from that movement's inattention to matters of race), CRT represented a reckoning with the white backlash against the civil rights legislation of the 1960s, and launched an ambitious reinterpretation

---

1. Its "first institutionalized expression," it is generally agreed, was the now-famous Alternative Course at Harvard in 1981 (xxi). After Derrick Bell left Harvard Law to become dean of the University of Oregon Law School in 1980, Harvard's administration refused to commit to replacing him with another scholar of color. In response, faculty and students organized a "student-led continuation of Bell's course which focused on American law through the prism of race" (xxi), centered on Bell's 1973 book, *Race, Racism, and American Law*. Kimberlé Crenshaw was "one of its main organizers" (xxi), as was Mari Matsuda. See the Introduction to the 1995 *Critical Race Theory* anthology for what is effectively the canonical account of the history of the founding of CRT.

of the function of mainstream legal traditions in the United States. The central proposition of CRT, as announced in the 1995 anthology *Critical Race Theory: The Key Writings That Formed the Movement* (edited by Crenshaw, Neil Gotanda, Gary Peller, and Kendall Thomas) involves the need "to understand how a regime of white supremacy and its subordination of people of color have been created and maintained in America, and, in particular, to examine the relationship between that social structure and professed ideals such as 'the rule of law' and 'equal protection'" (xiii). In the introduction to the 1993 volume *Words That Wound: Critical Race Theory, Assaultive Speech, and the First Amendment*, Matsuda, Lawrence, Delgado, and Crenshaw write that "[o]ur work presented racism not as isolated instances of conscious bigoted decisionmaking or prejudiced practice, but as larger, systemic, structural, and cultural, as deeply psychologically and socially ingrained" (5). Drawing on methodologies not typically deployed by legal theorists (such as personal narrative and, in a different vein, poststructuralism), critical race theorists explored the promise and the limitation of liberalism as an intellectual tradition capable of fostering racial justice.

To take one foundational example: in 1980, Bell published the landmark essay "*Brown v. Board of Education* and the Interest Convergence Dilemma," which argued that Black people make advances in civil rights only when their interests converge with those of white Americans. It is an argument that still makes some white people defensive today, since many (but not most) white people supported the civil rights movement. But it is, unfortunately, demonstrably true. The struggle against desegregation in the United States was always complexly intertwined with the Cold War: Jim Crow laws served as a powerful recruiting device for Soviet initiatives in decolonizing African states, as did news footage from the Bloody Sunday beatings of civil rights marchers at the Edmund Pettus Bridge in Selma, Alabama, or Bull Connor unleashing attack dogs and turning firehoses on peaceful demonstrators in Birmingham. Everything about the apparatus of segregation did considerable damage to the international reputation of the United States, belying our rhetoric of freedom and democracy; and every victory against segregation, beginning with *Brown v. Board*, was partly a matter of international public relations in the Cold War. "[T]he decision," Bell writes, "helped to provide immediate credibility to America's struggle with communist countries to win the hearts and minds of emerging third world people. At least this argument was advanced by lawyers for both the NAACP and the federal government" (23).

From the earliest moments of the civil rights struggle, American liberalism has ostensibly been defined by its support for the movement. But the biggest obstacle posed by liberalism, critical race theorists argued, is its inability to understand racism as a structural phenomenon rather than as the agglomeration of individual, intentional acts of bigotry:

> Racial justice was embraced in the American mainstream in terms that excluded radical or fundamental challenges to status quo institutional practices in American society by treating the exercise of racial power as rare and aberrational rather than as systemic and ingrained. The construction of "racism" from what Alan Freeman terms the "perpetrator perspective" restrictively conceived racism as an intentional, albeit irrational, deviation by a conscious wrongdoer from otherwise neutral, rational, and just ways of distributing jobs, power, prestige, and wealth. The adoption of this perspective allowed a broad cultural mainstream both explicitly to acknowledge the fact of racism and, simultaneously, to insist on its

irregular occurrence and limited significance. As Freeman concludes, liberal race reform thus served to legitimize the basic myths of American meritocracy. (*CRT* xiv)

Freeman's argument contrasted this "perpetrator perspective" on racism with the "victim perspective," from which "racial discrimination describes those conditions of actual social existence as a member of a perpetual underclass" (29). To understand how CRT challenged mainstream thinking on civil rights, it's worth looking at Freeman's reading of the Supreme Court case of *Griggs v. Duke Power Co.* (1971) and the idea of "disparate impact theory."

Griggs, writes Freeman, was "the Supreme Court's first substantive decision under Title VII of the Civil Rights Act of 1964," and "as close as the court has ever come to formally adopting the victim perspective" (37). Indeed, the finding in *Griggs* was such a departure from legal business as usual, and the idea of "disparate impact theory" so threatening to the edifices of structural racism, that the court almost immediately set about undermining and ultimately reversing it, in cases from *Washington v. Davis* (1976) to *Wards Cove Packing Co. v. Atonio* (1989)—the latter a backlash against disparate impact theory so sweeping that it provoked Congress to amend Title VII in the Civil Rights Act of 1991. The issue (without getting too deep into the weeds of these cases) is whether an employment practice can be prohibited as racially discriminatory regardless of whether the practice was instituted with the intent to discriminate.[2] If the practice has a demonstrably disparate impact on nonwhite employees or applicants, that

---

2. Disparate impact theory has been an important element of the recent controversies over the laws introduced by Republicans after Biden's election to try to restrict access to voting.

in itself provides sufficient reason to scrutinize it. Employers requiring high school diplomas or certain scores on general intelligence tests, as in *Griggs*, might thus be found in violation of Title VII when

> (a) neither standard is shown to be significantly related to successful job performance, (b) both requirements operate to disqualify Negroes at a substantially higher rate than white applicants, and (c) the jobs in question formerly had been filled only by white employees as part of a longstanding practice of giving preference to whites. (401 U.S. 424–25)

Freeman rightly sees *Griggs* as a breakthrough: "for the first time the court held that a neutral practice, not purposefully discriminatory, that nevertheless failed to admit blacks to jobs had to justify itself or else be declared invalid" (38). Moreover, Freeman credited the court with taking "one general swipe at the workings of meritocracy" (38), quoting its finding that "the facts of this case demonstrate the inadequacy of broad and general testing devices as well as the infirmity of using diplomas or degrees as fixed measures of capability. History is filled with examples of men and women who rendered highly effective performance without the conventional badges of accomplishment in terms of certificates, diplomas, or degrees" (38–39, quoting 401 U.S. 425–26).

The *Griggs* decision was unanimous. It seemed to inaugurate a new understanding, in legal circles, of how to seek remedies for institutional racism. Nonetheless, only five years later and by a 7–2 margin (with only liberal stalwarts William Brennan and Thurgood Marshall dissenting), the Supreme Court found in *Washington v. Davis* (1976) that a verbal acuity test for police officers, which produced a failure rate for Black applicants four times as high as that for whites, was legal. "While not quite obliterating *Griggs*," Freeman writes, "the court has so undermined it that it has ceased to be a credible threat" (43). Charles Lawrence III, likewise, concludes that by kneecapping disparate impact theory, the court foreclosed on any attempt to grapple with structural forms of racism: "By insisting that a blameworthy perpetrator be found before the existence of racial discrimination can be acknowledged, the Court creates an imaginary world where discrimination does not exist unless it was consciously intended" (239).

We take this brief detour into Title VII of the Civil Rights Act and its fate in the courts for two reasons. One, it offers a good snapshot of what CRT's founders were trying to do in the field of law and why that work remains so important today. Two, we hope it helps to provide intellectual and historical context for the early-1990s backlash against CRT, which was led mostly by traditional civil libertarians (including many with impeccable liberal credentials) and fought almost entirely over the CRT critique of free speech. (We will discuss the AAUP's contribution to that backlash in the following chapter.) That critique of CRT had merit in some respects, we think, but it needs to be revisited today—which is what we are about to do. But the broader initial point is that CRT wasn't exclusively or even primarily about free speech. It originated in law schools, yes, but it mounted a sweeping critique of structural racism in American culture and society—from schooling to employment to housing to voting to the institutions of law themselves, whether these be the admissions and hiring practices of law schools or, as in Richard Delgado's critique of "the imperial scholar," the citational practices of elite law professors (institutions that, CRT writers agreed, worked to marginalize nonwhite legal scholars). Some of the insights of CRT were rebuffed by the courts, as the post–civil rights judiciary moved steadily to the right (a phenomenon that was turbocharged in the Trump years); others were contested within academe, most notably by more centrist scholars of color such as Randall Kennedy ("Racial Critiques of Legal Academia") and Henry Louis Gates, Jr.

Gates's essay, "War of Words: Critical Race Theory and the First Amendment," is a long critique of the CRT position on free speech and hate speech, and though it contributed to the backlash that saw CRT in terms of censorship and speech codes rather than as an analysis of structural racism, it retains some value today.[3] For one thing, it serves as a useful reminder of why CRT-inspired speech codes were implemented and then roundly criticized on American campuses in the midst of the early-'90s hysteria over "political correctness" (of which speech codes were considered to be the enforcement mechanism); it also serves as a reminder of what we do *not* want to revisit or advocate today, such as CRT's early reliance on Catharine Mac-Kinnon's work to implement antipornography legislation, the Canadian version of which, Gates rightly notes, immediately empowered racists and homophobes in law enforcement to raid gay bookstores and confiscate copies of bell hooks's book *Black Looks* (43). Gates is also right to argue that even the very careful, narrowly worded speech code at Stanford, authored by law professor Thomas Grey, would treat "out of my face, jungle bunny" as hate speech (47) but not a full paragraph directed at Black students telling them that they do not belong at Stanford and will have difficulty meeting the university's

3. To be fair, Gates's essay is more or less a long review essay of *Words That Wound*, adapted from its two-part publication in *The New Republic* (September 20 and 27, 1993), so it makes sense that it would concentrate exclusively on the CRT challenge to liberal ideas of free speech. We will have more to say on that score when we discuss Ulrich Baer's work in the following chapter.

academic standards because "you're the beneficiary of a disruptive policy of affirmative action that places underqualified, underprepared, and often undertalented black students in demanding educational environments like this one" (46). This, Gates notes, "makes a mockery of the words-that-wound rationale" (47).

On the other hand, Gates's essay has its questionable moments. One occurs in the concluding paragraph, which turns Charles Lawrence's words against him in a way that seems not entirely fair. Predicting that CRT "will not have been without its political costs," Gates writes,

> I cannot put it better than Charles Lawrence himself, who writes: "I fear that by framing the debate as we have—as one in which the liberty of free speech is in conflict with the elimination of racism—we have advanced the cause of racial oppression and placed the bigot on the moral high ground, fanning the rising flames of racism." Though he does not intend it as such, I can only read this as a harsh rebuke to the hate-speech movement itself. (57, quoting Lawrence, *Words* 57)

Lawrence may be guilty of an infelicitous use of the first person plural here, because his "we," read in the context of his full essay, is pretty clearly "other people," and those other people are pretty clearly traditional civil libertarians: on the very next page, he writes, "*the way the debate has been framed* makes heroes out of bigots and fans the flames of social violence" (58; our emphasis). Lawrence's complaint seems to us justified, then and now: indeed, few things are so tiresome as the bigot who complains, as bigots almost invariably do, that *he* is the real victim, prohibited by PC or cancel culture from telling uncomfortable home truths. It is this phenomenon that has led some observers (including us) to conclude that these *soi-disant* heroes imagine that the First Amendment not only protects their speech but prohibits any criticism of their speech.

The other questionable moments of Gates's essay, though, are more interesting, insofar as they raise broad questions about historical and political context. We have in mind two passages. One is Gates's appeal to the history of First Amendment jurisprudence and his skepticism about CRT writers' attempt to dredge up precedents like *Chaplinsky v. New Hampshire* (1942) and *Beauharnais v. Illinois* (1952) in order to reanimate decisions involving fighting words and group defamation, respectively. The question at stake here—to which we will return in the following chapter—is the value of defending hateful speech on principle:

> [i]t may be that the sort of formal liberties vouchsafed by this process aren't the sort of liberties we need most. Maybe we've been overly impressed by the frisson of defending bad people for good causes, when the good consequences may be at best conjectural and the bad ones are real and immediate. Maybe, these critics conclude, it's time to give up the pursuit of abstract principles and defend victims against victimizers, achieving your results in the here-and-now, not the sweet hereafter.
>
> Now, there's something to this position, but like the position it is meant to rebuff, it is overstated. Nadine Strossen, a general counsel to the American Civil Liberties Union, can show, for example, that the organization's winning First Amendment defense of the racist Father Terminiello in 1949 bore Fourteenth Amendment fruit when it was able to use the landmark *Terminiello* decision to defend the free speech rights of civil rights protestors in the sixties and seventies. (36–37)

This may have been true in 1993, and in fact was axiomatic for traditional civil rights advocates. It is, in effect, the rebuttal to Charles Lawrence III's charge that "it becomes difficult for us to believe that fighting to protect speech rights for racists will ensure our own speech rights" because "our experience is that the American system of justice has never been symmetrical where race is concerned" (76). But one wonders if one can offer the same kind of assurance today. As we'll note in the next chapter, the terrain of First Amendment jurisprudence has been significantly transformed by decisions like *Citizens United v. Federal Elections Commission* (2010), *Burwell v. Hobby Lobby Stores, Inc.* (2014), and *Roman Catholic Diocese of Brooklyn, New York v. Cuomo* (2020), which have decisively tilted the First Amendment in the favor of corporations and religious conservatives. Moreover, we will see that for Ulrich Baer, the 2017 "Unite the Right" rally in Charlottesville—and the rise of groups like Identity Evropa, the Three Percenters, and the Proud Boys—raises the question of whether the sell-by date of this argument has expired, and whether we might consider that supporting free speech for Nazis is actually quite beneficial to Nazis and destructive of democracy to boot. Indeed, as Mari Matsuda wrote in her contribution to *Words That Wound* (in a passage left unaddressed by Gates), "The chilling sight of avowed racists in threatening regalia marching through our neighborhoods with full police protection is a statement of state authorization. The Klan marches because marching promotes the Klan and because of the terrorizing and inciting effect of its public displays. Open display conveys legitimacy. The government advances this effect when it protects these marches" (48).

The second passage we want to highlight seeks to find a paradox where we find none—though it speaks, as does the first, to a specific historical moment, the moment when CRT finds itself seeking institutional support:

Here, then, is the political ambiguity that haunts the new academic activism. "Our colleagues of color, struggling to carry the multiple burdens of token representative, role model, and change agent in increasingly hostile environments, needed to know that the institutions in which they worked stood behind them." *Needed to know that the institutions in which they worked stood behind them*: I have difficulty imagining that this sentiment could have been expressed by their activist counterparts in the sixties, who defined themselves through their adversarial relation to authority and its institutions. And that is the crucial difference this time around. Today, the aim is not to resist power, but to enlist power. (42, quoting *Words* 7)

And what, we would ask, is the least bit surprising or ambiguous about that? This is almost as if to say, bemusedly, *when you were a student, you occupied this building, but now that you have been hired as a faculty member, you want an office in it!* The "colleagues of color" described here are very familiar to us, as are their multiple burdens, none of which we, as white faculty, have been required to shoulder. They know all too well that they are made to serve as token representatives, role models, and change agents, usually by being given a truckload of extra committee work, being expected to mentor all students of color, and being asked to serve as diversity window dressing for the university's strategic communications apparatus. Faculty members of color have every reason to expect their institutions to have their backs for that extra work—which was, of course, one of the demands of the Princeton Faculty Letter to which its critics did not bother to attend.

What makes this passage objectionable, we think, is that in 1993, CRT had an especially tenuous hold on institutional power in American academe. It had developed a body of work and had begun to challenge academic business as usual outside law schools, but as we noted above, its critique of free speech was met with general hostility and its broader critique of structural racism had not even begun to seep into the cultural groundwater; though Crenshaw's idea of intersectionality is now well known to millions of undergraduates (and their instructors), it was still on the margins of mainstream academic discourse in 1993, and the things most white academics knew about CRT generally were the critiques of it. One index of CRT's lack of cultural capital is the very fact that Henry Louis Gates could write one of those critiques of it for *The New Republic*, where it would be unthinkable for someone like Lani Guinier to offer a reply, not least because the magazine had led a furious—and successful—campaign against Guinier's appointment to head the Civil Rights Division of the Department of Justice. (It is notable, on that score, that Kimberlé Crenshaw published "The Capitol Riots and the Eternal Fantasy of a Racially Virtuous America," from which the epigraph for this book was taken, in *The New Republic* in 2021.)

In 1995, Derrick Bell addressed himself to the mounting backlash in an essay titled (appropriately) "Who's Afraid of Critical Race Theory?" In it, he assessed the progress of CRT since its beginnings and diagnosed the apparent impasse it had reached by the time of his writing. White faculty, Bell explained, strongly resisted certain elements of CRT, especially its normative and methodological refusal of the putatively colorless and universal voice of reason and authority. "Critical race theory writing and lecturing," Bell writes, "is characterized by frequent use of the first person, storytelling, narrative, allegory, interdisciplinary treatment of law, and the unapologetic use of creativity" (899). CRT's critics argued in effect that unless and until the embodied voices of those with different histories and perspectives from their white peers could be translated into the putatively disembodied voice of authority, CRT would lack full legitimacy and acceptance in the university. This was a demand that CRT scholars were right to refuse. As

Mari Matsuda insisted in "Looking to the Bottom: Critical Legal Studies and Reparations," "those who have experienced discrimination speak with a special voice to which we should listen. Looking to the bottom—adopting the perspective of those who have seen and felt the falsity of the liberal promise—can assist critical scholars in the task of fathoming the phenomenology of the law and defining the elements of justice" (63). That special voice emphatically includes testimony— often offered by the scholars themselves—that can convey the structure of feeling of racism, the sense, as Lawrence writes, that "Black folks know that no racial incident is 'isolated' in the United States. That is what makes the incidents so horrible, so scary. It is the knowledge that they are *not* the isolated unpopular speech of a dissident few that makes them so frightening" (*Words* 73–74). CRT scholars wrote with a personal voice, one might say, in order to try to establish the fact, for their uncomprehending colleagues, that any Black man out for a casual jog knows that he might meet the fate of Ahmaud Arbery, murdered by white vigilantes in Georgia in February 2020. *That* is what makes such incidents so horrible, so scary. It is a lesson taught repeatedly, and yet a lesson many white people have never learned.

ASKING WHO IS afraid of critical race theory *today* takes us beyond the Ivory Tower to the White House. On September 4, 2020, the Office of the President of the United States of America issued a directive banning all trainings informed by critical race theory: "The divisive, false, and demeaning propaganda of the critical race theory movement is contrary to all we stand for as Americans and should have no place in the Federal government" (Vought). On October 30, anti-CRT crusader Christopher Rufo (about whom we will say more in a moment) tweeted, "Heading into @WhiteHouse to celebrate our victory against critical race theory," appending swords-crossing and

American-flag emojis to his words. The *New York Times* journalist Jamelle Bouie tweeted in response to Rufo: "it is still strange to me how 'critical race theory' became this bogeyman to the right. it is not that i think it's weird they conjured up a fake crisis to justify their desire to repress, but that of all the targets, a somewhat obscure set of ideas from the legal academy?" It is tempting to think that critical race theory drew the attention of the white-nationalist-in-chief and his advisers simply because it combines three words long considered suspect by the right. But the interesting thing is that the Trump administration was *right* to be threatened by this body of work, regardless of whether any member of the administration had read any of it.

A Black man living in the White House between 2009 and 2017 exposed how deep racism runs in the American tradition. By all accounts, the Obama years witnessed the widespread re-emergence and growth of white nationalist and white supremacist militia groups. That rise was accurately predicted by a report released on April 7, 2009, by the Department of Homeland Security's Office of Intelligence and Analysis, *Rightwing Extremism: Current Economic and Political Climate Fueling Resurgence in Radicalization and Recruitment.*[4] Many of them claimed to be motivated by a desire to protect the Constitution *from* the Executive Office and, when Trump was elected, their

4. Despite the accuracy of the report (or, perhaps, precisely because of that accuracy), the DHS was pressured by conservative and far-right groups into withdrawing it—and, according to Daryl Johnson, lead author of the team that wrote the report, dismantling its domestic terrorism unit in the ensuing months even as abortion provider George Tiller was killed and the Holocaust Memorial Museum in Washington was attacked by a neo-Nazi who shot and killed a security guard (see Ackerman). After the deadly neo-Nazi "Unite the Right" rally in Charlottesville, Johnson warned that white nationalist groups had become more powerful than ever (Johnson, "I Warned").

concerns seemingly shifted to protecting the Executive Office itself. In "Who's Afraid of Critical Race Theory?" Bell discusses the way racism often erupts when Black ability is centered. "History shows . . . that indications of black success and thus possible black superiority result in racist outrage," Bell writes. "Most of the many race riots in this nation's history were sparked by white outrage over black success."[5] More recently, Carol Anderson has made the same observation. Describing the backlash to the civil rights legislation and its expansion of educational opportunities for Black Americans, Anderson writes, "Just as with Reconstruction, the Great Migration, and the *Brown* decision, this latest round of African American advances set the gears of white opposition in motion" (99). This is the path by which an "obscure set of ideas" that had never gained full acceptance in the academy in the late twentieth century became a "bogeyman" in the second decade of the twenty-first century. It begins with Trump's birther conspiracy during Obama's presidency and moves through conservative think-tanks and institutes, where a narrative that turned scholars of social and racial justice into the culprits of so-called culture wars was found to suit the right's purposes remarkably well.

5.   Nothing bears this out so well as the destruction of so-called Black Wall Street in the Greenwood District of Tulsa, Oklahoma in 1921, an event of murderous white terrorism (organized with the help of Tulsa city leaders) that killed dozens and left an estimated 10,000 Black people homeless. The massacre was then expunged from official histories of Oklahoma and accounts of race relations in the United States, being brought to general consciousness only in 2019 by means of the updated science fiction/graphic novel classic *Watchmen*, which aired on HBO to widespread acclaim. Showrunner Damon Lindelof reported that he was inspired to orient the rebooted series around the Tulsa massacre by reading Ta-Nehisi Coates's 2014 essay "The Case for Reparations."

In the social environment fostered by Trump and his enablers, grifters and opportunists built careers out of making products for an audience sympathetic to Trump's race-baiting and fear-mongering but that sees itself as more intellectually engaged than the MAGA-rally regular. People like Helen Pluckrose and James Lindsay—people with a tenuous connection to academia (PhDs without university jobs; Lindsay's degree is in math)—wrote books like *Cynical Theories: How Activist Scholarship Made Everything about Race, Gender, and Identity—and Why This Harms Everybody* (2020) which peddles a grossly simplified narrative about how postmodern theory "mutated" in universities into "post-colonialism, black feminism . . . intersectional feminism, critical race (legal) Theory, and queer Theory, all of which described the world critically *in order to change it*" (emphasis in original, 46, 47). Speaking to that layperson who already resents what they consider the elitism of the university, they offered the news that "Critical Race Theory is literally a conspiracy theory that all of the liberal order, equality, rationalism, and the constitution are the conspiracy against non-white people in a hierarchical fashion," as Lindsay tweeted in November 2020.

In Pluckrose's and Lindsay's telling, you can draw a straight line from the late-twentieth-century academic work of critical race theorists like Bell, Delgado, Crenshaw, Matsuda and others to Black Lives Matter protests on the streets in 2020. And Pluckrose and Lindsay are far from alone. On the contrary, the belief that CRT is the intellectual foundation for BLM is now axiomatic on that wing of the right most sympathetic to white nationalism: as Peter Burfeind put it in the *Federalist*, "Black Lives Matter is the operational arm of 'critical race theory,' the postmodern philosophy of 'critical theory' applied to race."[6] As *City Journal* writer Max Eden explained in September 2020,

6. In addition to Burfeind's and Eden's essays, see Lindsay, "Do Better than Critical Race Theory," in *New Discourses*, the online journal founded by

CNN anchor Brian Stelter credited *City Journal* contributing editor Christopher Rufo for bringing this issue to the administration's attention through his investigative journalism, featured prominently on *Tucker Carlson Tonight*. Working with whistleblowers, Rufo documented that NASA spent half a million dollars on "power and privilege sexual education workshops," that the FBI was holding weekly "intersectionality" workshops, and that Sandia National Laboratories, which designs America's nuclear weapons, held a three-day reeducation camp to deconstruct "white male culture."

For outlets like *City Journal*, the house organ of the right-wing Manhattan Institute (which started out in 1978 as a free-market conservative think tank but has since 2015 devoted itself to legitimizing and defending Trump),[7] these workshops are prima facie outrageous, because in their worldview, structural racism and sexism simply do not exist. (Perhaps Col. Betsy Schoeller could teach them something about entrenched sexism in the armed forces.) Rufo himself, as the conduit between right-wing think tanks and Tucker Carlson, today's leading exponent of white nationalism in the United States, has an interesting professional trajectory that sheds necessary light on where the backlash against CRT is coming from. His *City Journal* author page

---

Lindsay, devoted to the goal of "pursuing the light of objective truth in subjective darkness"; and, at a considerably higher intellectual level for the right-wing web, John Murawski, "The Deeply Pessimistic Intellectual Roots of Black Lives Matter, 'the 1619 Project,' and Much Else in Woke America," *RealClearInvestigations*. Eden, we note, is laboring under the misconception that CRT "was largely pioneered in U.S. schools of education," but that does not prevent him from writing about it anyway.

7. See Sol Stern, "Think Tank in the Tank," subheaded "I spent two decades writing for City Journal, and I cherished it and the Manhattan Institute's independence. Then came the Trump era."

lists him as "a documentary filmmaker and research fellow at Discovery Institute's Center on Wealth, Poverty, & Morality" (he is currently the director of that center); the Discovery Institute, founded in 1990 as an offshoot of the right-wing Hudson Institute, is primarily an organization devoted to challenging the theory of evolution and promoting "intelligent design." In 2020, he joined the Heritage Foundation as a visiting fellow. Rufo is also an "Adjunct Fellow in California Reform" with the free-market conservative think tank the Pacific Research Institute, where his bio notes that he has also been a Lincoln Fellow at the Claremont Institute, which carries the same veneer of intellectual think-tank respectability but is now on the far-right fringe of the think tank world—which does not mean it is not influential; quite the contrary. And Claremont's response to the BLM protests of 2020 was nothing if not emphatic: under the headline, "America Is Not Racist," Chairman Thomas D. Klingenstein and President Ryan P. Williams write that "so many of our citizens believe that America is racist to its core" because "this lie has been preached by our universities and media like the Gospel for a generation. From there it has traveled throughout society, particularly among the elite." Remarkably, it has done so without opposition of any kind: "Even most leaders on the Right are unwilling to refute this destructive untruth."[8]

8. Phantasmic as this may sound, it is actually standard fare for right-wing victimology, in which conservatives are the hapless, powerless targets of a monolithic liberal-left intelligentsia that controls the American educational apparatus, mass media, and entertainment industry. The Claremont Institute statement needs to be read in full to get an adequate sense of its petulance and ignorance, but we will not reproduce all five paragraphs here. Suffice it to note that (a) Laura K. Field of the more moderate free-market conservative think tank the Niskanen Center called the statement "ugly and incoherent," and that (b) President Trump awarded the Claremont Institute a National Hu-

The backlash against CRT in 2020, then, points to three important features of American cultural and intellectual life. The first is that, like the firestorm of criticism that almost engulfed Damon Sajnani's course "The Problem of Whiteness" (with which, of course, it is continuous), the backlash dramatically bears out the central arguments of CRT, demonstrating the prevalence and virulence of weaponized whiteness. The second is that, even if CRT did have a direct, formative influence on BLM—say, if Opal Tometi, Patrisse Cullors, and Alicia Garza (the three women who started the BLM movement in 2013) had taken their inspiration from books like Bell's *Race, Racism and the American Law* and Patricia Hill Collins's *Black Feminist Thought* (1990)—the takeaway from the 2020 backlash should surely be that the road from academic theory to in-the-streets public practice is much more circuitous than the road from right-wing think tanks to the public airwaves and the Trump White House. (To our knowledge, no one asserting a link between CRT and BLM has acknowledged that protests against police brutality in the United States have a very long history independent of either movement.) The third is that the right-wing intellectual infrastructure of privately funded think tanks and policy factories—the source of what is sometimes bitterly referred to by liberals as "wingnut welfare"—is operating precisely as designed. It was meant to be a counterweight to comparatively liberal institutions such as universities, and it is providing steady employment and publicity for a deep roster of intellectuals willing to

---

manities Medal in 2019. The Claremont Institute is also the outfit that, in 2016, published the incendiary screed "The Flight 93 Election" (under the byline Publius Decius Mus, later revealed to be Michael Anton), which was immediately promoted by Rush Limbaugh. Few think tanks have been more influential in the rise of Trumpism.

devote themselves to a range of toxic enterprises ranging from white supremacism to climate change denial to intelligent design to (at an extreme, in the work of the Pioneer Fund), neo-Nazi beliefs in race and intelligence.[9] Were Amy Wax, Bruce Gilley, or Lawrence Mead ever to lose their academic positions, there would be a flotilla of think-tank lifeboats ready and waiting to pick them up.

Indeed, though the Claremont Institute's self-described "salvo" "America Is Not Racist" did not take off the way its framers clearly wanted it to when they released it in multiple forms on June 3, 2020, the backlash against critical race theory *is* working as a strategy to mobilize efforts to suppress knowledge of America's history of racism. Rufo forthrightly admits that his characterization of critical race theory has nothing to do with critical race theory itself, and everything to do with combating antiracist initiatives and factually accurate histories of the United States. For him, it is a matter of "branding," as he put it in a pair of tweets from March 15, 2021:

> We have successfully frozen their brand—"critical race theory"—into the public conversation and are steadily driving up negative perceptions. We will eventually turn it toxic, as we put all of the various insanities under that brand category.
>
> The goal is to have the public read something crazy in the newspaper and immediately think "critical race theory." We have de-

9. The Pioneer Fund, founded in 1937 for the "improvement of the white race," has funded eugenics for decades, and provided much of the research on which Herrnstein and Murray relied for *The Bell Curve*. See, for a short introduction, Adam Miller, "The Pioneer Fund: Bankrolling the Professors of Hate"; for an update on how its work is being adopted by white nationalists worldwide, see Quinn Slobodian, "The Globalization of the IQ Wars."

codified the term and will recodify it to annex the entire range of cultural constructions that are unpopular with Americans.

By "Americans," we suspect, Rufo means "white Americans," and perhaps more specifically "white Americans who live in the Fox News Universe." But there is no ambiguity about his commitment to making things up as he goes.

PERHAPS WE SHOULD thank Rufo and his ilk for directing everyone's attention to critical race theory, because it turns out that what critical race theorists had to say about America in the 1980s tells us a lot about the state of the union in the first decades of the twenty-first century. "The Trump movement," Jamelle Bouie writes, "has never been about 'populism' or 'nationalism' or the interests of working-class Americans." He continues:

> It has always and only been about the contours of our national community: who belongs and who doesn't; who counts and who shouldn't; who can wield power and who must be subject to it.
>
> And the answers, no matter how much the president's defenders and apologists pretend otherwise, have race at their core. Yes, Trump will take support from anyone who gives it to him, but the Americans that matter—whose votes must be counted, whose wishes must be heard, respected and fulfilled—are the white ones, and of them, only a subset. ("It Started with Birtherism")

Trump has forced many white liberals—complacent in the belief that their country fulfilled the promise of its Revolution when it passed civil rights legislation and became "post-racial" with the election of Obama—to think again. Just as the whites responsible for "Southern

Redemption" after the withdrawal of Federal troops from the South in 1877 sought to undo the outcome of the Civil War and reestablish a neo-Confederate regime devoted to Black disenfranchisement and the ideological rehabilitation of Confederate leaders, the whites who opposed the Civil Rights Act and the Voting Rights Act never gave up after 1965, devoting an entire legal industry to the project of rolling them back.[10] They/we also have to acknowledge that "Trumpism" didn't begin with Trump. Bouie writes:

> Trump did not force the Republican Party in Michigan and Wisconsin to create districts so slanted as to make a mockery of representative government in their states; he did not tell the North Carolina Republican Party to devise and pass a voter identification bill targeting the state's Black voters for disenfranchisement with "surgical precision"; he didn't push Republican election officials in Georgia to indiscriminately purge their voter rolls or pressure Florida Republicans into practically nullifying a state constitutional amendment—passed by ballot measure—to give voting rights to former felons.

Revisiting the work of critical race theorists reminds us that the Reagan years were, in important respects, harbingers of the Trump ones. Many of the foundational works of CRT were written in the context of a Reagan presidency in which the successes of the civil

---

10. The conservative attack on the Voting Rights Act arguably reached its apotheosis with the Supreme Court's decision in *Shelby County v. Holder* (2013), which struck down Section 4(b) of the act, pertaining to the formula by which jurisdictions are assessed for their history of racial discrimination in voting. But perhaps there is still more damage yet to come.

rights movement were diminished and deprived of oxygen. This was largely achieved by circumscribing the Civil Rights Act and the Voting Rights Act such that they were viewed through a lens of strictly formal equality; as Lani Guinier wrote in *Lift Every Voice* (1998), "instead of a moral crusade led by the people, the civil rights movement became an almost purely legal crusade" (227). The right was more than happy to shift to those grounds, as Crenshaw pointed out in her 1988 *Harvard Law Review* article "Race, Reform, and Retrenchment: Transformation and Legitimation in Antidiscrimination Law": "The principal basis of [the Reagan administration's] hostility was a formalistic, color-blind view of civil rights that had developed in the neoconservative 'think tanks' during the 1970's" (1337). The gains made in the 1960s were quickly contained by narratives of a colorblind and "postracial" America.

Crenshaw argued in that article that "antidiscrimination discourse is fundamentally ambiguous" (1335) and that "the civil rights constituency cannot afford to view antidiscrimination doctrine as a permanent pronouncement of society's commitment to ending racial subordination" (1335). Instead, she said, "antidiscrimination law represents an ongoing ideological struggle in which the occasional winners harness the moral, coercive, consensual power of law" (1335). Crenshaw's essay explains the necessary ambivalence toward the law animating most work in CRT when history repeatedly shows that the law can be interpreted and enforced in ways that serve different interests rather than all interests equitably. Indeed, this insight is what drew critical race theorists to Critical Legal Studies in the first place: as Mari Matsuda wrote, "this movement [CLS] is attractive to minority scholars because its central descriptive message—that legal ideals are manipulable, and that law serves to legitimate existing maldistributions of wealth and power—rings true for anyone who has experienced life in nonwhite America" ("Looking to the Bottom" 64). Or, as Bell put it in "Who's Afraid of Critical Race Theory?", "There is . . . a good deal of tension in critical race theory scholarship, a tension that Angela Harris characterizes as between its commitment to radical critique of the law (which is normatively deconstructionist) and its commitment to radical emancipation by the law (which is normatively reconstructionist)" (899). The hope of the critical race theorists, Crenshaw wrote, is that "engaging in rights rhetoric can be an attempt to turn society's 'institutional logic' against itself—to redeem some of the rhetorical promises and the self-congratulations that seem to thrive in American political discourse" (1366). To put this another way, conditions for public discourse, broadly, and academic discourse, narrowly, will improve if sentiments like "We can disagree and still love each other as long as your disagreement is not rooted in my oppression and denial of my humanity and my right to exist" become more ubiquitous than "I disapprove of what you say but I will defend to the death your right to say it."[11]

When Bell wrote about the academy's failure to embrace critical race theory in 1995, he struck a poignant note—a note sounded in the work of many critical race theorists in the 1990s when they suggest that they write for themselves and for one another with little expectation of persuading their critics. "The critical race theory perspective," Bell wrote, "offers blacks and their white allies insight, spiked with humor, as a balm for this latest insult, and enables them to gird

---

11. The first passage is often attributed to James Baldwin, most likely because the person who tweeted it in 2015, Robert Jones, Jr., goes by the Twitter handle "Son of Baldwin" (and to be fair, it *does* have a Baldwinian ring to it). The second is almost always attributed to Voltaire but was in fact written as an encapsulation of his beliefs by one of his biographers, Evelyn Beatrice Hall, in her 1906 book, *Friends of Voltaire*.

themselves for those certain to follow" (898). The latest insult to which Bell referred was the 1994 publication of Richard J. Herrnstein and Charles Murray's *The Bell Curve*. Fast forward twenty-plus years: Charles Murray is invited to speak at Middlebury College in 2017. It is as if the country were determined to rehearse every last scene of the 1990s culture wars, having learned nothing the first time. But because of the student protest that ensued, Murray's tumultuous visit is one of the key events—like the Christakis incident discussed at the outset of chapter 1—that was successfully framed by the liberal center and the conservative right as a "free speech" issue, thus fueling a national discourse about snowflakes and coddled minds. Peter Beinart, for example, wrote "A Violent Attack on Free Speech at Middlebury" for the *Atlantic*. The "violent attack" (violence perpetrated on the abstraction "free speech") took place in March 2017.[12] Trump had been in office for little more than one year and yet hate crimes had already increased by 17 percent from the average in 2015 (see Hanci, "Hate Crimes Increase"). The Unite the Right rally in Charlottesville was only five months in the future. Were the students attacking free speech or were they attacking racism? Why, they wondered, should

12. The actual violent attack—as Beinart notes—happened when Professor Alison Stanger was assaulted by a protestor after the event; she went to the hospital and received a neck brace, and reportedly sustained a concussion. Since Stanger had agreed to moderate a question-and-answer session that would have ensured that Murray would have taken hostile questions, the assault seemed to many commentators prima facie evidence of the illegitimacy of the "intolerant left." See Katharine Q. Seelye, "Protestors Disrupt Speech by 'Bell Curve' Author at Vermont College."

To his credit, Beinart acknowledges that "Before I began working there full-time, my old magazine, *The New Republic*, published an excerpt of [*The Bell Curve*], along with rebuttals, and thus gave it a legitimacy it did not deserve." We agree that that exposure was decisive. See note 13 below.

racism get a platform on a university campus? They were joined by over 450 Middlebury alumni, who signed an open letter arguing that Murray's talk was "not a matter of free speech," insofar as "his views were offensive and based on shoddy scholarship." Our own view is close to this; although we believe that Murray's talk is a matter of free speech, we also believe—as we will argue at greater length in the next chapter—that because it is based on the shoddy scholarship underlying racist pseudoscience, it should not be taken seriously and legitimated on a college campus.

We note, however, that there is a good argument for seeing Murray's talk as something other than free speech: as Ibram X. Kendi writes, racist untruths might be better characterized as "unfree speech."

> Just like we should not have the freedom to enslave people, we should not have the freedom to publish untruths about people. When the press publishes false or unproven racist ideas in news stories or columns without informing readers there is no truth to those claims and tales, that is not an exercise in free speech. That is unfree speech. . . . We should have the freedom to offer in the press varying controversial and provocative racial thoughts from the ground of evidentiary truth. That's free speech. At the same time, we must recognize and take seriously the difference between unfree speech based on falsehoods, and free speech based on facts, while never conflating the two. Free speech—in its open-minded search for truth—produces lively debates, growing intelligence, and mutual love. Unfree speech—in its close-minded defense of falsehoods—produces arguments, ignorance, and hate.

Indeed, from this angle, the phrase "free speech" is itself deeply ideological because all speech is not equally free. It also does not make, to quote Princeton undergraduate Brittani Telfair, "symmetric asks" of each of us. In a 2020 op-ed for the *Daily Princetonian* titled "You're not entitled to 'civility,'" Telfair explains how "civility" requires one to divorce one's personhood from the conversation by debating a question in the abstract. She was asked in one class, she says, "if Brown v. Board of Education 'should have happened.'" "Over the years," I've heard innumerable racist stereotypes recounted as though they were fact," she continues; "My academic experience has not been enriched by any of this." Telfair remained *civil* on these occasions: "I carefully monitored the tone of my responses but the expectation to do so shouldn't be on me."

We will return to this dynamic in chapter 5 by way of Ulrich Baer's work—the dynamic in which some speakers begin from the position of having to justify their legitimacy to speak at all. But we could find very similar words and points by returning to Bell's essay, one discussing the original publication of the book at the heart of the Middlebury controversy. Here's Bell on Murray in 1995:

> There is, critics maintain, no basis for a finding that intelligence is inherited and, indeed, no accepted definition of the vague term "intelligence." There is, on the other hand, a depressingly strong and invariant correlation between resources and race in this country, and resources and success—including success in taking I.Q. tests. These are settled facts. (894)

So why did *The Bell Curve* secure a publisher and why did it sell so many copies and receive so much attention?[13] "*The Bell Curve,*" Bell wrote,

13. As Peter Beinart noted, *The New Republic*, under Andrew Sullivan's leadership, gave the book a mainstream legitimacy it would not have had if

"captured the nation's fascination precisely because it laid out in scientific jargon what many whites believe, need desperately to believe, but dare not reveal in public or even to their private selves" (898). It served some white people's interests to revisit a tired debate and to revisit it in the allegedly universal voice of science and reason. Is it an accident, then, that in the Trump era, we would find Murray back at the center of the culture wars?[14]

it had been consigned, as it should have been, to the toxic regions of the *National Review* where virulent racists like John Derbyshire and Peter Brimelow were still writing. Sullivan, of course, remains a caustic participant in the campus culture wars, writing screeds like "We All Live on Campus Now" (in which he notes with unhinged alarm that "the very word *intersectional* is a function of neo-Marxist critical race theory") as if he has nothing to answer for in the history of American race relations. As Louis Menand put it in his review of Dinesh D'Souza's *Illiberal Education* in 1991, "it is not pleasant to see a man who did so much to poison the wells now turning up dressed as the water commissioner" (107).

14. Were he alive today, Stephen Jay Gould would certainly say no, it's no accident at all. He published *The Mismeasure of Man* in 1981 to try to drive a stake through the racist pseudoscience of Arthur Jensen and William Shockley, only to witness the return of the undead with the publication of *The Bell Curve* thirteen years later. His introduction to the revised 1996 edition of the book bears rereading today:

> critiques of biological determinism are also timely at certain moments (including the present) because—and you may now choose your favorite image, from heads of the Lernaean Hydra if your tastes be classical, to crabgrass on suburban lawns if you favor vernacular modernity—the same bad arguments recur every few years with a predictable and depressing regularity. No sooner do we debunk one version than the next chapter of the same bad text emerges to ephemeral prominence.

"The problem," Bell wrote, "is that not all positioned perspectives are equally valued, equally heard, or equally included. From the perspective of critical race theory, some positions have historically been oppressed, distorted, ignored, silenced, destroyed, appropriated, commodified, and marginalized-and all of this, not accidentally" (901). This is why the embodied voice is central to critical race theory. Charles Lawrence, for example, opened his analysis of *Washington v. Davis* for the *Stanford Law Review* in 1987 by telling his readers about his experience in kindergarten in the late 1950s. When his kind, white teacher read *Little Black Sambo* to him and his all-white classmates, his stomach twisted into knots and he wanted to hide. He doesn't tell us what he feels when, thirty years later, he encounters the same book

---

No mystery attends the reason for these recurrences. They are not manifestations of some underlying cyclicity, obeying a natural law that might be captured in a mathematical formula as convenient as IQ; nor do these episodes represent any hot item of new data or some previously unconsidered novel twist in argument, for the theory of unitary, rankable, innate, and effectively unchangeable intelligence never alters very much in each sequential formulation. Each surge to popularity works with the same fallacious logic and flawed information.

The reasons for recurrence are sociopolitical, and not far to seek: resurgences for biological determinism correlated with episodes of political retrenchment, particularly with campaigns for reduced government spending on social programs, or at times of fear among ruling elites, when disadvantaged groups sow serious unrest or even threaten to usurp power. What argument against social change could be more chillingly effective than the claim that established orders, with some groups on top and others at the bottom, exist as an accurate reflection of the innate and unchangeable intellectual capacities of people so ranked? (27–28).

but now at his daughter's preschool and about to be read to her. We are the ones now who feel sick, for him and his daughter. This is how Lawrence prepares us for the argument about unconscious racism and the law that follows. He understands, as Bell puts it, that "a neutral perspective does not, and cannot, exist—that we all speak from a particular point of view, from what he calls a 'positioned perspective'" (901).

Did the Middlebury students protesting Charles Murray's invitation understand the lessons that CRT professors had been teaching for decades, lessons that some white Americans appear to be learning only by way of the national reckoning with George Floyd's murder? We think it is entirely possible, regardless of whether they were familiar with specific texts. The right-wing outlet *Minding the Campus* (formerly published by the Manhattan Institute but now markedly lower on the wingnut welfare food chain, having been acquired by the National Association of Scholars in June 2020) published an article titled "Young Americans Are Too Sensitive about Speech" in November 2020, an article sounding the same alarm that has been ringing non-stop since the Middlebury affair. In it, Samuel J. Abrams reported that data from American Enterprise Institute's Survey Center on American Life shows:

> Those in Gen Z—the youngest adult generation now in college—are appreciably more likely to be offended and overly sensitive to speech. More specifically, a national sample of over 4,000 Americans was asked to select between two statements about speech: either people need to be more careful about the language they use to avoid offending those with different backgrounds OR too many people are easily offended these days over the language that others use. The results show that the nation is fairly split on this issue, with 47% of respon-

dents stating that people should be more careful with their language, compared to 52% holding that the country is too sensitive. Unsurprisingly, some differences emerge in response to the speech choices between specific demographic groups. For example, blacks are the most worried about offensive language (71%), while whites and Latinos are far less concerned (40% and 51%, respectively).

"Blacks are the most worried about offensive language." The article does not pause here and consider this in its historical context of a MAGA crowd chanting "send her back," referring to a Black congresswoman, while the white president of the United States stands smirking, soaking it in for a full 13 seconds. Instead, it pivots immediately to what it calls "the real issue here" which "is the significant difference in response between generations." It continues:

> Almost 60% of those in Gen Z are worried about offending others—24% greater than the national average. This changes almost immediately as older generations are considered. Just 48% of Millennials and 44% of Gen Xers, by comparison, were as worried about offending people with different backgrounds. Both Boomers and Silents—the grandparents of Zers—were in the mid-forty percentile range as well.

What is the lesson to be drawn from this generational difference, according to *Minding the Campus*? Is it that the rising generation is more prepared than the declining one to consider that the same words indisputably affect different people differently? That they are more willing to consider that perspective, position, context, and history matter when exercising one's right to free speech? (One could, and should, ask the same questions about the Christakis incident.)

No. *Minding the Campus* does not think there is anything to learn from Gen Z because *their* speech cannot be taken at face value. When they exercise their right to free speech, they only parrot what they've been told. "Young Americans are conditioned to find harm in practically everything," the article explains. After all, "when identity politics and intersectionality dominate high school and higher education, students will find 'discrimination' in every corner."

At the end of the twentieth century, critical race theorists pressed on with their work despite the growing sense that the academy was responding largely with hostility. Today, the culture-war right is convinced that CRT has replaced fluoride in the drinking water. As we noted above, we suspect that this is not entirely wrong, even if the critics' understanding of CRT amounts to little more than a mantra of "postmodernist neo-Marxist Frankfurt School deconstruction bad." Certainly, as we noted above, the term *intersectionality* has a currency and ubiquity almost unimaginable thirty years ago. But there is another explanation ready to hand. If, as the *Minding the Cam*pus piece concludes, "the data clearly show that Gen Zers are more sensitive to words and have a more encompassing definition of discrimination," might this be the result of numerous cultural, social, and political factors, only a few of which may have been learned in school? One such factor might simply be the banal reality of this generation's experience with racism, with gender and sexual harassment, with transphobia, with social media. Do even the white kids have a more sensitive relationship to "speech" because the rise of social media has demonstrated to them just how badly words can wound? how powerful words are at creating in and out groups? at determining who belongs and who doesn't?

John Murawski's skeptical take on CRT in *RealClearInvestigations*, which we referenced in note 6, includes some interesting testimony from the targets of the backlash, who claim that their ascendancy is just history unfolding before us:

> "I've always laid it at the doorstep of the millennials, who were by and large highly receptive to our message, and maybe, as well, Trump for the opposite reason—because he's so crude and awful," said University of Alabama law professor Richard Delgado. . . .
>
> "Is it society that has come around to us?" Delgado, who identifies as Chicano, said in a phone interview. "Because the world is so terrible, that they've hit upon us and our ways of describing it? Because it rings true?"
>
> Angela Onwuachi-Willig, dean and professor at the Boston University Law School and the daughter of Nigerian immigrant parents, says the country is in the midst of a "generational shift" among students who have grown up in "pervasive segregation in their residential lives." She said she is continually surprised by her students' fluency in the argot of critical race theory.
>
> "You've got this open generation that grew up exposed to this language in middle school, high school and certainly in college," said Onwuachi-Willig, who identifies as black and specializes in critical race theory, gender matters, race and law, and related issues. "It's not called critical race theory—it's just something you know."

So in an important sense, the Return of Charles Murray was not just another tired reboot of a 1990s meme. It offers an index of what has changed since the mid-1990s. Many people, including presumably the students themselves, saw in the Middlebury protest an acknowledgment of the damage done to people's sense of fair play when a university platform is given to someone who had been promoting pseudoscientific racism long after it had been discredited.

Perhaps, after all, there is an emergent dispensation on campus. Carolyn Rouse, chair of the Department of Anthropology at Princeton, suggested as much in a roundtable assembled by the *Princeton Alumni Weekly* on the subject of "The University, Social Justice, and Free Inquiry":

> There are limits in the classroom. We could relitigate whether the Earth is round or whether Blacks are a different species than whites, but that is a huge waste of time, from my perspective. I hope, by the way, that during the Trump era people understand what it feels like to have your time wasted by having to disprove things that have already been disproven.
>
> When I first came to Princeton 20 years ago, there were very openly racist students who would say publicly, for example, that we know all Black people are drug users. Of course, that is a false statement. But do I allow a student to bring an opinion like that into a classroom conversation? Do I, again, have to keep relitigating things that we already know?
>
> When people say, "Is there some sort of conflict between free speech and inclusivity?" oftentimes what they're really saying is, "We want to relitigate old racist, sexist, classist arguments," and I just think that that is not my job to debunk those arguments over and over again. . . .
>
> I'm not trying to shut down debate, but oftentimes when people demand free speech and inclusivity, it's code for, "Can we let vile opinions be subjects for discussion in a classroom?" From my perspective, the answer to that is no. (See Bernstein)

If indeed a sense is spreading that we need not relitigate vile opinions, then perhaps, in some quarters, the CRT critique of free speech absolutism is starting to become common sense. And that, surely, is what is driving the racist right to its paroxysms of rage.

IN "FEELING THE PROBLEM: Working through Diversity Work," Molloy College professor of humanities Mark S. James discusses his experience teaching at a predominantly white university during the Trump years when many faculty on his campus "responded to the backlash against 'political correctness' on campus by promoting a posture of tolerance for all ideas—including ideas that silence and justify violence against those of us from marginalized groups" (218). James writes:

> Some of my colleagues have argued that a position of neutrality makes room for those with potentially oppressive opinions to express them rather than feeling shut down, which allows us to expose their ideas to critical examination and to counter them with evidence and facts. They suggest that if this is done with enough deference and civility, then those who would otherwise shut down will be more likely to listen and, in time, recognize the error of their ways. Failing that, we can always insist that experience with diversity makes them more marketable to future employers. So if reason doesn't bring them around, self-interest might, but as long as we keep the faith that they will come around on their own time, then we can't be accused of unfairly imposing our views on them. (218)

This approach, James goes on to say, amounts to "institutionalizing an affect of tolerance and civility" (218). This—an institutionalized affect—does not suggest the dogged pursuit of truth that conservatives and classic liberals claim to champion. Rather, it is the predictable consequence of all their many charges of "political indoctrination": for what this affect translates into, James argues, is a situation in which BIPOC faculty and students "must allow their experiences to be rationalized, trivialized, and dismissed to keep from triggering the defensive reaction that occurs when white privilege is named or challenged" (218). "Thus," James continues, "out of the expressed concern not to appear biased against 'conservative' points of view and in the interest of promoting 'free speech,' the aggrieved voices of those in positions of power and privilege once again dominate the discourse, which calls into question our institutional commitment to the pursuit of truth and justice in general, to say nothing of our commitment to listen to and provide support for those who continue to be silenced or worse just about everywhere else" (219).

The question keeps getting posed as, *Do we have to choose between inclusivity and academic freedom?* James's essay shows us that the answer to this question is "no," but that the answer to the question, *Do we have to choose between free speech and academic freedom?* might well be "yes," at least when we're speaking within the university and in its name. James writes:

> [It] may be a mistake to assume that we all share compatible notions of what democracy in America means or how it should work. Perhaps the greatest source of tension is an insistence that these differences are negotiable. Perhaps it is time to finally acknowledge that the true diversity of views includes those that reject the basic premise that our democracy does or should include everyone. By breaking through this wall of denial, we may be in a better position to fully appreciate the stakes of our teachings and clarify our aims and purposes as educators. (218)

After Trump, even many white academics understand that, as James puts it, "the fiction that everyone is making a good-faith effort to find a way to share this country [has become] impossible to sustain" (218). By abandoning the liberal fantasy that all differences are surmountable given enough speech and counter-speech, we can more honestly defend academic freedom rather than succumbing to the temptation to subordinate it to free speech.

"The reality is," Telfair, the Princeton student quoted earlier, writes, "civil discourse does not always have symmetric asks of everyone." We consider this to be one of the most important insights to be gained from the culture wars of the last decade; it succinctly explains how American politics made it difficult and downright *wrong* to try to navigate the classroom by way of standard liberal platitudes. And though it is only one sentence, it draws on a deep well of scholarly work on the structural inequalities that are built into ostensibly open debates. Some things are not worthy of entertaining as if we could pretend they were bloodless. Whether *Brown v. Board of Education* "should have happened" is one. Bruce Gilley's cost-benefit approaches to American slavery and Western colonialism that conveniently subtract the "cost" to Africans and the colonized are others. Telfair provides yet another: "The basic and fully-answered question of whether or not racism is real is a distraction from talking about how to handle its innumerable impacts." If we internalize the insight of asymmetry, we can bring that to bear on an inadequately content-neutral and ahistorical conception of academic freedom.

We have turned to Charles Mills because that's what Mills explains—that what has long been understood as an ahistorical liberalism is in fact a racial liberalism.[15] It is no accident that Mills often remarks on the whiteness of his field—political philosophy—when talking about the dominance of Rawlsian liberalism within it.

15. Sara Ahmed's work in this vein is also indispensable. See, in particular, "Whiteness and the General Will: Diversity Work as Willful Work."

Who contributes to the discussion affects where that discussion leads. What Mills calls "the myth of an all-inclusive contract creating a socio-political order presided over by a neutral state equally responsive to all its colorless citizens" (41) stands in the way of our acknowledging this basic point. Even when the majority of us (faculty) recognize that the "all-inclusive contract" is a myth, we've still been slow to thoroughly digest just how much it matters who is at the table when theorizing concepts like academic freedom. "What if, after long political struggles," Mills asks, "there developed at last a seeming equality that later turned out to be more nominal than substantive, so that justice and equal protection were still effectively denied even while being triumphantly proclaimed?" (30) "It would mean," he answers, "that we would need to recognize the inadequacy of speaking in the abstract of liberalism and contractarianism" (30). Abstractions spoken in a universal (white) voice lead to bloodless calculations like cost-benefit analyses of slavery and empire. From a less philosophical and more journalistic vantagepoint, Pankaj Mishra does work on liberalism that is comparable to that of Mills. In *Blind Fanatics: Liberals, Race, and Empire*, Mishra examines liberalism's complicity in western imperialism.[16] He spotlights those thinkers who saw through liberalism's bad faith from the beginning because they were members of the empire's subjugated rather than ruling classes. When the history of colonialism is written by the once-colonized as well as by the colonizer, that history is

16. For a more theoretical deconstruction of the vantage point of Western imperial knowledge, see Walter D. Mignolo's work. His essay "Epistemic Disobedience, Independent Thought, and De-Colonial Freedom" offers a critique of the disembodied voice of knowledge that resonates powerfully with CRT but takes the colonial context as its frame of reference.

considerably more complete.[17] Nobody can now revert to the Kipling version and expect to be taken seriously in the academy—at least not by all those sectors of the academy that are not centers and institutes propped up by right-wing money, unanswerable to academic standards.

In a 2017 essay, "Academic Unfreedom, Unacademic Freedom," Amherst law professor Adam Sitze writes:

> The biologist is not free to speak as though evolution were not the decisive premise for the study of life on earth. The climate scientist is not free to pretend that climate change is not human-caused. The historian is not free to pretend that slave labor does not account for the genesis and basis of American culture, society, and politics. (598)

We note, ruefully, that the right-wing foundations we have discussed above, the ones offering sinecures to people like Christopher Rufo, are working precisely this terrain: challenging evolution, denying climate change, and insisting that slave labor does not account for the genesis and basis of American culture, society, and politics. In closing, we'd like to turn to the last of these, by way of a brief look at the backlash to the 1619 Project. For the 1619 Project can be seen as a CRT perspective on American history—and again, we think that even though the backlashers have an inadequate understanding of what they're backlashing against, the interesting thing is that they're not entirely wrong: the threat of CRT to white supremacy and jingoistic American triumphalism is quite real.

17. This principle is practically axiomatic in postcolonial theory; one now-canonical and highly generative example is Dipesh Chakrabarty's *Provincializing Europe*, published in 2000.

The premise of the 1619 Project, we think, is unassailable: what Nikole Hannah-Jones and a group of *New York Times* journalists presented was an account of America in which 1619 displaces 1776, in order to make the case that slavery is foundational to the history of what became the United States, subtending and deforming the egalitarian promise that all men are created equal, and informing the post–Civil War institutions of white supremacy to this day. The most controversial of its claims—that is, the arguments that provoked heated debate among legitimate historians, as opposed to the indiscriminate denials of the entire project characteristic of the whitelashing right—seem to us matters of emphasis rather than outright errors: the question of whether, as Hannah-Jones wrote, "one of the primary reasons the colonists decided to declare their independence from Britain was because they wanted to protect the institution of slavery," and the question of whether Black freedom fighters have "for the most part . . . fought alone." (Hannah-Jones, "Our Democracy's Founding Ideals").

As to the second question, we understand (being white people) that white people constantly need to be reassured that even in the depths of American slavocracy, there were some good white people. We all like to imagine we would be Huckleberry Finn, not some random plantation overseer.[18] But the sorry fact is that a lot of the time, there weren't *enough* good white people, or enough good white people within, say, a fifty-mile radius. In one of the most judicious parsings of the debate, *Atlantic* writer Adam Serwer observes,

18. This is of course not to say that Huck Finn himself is an anti-racist figure; he never wavers from his belief, taught to him by every adult he knows, that abolitionism is wrong. He is simply making an exception for Jim, whom he has grown to respect. But his decision has long been hailed as heroic by white readers.

[L]ooking back to the long stretches of night before the light of dawn broke—the centuries of slavery and the century of Jim Crow that followed—"largely alone" seems more than defensible. Douglass had Garrison, but the onetime Maryland slave had to go north to find him. The millions who continued to labor in bondage until 1865 struggled, survived, and resisted far from the welcoming arms of northern abolitionists.

"I think one would be very hard-pressed to look at the factual record from 1619 to the present of the black freedom movement and come away with any conclusion other than that most of the time, black people did not have a lot of allies in that movement," Hannah-Jones told me. "It is not saying that black people only fought alone. It is saying that *most of the time* we did."

The argument is not only true; it is a long-overdue antidote to narratives like *The Long Walk Home* (1990) and *Mississippi Burning* (1998), with sympathetic white people front and center in the struggle against Jim Crow. The persistent appeal of those narratives for white people, we suspect, accounts for some of the vehemence with which this argument was met.[19]

19. This was, in fact, the claim to which Arkansas newspaper publisher and University of North Carolina alumnus and donor Walter Hussman Jr. objected when Hannah-Jones was offered a tenured position as the Knight Chair in Race and Investigative Journalism at UNC-Chapel Hill. "I think this claim denigrates [!] the courageous efforts of many white Americans to address the sin of slavery and the racial injustices that resulted after the Civil War. Long before Nikole Hannah Jones won her Pulitzer Prize, courageous white southerners risking their lives standing up for the rights of blacks were winning Pulitzer prizes, too." UNC's journalism school is named after Hussman, who donated $25 million to the university. See Julia Craven, "The Newspaper Baron Who Lobbied against Nikole Hannah-Jones," *Slate*, June 4, 2021.

As for the role of slavery and its defense in the American Revolution, this is not an issue we will attempt to settle here; we will, instead, outsource the question to David Waldstreicher, who in early 2020 wrote what we believe is the best single guide to the controversy. Noting that "these are perennial issues in the history of emancipation and civil rights," Waldstreicher rehearses decades of debates among historians, and notes along the way that there is a good reason why researchers haven't turned up any hidden documents in which the architects of the Revolution write, "in truth, we seek freedom in order to sustain slavery":

> When Gordon Wood complains that no American founders said they were declaring independence in order to keep their slaves, he neglects the fact that most revolutionaries who tried to explain American protest were embarrassed about slavery. Long before anyone stated why they chose sides in '76, they all learned that saying that they wanted to protect *that* property would have undermined their claims against the British by exposing them as hypocrites. It wasn't a selling point in the pamphlet war; it was something to be defensive and quiet about.

At one point, Waldstreicher offers a corrective to Serwer's overview—an important one, since so much of the professional historians' backlash against the 1619 Project has tried to cast it as the work of mere journalists trying to punch above their weight (and in the following paragraph, we will see a journalist attempting the same move):

> What Serwer misses is that this is not simply a clash between the *Times* authors and a group of historians: it is also a pre-existing

argument between historians themselves. ([Sean] Wilentz, in his subsequent reply to Serwer in *The Atlantic* this week, tries to perform a magician's act and render invisible the very existence of that debate, much as he ignores the scholarship when he is not mischaracterizing its substance.) The arguments made by the 1619 Project are largely based on the work of scholars such as [Gerald] Horne, [Woody] Holton, [Alan] Taylor, myself, and others (indeed, Hannah-Jones and Silverstein have acknowledged as much). By bringing the critical ideas of these scholars to a wide audience, the 1619 Project essentially drew back the curtain on a vital debate within the field of U.S. history. By responding with such force, critics of the project have helped define the contours of this debate. It is an important one for us to have, in part because this is an argument that goes all the way back to the founding itself.

Despite the (well-deserved) swipe at Wilentz, this is a gracious response to the critics of the 1619 Project, almost thanking them for their contribution to it—but here Waldstreicher is talking only about critics among other professional historians. Outside academe, conservatives have generally responded with vitriol or bad faith or both.

We will close with two minor but telling examples—one of bad faith, the other of vitriol. The first is that of *New York Times* opinion writer Bret Stephens, who, in an October 2020 op-ed ("The 1619 Chronicles"), declared the project to be a "failure"—and, more broadly, that journalists need to stay in their lane and let academics have the final word on history, because his fellow *Times* writers "are not in a position to adjudicate historical disputes." After reiterating Wilentz's complaint that the desire to preserve slavery was not one of the "primary reasons" for the Revolution, Stephens turns to a female historian of color for further support:

> Then there was an essay in Politico in March by the Northwestern historian Leslie M. Harris, an expert on pre–Civil War African-American life and slavery. "On Aug. 19 of last year," Harris wrote, "I listened in stunned silence as Nikole Hannah-Jones . . . repeated an idea that I had vigorously argued against with her fact checker: that the patriots fought the American Revolution in large part to preserve slavery in North America."

That is, indeed, the first sentence of Harris's essay. And although Stephens acknowledges that Harris expressed "sympathy with the project's moral aims," he does not bother to take stock of any of the roughly 2,500 words that followed that sentence, in which Harris explains, "I was concerned that critics would use the overstated claim to discredit the entire undertaking. So far, that's exactly what has happened." Here's more of what Stephens missed:

> The United States was not, in fact, founded to protect slavery—but the *Times* is right that slavery was central to its story. And the argument among historians, while real, is hardly black and white. Over the past half-century, important foundational work on the history and legacy of slavery has been done by a multiracial group of scholars who are committed to a broad understanding of U.S. history—one that centers on race without denying the roles of other influences or erasing the contributions of white elites. An accurate understanding of our history must present a comprehensive picture, and it's by paying attention to these scholars that we'll get there. ("I Helped Fact-Check")

Interestingly, a week after the appearance of Stephens's op-ed, Harris, together with Karin Wulf, director of the Omohundro Institute of Early American History and Culture and a professor of history at the College of William and Mary, wrote back—not to Stephens, but to a long essay in the *Washington Post* Style section by Sarah Ellison, "How the 1619 Project Took over 2020" (though we wonder if it wasn't aimed at Stephens as well). We cite it in full:

> Over the year since its launch, headlines and commentary about a few factual and interpretive errors in the 1619 Project have sidelined the critical histories of enslavement, segregation, racism and African Americans' contributions to the nation that it sought to highlight. The critiques have demanded a level of perfection that few publications of any kind achieve, and in doing so, have obscured much of the correct and important history that is contained in the project. The continued focus on these critiques also obscures the work of generations of scholars who have and continue to work to create a history more reflective of our nation.
>
> Many scholars and teachers have engaged with the 1619 Project for two reasons: because respectful exchange is productive, even when we disagree; and because we understand the aim of the project is to focus on those histories that have remained marginal to our national narrative. The 1619 Project has not provided all the answers about these histories—no single publication could. But it is pushing to the fore new ways of thinking about our shared histories. In turning back a century or more of historical error around the histories of slavery and African Americans, it's not surprising that some things are wrong, unresolved or in process. Yet the continued attention to a handful of issues in the 1619 Project should not impugn the larger effort. ("The 1619 Project's Greatest Contribution")

We think it's fair to conclude that Stephens quoted Harris out of context. We also think it's fair to conclude that for journalists and historians alike, this is a bad thing to do.

And then there is the vitriol. As with so many of the evils of the Trump era, it came from the top, with Trump himself, in mid-September 2020, using the occasion of a speech at the National Archives Museum to do what he does best, bloviate and lie: "the left has warped, distorted and defiled the American story with deceptions, falsehoods, and lies. There is no better example than the New York Times's totally discredited 1619 Project." And as in so many other areas of American political and cultural life, Trump has his admirers, epigones, and lickspittles on the fringes of academe. Thus it was that in October 2020, the National Association of Scholars issued a public letter demanding that the Pulitzer Prize Board revoke the prize it had awarded to Nikole Hannah-Jones earlier in the year. Given "the glaring historical fallacy at the heart of its account," the letter declares, "and the subsequent breaches of core journalistic ethics by both Hannah-Jones and the Times . . . the Board should acknowledge that its award was an error. It can and should correct that error by withdrawing the prize" (Wood, "Pulitzer Board"). For good measure, there is also an element of bad faith: in support of its attempt to besmirch Hannah-Jones and the 1619 Project, it cites a historian named Leslie M. Harris.

We trust that Nikole Hannah-Jones, and the 1619 Project, will be remembered long after the backlash has been consigned to the ash heap of history, hopefully along with the junk pile of Confederate statues erected after the rollback of Reconstruction. It is still possible, despite the resurgence of white nationalism in the United States and its enablers in the intelligentsia, that the arc of the moral universe will bend toward justice. Derrick Bell ended "Who's Afraid of Critical Race Theory?" a quarter of a century ago by encouraging critical race theorists not to be too disheartened by the lukewarm reception CRT had thus far received. He urged them to recall Beethoven's words when confronted by his critics: "It was not written for you, but for a later age" (910). In the following chapter, we'll try to suggest how we can rethink academic freedom for that age that might now, at long last, be upon us.

CHAPTER 5

THE LIMITS OF ACADEMIC FREEDOM

Up to this point, we have taken pains to disentangle academic freedom from freedom of speech, on the grounds that the former requires a degree of scholarly expertise and protocols of professional credentializing that are irrelevant to the latter. In this chapter, we will mount the argument that academic freedom *itself*, as traditionally understood, requires the same kind of rethinking that Charles Mills applies to liberal ideals more generally. But before we get there, we need to acknowledge that the AAUP itself has sometimes confused the issue, and we need to explain why we believe this confusion is a bad thing. Nowhere is this more apparent, or more questionable, than in the Association's 1994 statement, "On Freedom of Expression and Campus Speech Codes," which concludes with the ringing words, "Free speech is not simply an aspect of the educational enterprise to be weighed against other desirable ends. It is the very precondition of the academic enterprise itself" (362). The political pressures of that moment are still legible today: the AAUP's response to the advent of speech codes was not merely a response to the advent of speech codes, but to the broader phenomenon of "political correctness" as allegedly instantiated by those speech codes. But for us, rereading the statement now, these ringing words ring false. To be sure, some version of free speech is indispensable to the academic enterprise: universities must be intellectually autonomous from the state in that respect, and faculty members intellectually autonomous from university administrators, trustees, and donors. That is the rock on which the AAUP is founded. Students, for their part, may not enjoy academic freedom as we understand it, but they must be free to pursue and to contribute to their education in any manner that does not violate or jeopardize the educational mission of the university.

So what would it mean to act in a manner that violates or jeopardizes the educational mission of the university? That is one of the difficult questions "On Freedom of Expression and Campus Speech Codes" sought to answer, though the difficulty of the question is acknowledged more fully in the original version of the statement released in 1991, and the debate within the AAUP that followed its release, than in the final version published in *Academe* and in the AAUP "Redbook," *Policy Documents and Reports*.[1] That final version, we

1. See "A Preliminary Report on Freedom of Expression and Campus Harassment Codes" and "More on Campus Harassment Codes." The original report is deeply critical of speech codes, insisting that "within a college or university committed to the principles of academic freedom there can be no forbidden ideas" (24) and "experience demonstrates that, to be free, speech requires breathing space" (25). In line with First Amendment jurisprudence, the report draws the line only at "threats of violence and other forms of intimidation" (24), and argues that "except in the most egregious instances, when abusive status epithets or similar language, symbols, and representations are deliberately employed to degrade or humiliate those to whom they are directed, disciplinary proceedings are too blunt an instrument for the delicate task of distinguishing between impermissibly offensive speech and the expression of ideas to which academic institutions must

believe, needs to be revisited today for a number of reasons. The first is its surprising insistence that

> An institution of higher learning fails to fulfill its mission if it asserts the power to proscribe ideas—and racial or ethnic slurs, sexist epithets, or homophobic insults almost always express ideas, however repugnant. Indeed, by proscribing any ideas, a university sets an example that profoundly disserves its academic mission. (361)

Why did the AAUP accede to the argument that racial or ethnic slurs, sexist epithets, or homophobic insults constitute or express "ideas"? We see no value in dignifying insults by calling them "ideas." The "ideas" they express are typically limited to the literal terms of the utterance itself. (The earlier version of the statement explicitly made exceptions for hate speech directed at individuals; the final published version does not.)[2]

---

remain open. Reliance upon penal sanctions to curb the former will, therefore, almost inevitably chill the latter" (25).

However, the report also opened with a statement that takes on board at least some of the CRT critiques of free speech absolutism: "Academic institutions have an obligation to their students to maintain an environment conducive to the pursuit of the latter's education. They are obligated to faculty members to promote conditions conducive to teaching and to research or scholarly activity. Neither obligation is met in an environment in which some students and faculty are made to feel unwelcome and are thereby inhibited from fully participating in the life of the community for reasons unrelated to their capacity to benefit from or contribute to it" (23). No such passage survives in the final version of the statement published in 1994.

2. In his contribution to *Words That Wound*, Richard Delgado had noted that "most people today know that certain words are offensive and only calculated

But even more mistaken, we think, is the final sentence's insistence that "by proscribing any ideas, a university sets an example that profoundly disserves its academic mission." This dogmatic proscription of proscription suffuses the document and leads us to the second reason it needs to be revisited: it manifestly defaults on one of the primary responsibilities of institutions of higher education. "A college or university," it claims, "sets a perilous course if it seeks to differentiate between high-value and low-value speech" (361–62). (No version of this sentence is to be found in the 1991 draft.) On the contrary, it is one of the primary functions of a college or university, if not *the* primary function, to distinguish between high-value and low-value speech. This what professors do every time they grade student papers, write student recommendations, evaluate the work of their colleagues (especially for tenure and promotion), or participate in routine committee work. What is the intellectual mission of the university, we wonder, if it abandons the obligation to exercise critical judgment about the value of speech acts?

That abnegation of critical judgment, in the end, is the most important feature of the 1994 statement. It is announced in the document's short, emphatic second paragraph, which reads like a pull quote for the statement as a whole (and has often been cited that way): "On a campus that is free and open, no idea can be banned or forbidden. No viewpoint or message may be deemed so hateful or disturbing that it may not be expressed."[3]

---

to wound. No other use remains for such words as 'nigger,' 'wop,' 'spick,' or 'kike'" (94). This does not seem to us to be a controversial position, and we are at a loss for why the AAUP did not take it into consideration.

3. In *The Future of Academic Freedom*, Henry Reichman cites this passage of the 1994 statement approvingly, together with the passage on the proscription

This is a noble sentiment, resonating with echoes of Voltaire, Thomas Jefferson, and John Stuart Mill. It boldly and emphatically announces a commitment to radical open-mindedness, sure in the conviction that the best antidote to hate speech is more speech, and that the good will inevitably drive out the bad in the free marketplace of ideas. With that in mind, then, we would like to propose a number of lecture topics. Either or both of us will be happy to travel to your university, for a modest honorarium and reimbursement of travel and lodging expenses, to elaborate on any of the following ideas:

1. *The Jews had it coming.* Liberal orthodoxy has established that the Holocaust was a great evil, but few commentators are willing to admit that from 1880 to 1940, the domination of the world banking system, the universities, and the media by European Jews laid the grounds for an understandable, if not inevitable, resentment and backlash from people who felt excluded from and oppressed by the international order established by the Rothschilds and their associates.

2. *Vaccines cause autism.* Drawing on extensive ethnographic research into families around the world, we will contest the so-called "consensus" of experts that there is no link between compulsory vaccination and autism, and argue that the Brit-

---

against the proscription of ideas we have cited above, writing, "Although academic freedom may be limited by professional standards in ways that freedom of speech is not, it is difficult to imagine the faculty's academic freedom thriving where the freedom of expression of students and others is restricted" (24). For the reasons we are setting forth in this chapter, we think it is a serious mistake to link academic freedom to such a broad and indiscriminate endorsement of the value of *all* ideas (including epithets).

ish medical journal *The Lancet* was pressured into retracting its 1998 article on the subject by an international smear campaign waged by the medical establishment against Dr. Andrew Wakefield.

3. *Phrenology has much to teach us.* The groundbreaking work of Italian physician and criminologist Cesare Lombroso (1835–1909) has been deliberately neglected and maligned for decades by a woke orthodoxy forbidding the exploration of the links between physiognomy, congenital defects, and criminality. In this lecture, we will demonstrate why Lombroso's work remains important today, using calipers of our own design to determine, by precise measurements of the skulls of audience members, who among us is most likely to become a perpetrator of violent crime.

4. *Climate change is a hoax.* Driven by foundation funding and anticapitalist sentiment, *soi-disant* "climate scientists" have established a stultifying atmosphere—a chilly climate, one might say—that discourages skeptical thought and inquiry into the bases of the left-liberal belief that carbon emissions tied to fossil fuels are adversely affecting Earth's ecosystems. In this lecture, we will explore how, in the words of one observer, the "attempt to keep debate away from the general public and restrict it to academic experts" has enforced a lockstep conformity of thought within the ranks of an "unelected clique" of scientists.

5. *Black and brown people are incapable of self-government.* Drawing on the extensive archive of material we mentioned at the end of chapter 3, we will challenge the fashionable belief in political "self-determination" in two ways: first, by adducing contemporary examples in which Black self-government has

been self-undermining, and second, by developing counter-factuals in which we show that over the past five hundred years, Black and brown people would have been worse off, in the aggregate, if they had not been enslaved and colonized by the European powers.

We realize that in topic 5, we are poaching on Bruce Gilley's turf; in topic 4 we are encroaching on the territory of British climate change denialist Joanna Williams, who writes in *Academic Freedom in an Age of Conformity* that "the formal privileging of some ideas over others and some social groups over others is dependent upon the political biases of an unappointed academic elite" (14) and that "in some cases, such as climate change, this is because the science is presented as settled" (19). (In fact, the quotes in the final sentence of that paragraph above are from Williams, 9.)[4] Nevertheless, we think we might be plausible speakers on these topics. When it comes to

4. It is not too much to say that one of Williams's aims is to advance an extreme libertarian idea of academic freedom so as to smuggle in an argument for climate change denial. That argument runs throughout her book, and leads to some unintentionally comic moments, as when she writes, "over recent years funding into climate change has increasingly been made available for projects which consider ways to reduce carbon emissions and promote sustainability, rather than those that aim to use science to counteract anthropocentric global warming and promote industrial development (see National Association of Scholars 2015)" (57). The citation here is to a 2015 NAS report, "Sustainability: Higher Education's New Fundamentalism," the content of which bears out the trollish premise of its title (Wood, "Sustainability"). Leaving aside Williams's insinuation that projects that promote reductions in carbon emissions are *not* making use of science, and that there is something suspect about the flow of funds to such projects, we

other controversial ideas, however, such as "torture is sometimes necessary and useful in matters of national security" and "people with significant intellectual disabilities are inherently less valuable than other humans and at an extreme should not be considered rights-bearing 'persons' at all," we feel that we are very likely out of our depth, and refer our readers to the seminal work of, respectively, John Yoo, Emanuel S. Heller Professor of Law at the University of California at Berkeley, and Peter Singer, Ira W. DeCamp Professor of Bioethics at Princeton University.

---

remain skeptical that someone who speaks of "anthropocentric" global warming has anything very useful to say about anthropogenic global warming.

Lest this seem a pedantic point about a possible error in copyediting, we could turn to Williams's badly mistaken reading of the AAUP's 1940 Statement of Principles, in which she claims that "one way in which the 1940 *Statement* limits academic freedom is in the instruction to faculty to avoid 'controversial discussion unrelated to their subject.' Far from freedom of extramural utterance, this restricts academics to speaking or writing only on topics relevant to their immediate professional specialization" (44). Passages like this make us wonder whether Williams's book received any meaningful editorial oversight at all. The language of the 1940 Statement is as follows: "teachers are entitled to freedom in the classroom in discussing their subject, but they should be careful not to introduce into their teaching controversial matter which has no relation to their subject." Williams's quote is inaccurate, and, more to the point, the 1940 statement (as we hope we made clear in chapter 2) has no bearing whatsoever on extramural speech. And lest anyone think the AAUP was trying to discourage controversy *per se*, the 1970 Interpretive Comment should have put that worry to rest: "The intent of this statement is not to discourage what is 'controversial.' Controversy is at the heart of the free academic inquiry which the entire statement is designed to foster. The passage serves to underscore the need for teachers to avoid persistently intruding material which has no relation to their subject."

We adduce Yoo and Singer in order to remind our readers, should they need reminding, that American universities not only employ people with odious views but reward them with prestigious named chairs at elite institutions. In the case of Singer, we can only suggest that people should ignore his views on human beings with significant intellectual disabilities, a topic about which, despite the volume of his writings on it, he remains underinformed and remarkably incurious. His work on animal rights and on inequality, by contrast, remains extremely important.[5] Similarly, we imagine that John Yoo can be defended for his work in other areas of law, areas that do not involve the commission and justification of crimes against humanity. As for our other proposed ideas for discussion, we believe there is a plausible case that topics 2 and 4, involving vaccination and climate change, might serve as foils for a more serious debate about how various scientific communities achieve consensus: that is, how, whether one subscribes to the philosophy and history of science associated with T. S. Kuhn or with Karl Popper, scientific paradigms are established, maintained, and challenged. We would consider it a dereliction of a university's educational mission, however, if antivaxxers and climate change denialists were permitted to speak without that kind of contextualization, as if their claims on the world were as valid as any other. And finally, with regard to topics 1, 3, and 5—involving Holo-

5. Michael has addressed Singer's shortcomings in this respect elsewhere, in "Equality, Freedom, and/or Justice for All: A Response to Martha Nussbaum" and *Life as Jamie Knows It: An Exceptional Child Grows Up*. See also Licia Carlson, *The Faces of Intellectual Disability: Philosophical Reflections* and Sunaura Taylor, *Beasts of Burden: Animal and Disability Liberation*, which does an admirable job of disarticulating Singer's work on animals from his work regarding humans with intellectual disabilities.

caust apologetics, phrenology, and white supremacy—we cannot imagine any legitimate educational purpose whatsoever.

When, in the course of writing this book and talking with colleagues, we have offered phrenology as an example of the kind of thing that should not be covered by the declaration that no idea should be banned or forbidden, we have met with skepticism as to whether there are any practicing phrenologists in the United States. We doubt it. But our point is, of course, that phrenology is one more rotten fruit of the rotten branch of white supremacist pseudoscience that formed the intellectual bulwark of theories of white supremacy from roughly 1850 to 1950 and gave us the era of eugenics. And though phrenology may be decaying in the junk bin of ideas today, yet another strain of that rotten fruit, research purporting to show a link between "race" and IQ, continues—as we noted with regard to Charles Murray and Gregory Christainsen—to survive at the margins of respectable discourse.[6] Indeed, it is striking that the physical sciences have managed to discredit phrenology altogether, for roughly the same reason that no practicing scientists today are investigating phlogiston or attempting to transmute lead into gold. In the social sciences, by contrast, zombie ideas involving race and IQ have proven exceptionally difficult to kill.

The quick and decisive reply to the libertarian absolutism of the 1994 statement is that of Stanley Fish, who asserts simply (and, we believe, correctly) that "Freedom of speech is not an academic

6. As Alex Shephard argues in "Charles Murray Is Never Going Away": "It doesn't matter that his research has been discredited—it all falls under a 'controversial' viewpoint that, for uncurious publishers, is indistinguishable from the usual conservative dreck. Far from being destroyed . . . Murray is seemingly always in the midst of a resurgence."

value. Accuracy of speech is an academic value; completeness of speech is an academic value; relevance of speech is an academic value. Each of these values is directly related to the goal of academic inquiry: getting a matter of fact right" ("Free Speech"). Fish's understanding of academic freedom is ultimately too narrow, we believe, because it would wrongly exclude legitimate work that leads to overtly political conclusions (of whatever stripe). Fish famously admonishes professors to "save the world on your own time"—the title of his 2008 book—as if professors seeking to contain the effects of climate change, for example, should not be trying literally to save the world in their professional capacities. However, we think his insistence on "accuracy of speech" is vastly preferable to the abdication of intellectual responsibility entailed in the AAUP's 1994 statement. One wonders why college professors would be so reluctant to affirm that the purpose of institutions of higher education is not to ensure that all views be heard, but to determine, by careful and impartial review, which views merit a hearing and which serve no conceivable educational mission. More to our immediate point, one wonders why college professors are so selective in their insistence that all views be heard: as Ulrich Baer writes in *What Snowflakes Get Right*, "Once scholars have accepted a set of facts by reaching a consensus, for example the theory of the Big Bang, the reasons for the extinction of the dinosaurs, or the financial situation of France at the time of the Louisiana Purchase, it is included as an indisputable ground rule for proceeding. The range of examples can be expanded greatly to show that the exclusion of some ideas as outright silly or absurd is standard procedure but that people tend to make absolutist exceptions when it comes to racial pseudo-science" (12). This, we believe, is precisely how ostensibly principled free-speech absolutism has worked in American academe. The AAUP should not be a party to it.

THOUGH BAER'S CRITIQUE of free speech absolutism on campus is principally concerned with controversies over invited speakers and student protests, and not with academic freedom, we will walk through his argument here because, like critical race theory, it has profound implications for how we think about freedom *as such*—and we find that his arguments about the limits of free speech on campus can be applied *a fortiori* to the principle of academic freedom. Baer's position rests on two premises usually overlooked or implicitly denied by free speech absolutists: one, the university is not a public square, but an educational institution with a mission to foster robust and legitimate intellectual exchange (he shares this position with Fish); two, the advent of Trumpism, and the increasingly open expressions of fascism and neo-Nazism in the United States, place unbearable pressure on liberal shibboleths about how the so-called marketplace of ideas actually works in reality.

For Baer, the defining moment for reevaluating free speech absolutism arrived in August 2017, with the neo-Nazi "Unite the Right" attack on Charlottesville and the University of Virginia:

> In the wake of the events in Charlottesville, it has become more evident that hate speech cannot be simply defeated with more speech. It has also become more evident that defending an absolute principle of free speech only works for everyone when the principle of equality is defended vigorously at the same time. Defending free speech as an absolute right, without also rejecting the content of virulent racist and misogynist speech, creates a moral vacuum. (xiv)

Notoriously, Donald Trump refused to condemn the rally, affirming the neo-Nazis' right to speak even though one of them had killed a counterprotestor, Heather Heyer. Baer writes:

> In legal terms, such viewpoint neutrality is a cherished principle. In the academy and real life, as President Trump's remarks showed, such abstractions do not really work. Defending an abstract idea of speech, without considering the content and context of the speech, does not work outside of the law. The events in Charlottesville, then, are perhaps less about free speech than about violence, intimidation, and terror. (xvi)

We think this is a good way to think about the "Unite the Right" rally; each of us would argue, on our home campuses (and Michael has, at Penn State), that an invitation for neo-Nazi Richard Spencer to speak should be seen not as a matter of free speech but as a tacit incitement to violence. And we agree with Baer that the reemergence of American neo-Nazis into public view raises unavoidable questions for people who believe, in the oft-cited words of Justice Brandeis, that "sunlight is the best disinfectant" for hate speech.

Revisiting the famous 1977 decision of the American Civil Liberties Union (ACLU) to defend the right of neo-Nazis to march in the largely Jewish suburb of Skokie, Illinois, Baer writes,

> If Skokie was a victory for free speech, did the neo-Nazis' march expose vile ideas of virulent racism to sunlight, where they withered and died? . . . That is the question at the heart of today's campus controversies: is our country better off in 2018 because the courts have protected hate speech above other types of speech? Or is the country worse off in 2018 because hate speech and anti-democratic

activism have been granted special protection not accorded to other types of speech? (69–70)

These are the right questions to ask—not only about Skokie and Charlottesville but about Nazism in general, starting with the original phenomenon a century ago, before it entered its neo- phase: "did permitting Adolf Hitler to speak after he had been forbidden from political agitation in the 1920s, and permitting the Nazis to promulgate anti-democratic ideals in 1930's Germany through marches and speeches, provide a benefit to the world?" (133) And the clear and unambiguous answer, we believe, is no, the promulgation of antidemocratic ideals in Weimar Germany did not provide a benefit to the world, and the United States is in many respects worse off because hate speech and antidemocratic activism have been granted special protection not accorded to other types of speech. It turns out that sometimes sunlight is not the best disinfectant. On the contrary, sometimes sunlight makes things grow, and little shoots of neo-Nazism begin to flower and bear fruit everywhere. Bleach, perhaps, might be a better disinfectant.

Baer notes that American support for absolute free speech is strongly bipartisan: where conservatives and libertarians are distrustful of government regulation in general, and especially with regard to the expression of belief (religious or otherwise), liberals' support is premised partly on the "worry that restrictions on speech will eventually limit them" (114), and partly on a faith in the power of reason and democratic deliberation. That faith, argues Baer, leads liberals to see their tolerance of hate speech as a virtue:

Defending the neo-Nazis is proof of their moral fortitude. They also believe that disputes will be settled on the basis of what is *true*, *reasonable, and just*, rather than what is persuasive, popular, better phrased, or backed by force. Extremist positions, progressive speech advocates maintain, will be defeated in the marketplace of ideas, which extends all around the college lectern, by refutation, reasoned critique, or ridicule. The Nazis will be laughed out of the lecture hall; the Holocaust deniers will scurry off when their lies are examined in the light of day; the racial supremacists will recognize the wrongness of assaulting the dignity of minorities and the rightness of America's bedrock principle of equality, once they've been exposed to reasoned argument and more speech from the other side. More speech! This, liberals hope, will yield the truth. (115)

Indeed, Baer writes, some liberals go so far as to argue that exposure to hate speech is beneficial *for the targets of hate speech themselves*. His paraphrase of this position may seem, at first, mildly snarky: "It might be a rocky ride for some, but with a sufficiently thick skin and a few political bruises, and the option to stay home when the Nazis come to town, everyone will be better off in the end, as long as we grant a hearing to even the worst ideas. In fact, exposure to hateful ideas will increase society's overall capacity for the toleration of difference" (116–17). A few pages later, however, Baer reveals that this characterization of the liberal position is in fact thoroughly fair, when he quotes Columbia University president and First Amendment scholar Lee Bollinger, who, in his 1986 book *The Tolerant Society*, wrote that encountering hate speech leads to an "increase in our capacity for toleration generally" (134, quoting Bollinger 182).

More astonishing, perhaps, is Baer's citation of Nadine Strossen's 2018 book, *Hate: Why We Should Resist It with Free Speech, Not Censorship*, which immediately follows his citation of Bollinger. "Nadine Strossen," Baer writes, "president emerita of the ACLU, entertains the idea that 'hearing hateful speech . . . [can constitute] opportunities for positive personal development'" (134, quoting Strossen 126). Here Baer is subtly pulling a punch; the original passage in Strossen's book is actually worse. Here's what the ellipsis elides: "the best strategy for both mental and physical health is *education about the fact that such speech is not necessarily harmful*, and about how to perceive such stressful situations as opportunities for positive personal development" (126; emphasis added). We have admired Nadine Strossen's work for decades and are at a loss to account for the extraordinary arrogance and condescension involved in the words we have highlighted. Not only is exposure to hate speech ultimately good for its targets; more than this, it provides an opportunity for someone (who?) to step in and inform the person targeted by hate speech of "the fact"—the fact!—"that such speech is not necessarily harmful." We doubt very much that anyone on the receiving end of hate speech will find this counsel comforting or persuasive. We suspect that Mari Matsuda had a far better sense of what is at stake when she wrote, in *Words That Wound*, that "tolerance of hate speech is not tolerance borne by the community at large. Rather, it is a psychic tax imposed on those least able to pay" (18). Baer, for his part, remarks drily, "there is no evidence that our society has grown more tolerant because hate was permitted to flourish. I also cannot locate evidence that hate speech always provides opportunities for positive development for minority communities" (134).

This aspect of Baer's argument clearly reaches beyond the issue of controversial campus speakers, making claims about the shortcomings and blind spots of free speech absolutism in general; indeed, as we will see below, one prong of that argument goes to the very heart of American self-definition. But we are spelling it out here because we believe that Baer, unlike most commentators in the mainstream of debates over the First Amendment, has correctly realized that libertarian beliefs in the reliability of the free marketplace of ideas have been revealed to be without foundation. (Whether that realization is due to his learning from the work of CRT, his deep familiarity with Germany's history, or the advent of Trump is unclear, though he tends to stress the latter.) That belief in a marketplace of ideas is the intellectual counterpart to the libertarian belief in the invisible hand of the free market in economics, a belief that has survived more than a century and a half of catastrophic boom-bust cycles in capitalism that revealed (at least for Keynesians and people concerned with basic issues of equity) the need for a more tightly regulated mixed economy. The belief in a free marketplace of ideas cannot account for the zombie afterlife of ideas that should have died a natural death, whether in the form of neo-Nazism worldwide or the neo-Confederate enclaves in the United States. For Baer, that is why the "Unite the Right" rally in Charlottesville was decisive.[7]

But we could add two more reasons to be skeptical of that free marketplace. We have mentioned them above: the first is the ascen-

7. Of course (and it needs to be said more than once), CRT had made similar arguments long before the "Unite the Right" rally made them inescapable. Charles Lawrence in *Words That Wound*: "Blacks and other people of color are equally skeptical about the absolutist argument that even the most injurious speech must remain unregulated because in an unregulated marketplace of ideas the best ideas will rise to the top and gain acceptance. Our experience tells us the opposite. We have seen too many demagogues elected by appealing to U.S. racism. We have seen too many good, liberal politicians shy away from the issues that might brand them as too closely allied with us. The American marketplace of ideas was founded with the idea of the racial inferiority of nonwhites as one of its chief commodities, and ever since the market opened, racism has remained its most active item in trade" (76–77).

dancy in the twenty-first century of an extreme libertarian interpretation of the First Amendment that tilts the field toward corporations and religious conservatives, which some legal theorists have dubbed "First Amendment Lochnerism."[8] As Tim Wu, Isidor and Seville Sulzbacher Professor of Law at Columbia Law School, has written,

> The First Amendment was once thought of as the law of the political underdog. Its archetypal beneficiary was the humble pamphleteer whose unpopular ideas eventually gain majority support. . . . Today, however, the First Amendment's role in the American political process has changed decisively. It can longer be described as a law that protects unpopular speakers or other politically weak actors. . . . If the First Amendment could once be described as a remedy for defects in the political process, it has now as often become the cause of such defects. For today's First Amendment is regularly deployed not to promote or facilitate political debate but to end it. Across broad areas of public regulation, the judiciary has intervened to shut down active political debate in the fields of privacy, telecommunication, securities, false advertising, and health and safety regulation, among others. ("Beyond")

The second reason, loosely related to the first, is the rise of social media, which, according to media theorist Siva Vaidhyanathan (and many other observers), "has fostered the deterioration of democratic

8. For those of you not steeped in the law, "Lochnerism" derives its name from the 1905 Supreme Court decision *Lochner v. New York*, which was the centerpiece of decades of overreaching legal decisions that sought to strike down any regulations, contracts, or laws that were perceived to infringe on the free market.

and intellectual culture around the world" (3).[9] There is a case to be made that Facebook is especially susceptible to pressure from the extreme right wing: in 2020 alone, the social-media behemoth was revealed to have tweaked its algorithms specifically to support the far-right *Daily Wire* and harm the venerable left-wing *Mother Jones*, and in the wake of the election, Mark Zuckerberg himself said that extreme-right conspiracy theorist and white nationalist Steve Bannon had not violated enough Facebook policies to justify a ban—after Bannon had posted a call for the beheading of Dr. Anthony Fauci, director of the National Institute of Allergy and Infectious Diseases. (It helps, no doubt, that Facebook's vice president of global public policy, Joel Kaplan, has numerous ties to alt-right outlets like the Daily Caller and the Daily Wire.)[10] But even if that were not the case, Facebook would still be a menace; as Vaidhyanathan puts it, "Facebook is explicitly engineered to promote items that generate strong reactions," and "[t]his design feature—or flaw, if you care about the

9. See also the Freedom House report, "Media Freedom: A Downward Spiral." Social media "can certainly help pro-democracy movements at times, but they overall give far-right parties and authoritarians an advantage."
10. For the tweaking of Facebook's algorithms, see Bauerlein and Jeffery, "Facebook Manipulated the News You See to Appease Republicans, Insiders Say"; for Zuckerberg's refusal to ban Bannon, see Guynn, "Mark Zuckerberg Defends Not Banning Steve Bannon from Facebook for Beheading Comments"; for Kaplan's connections to and promotion of the alt-right, see Weissman, "Facebook Kowtowed to Conservatives and Got Nothing in Return." It is diagnostic of the mendacity and chutzpah of American conservatives that they continue to complain that social media are biased against *them*. But now that Trump has been banned from Facebook at least until 2023 and indefinitely suspended from Twitter (long overdue actions, we believe), they do have a martyr to celebrate.

quality of knowledge and debate—ensures that the most inflammatory material will travel the farthest and the fastest. Sober, measured accounts of the world have no chance on Facebook. And when Facebook dominates our sense of the world and our social circles, we all potentially become carriers of extremist nonsense" (5).

Liberal theorists of democracy have not yet taken on the full implications of this latter development. We still cling to the wreckage of Habermasian beliefs about the public sphere, originating in early eighteenth-century coffee shops in England and evolving into systems of global mass communication that make it possible, in theory (and largely in practice, in the industrialized world), for anyone to contribute to public discourse. We imagined that this revolution in communications would be the equivalent and the enabler of the project of human emancipation that began with the Enlightenment, in which all humans would eventually be seen as free and equal regardless of rank or station. And we say "we" because we ourselves believed some version of this creed.

But now we have learned that a global system of mass communications that connects two billion humans worldwide is not like a great big coffee shop in which people exchange reasoned ideas about the good life and the just society. It is more like an internet comment thread from hell, continually hijacked by trolls who have no interest whatsoever in reasoned ideas about anything. Social media have revealed—decisively and irrevocably, we believe—that not everyone at the table is operating in good faith. The free marketplace of ideas, realized most fully in Facebook, turns out not to be a seminar for the promotion of democracy. It turns out to be an anarchic free-for-all that affords both sunlight and oxygen to the most noxious ideas humans have yet devised, and leads directly to the circulation of elaborate, supercharged fantasies about child-abduction-and-molestation networks run by Democratic officials operating out of a Washington pizza parlor and masses of tiki-torch-wielding white supremacists marching through the grounds of the University of Virginia chanting "Jews will not replace us."

Under these circumstances, the claim that a university "sets a perilous course if it seeks to differentiate between high-value and low-value speech" (to return to the language of the 1994 AAUP statement on speech codes) looks more and more absurd with each passing year. This is rather a mission statement for the College of Facebook or Troll State University. The lesson of the past decade, we believe, is that it is more imperative than ever for universities to differentiate between high-value and low-value speech, or, if you prefer, legitimate ideas and utter bullshit. That is why we find so refreshing Baer's emphatic insistence that "the university's purpose is to vet ideas" (10); it was always true, even in the early 1990s when the AAUP statement was being composed, but it has become especially urgent in the age of social media.

REGARDLESS OF OUR enthusiasm for Baer's argument, however, we strongly suspect that despite his cogent criticisms of free speech absolutism, Baer is unlikely to make any real inroads on the past century of First Amendment jurisprudence.[11] Whatever the merits of his argument, and we believe they are many, it may never gain a sufficiently sympathetic hearing in the United States to affect policy, just as

---

11. The mainstream appetite for Baer-like arguments is clearly growing, though, as indicated by Emily Bazelon's October 2020 *New York Times Magazine* cover article "Free Speech in an Age of Disinformation." See also Thomas Edsall, "Have Trump's Lies Wrecked Free Speech?"—published, as fate would have it, on the morning of the day Trump loyalists stormed and desecrated the US Capitol in what was billed as a "First Amendment Protest."

the profusion of mass-murder shootings may never dislodge the American belief in the right to own weapons that make mass-murder shootings possible. Baer takes pains to point out that other developed nations—including, notably, Germany—have limitations on hate speech that somehow have not plunged their citizens into totalitarian dystopias. But we Americans seem to think—or have until Trump's presidency—that those limitations are not suitable for us. We are exceptional. There is, we are finding to our collective horror, a destructive and potentially murderous libertarianism baked into the country's very foundation.[12] We worry that, off campus and in the courts, Baer's argument has a snowflake's chance in hell of catching on.

But on campus, it's another story. Because universities have educational missions, regulation of speech goes with the territory. This is why, when critics of "political correctness" and "cancel culture" become agitated, they write columns like Andrew Sullivan's "We All Live on Campus Now": it is understood, in those quarters, that the attempt to marginalize or exclude speech that does not contribute to the educational mission is a *bad* thing, and campuses should accordingly be mocked or reviled. But for Baer, that attempt is necessary as a precondition for meaningful intellectual exchange:

> when someone has a record of eschewing the rules of debate, of
> lying deliberately in order to undermine others' faith in reason,
> and refusing the overall goal of reaching a consensus on truth and

12. Examples are legion, but for sheer barking lunacy, it's hard to beat the decision of the National Association of Radio Talk Show Hosts giving their 1995 Freedom of Speech Award to G. Gordon Liddy in 1995 in honor of his suggestion that Americans should resist agents of the Bureau of Alcohol, Tobacco, and Firearms by shooting for the head.

falsehoods, *any rented hall but not the university is a perfect setting for his or her speech.* The liberal commitment to reason is admirable. It is also politically naïve. It assumes that in the plurality of values found in our society, there are no speakers who dispute and want to destroy the values of debate, argument, and reason. (117; emphasis added)

For Baer, then, there are finally two reasons to exclude white supremacists from the conversation. We have already addressed the first: the belief in white supremacy is founded on racist pseudoscience that has long been discredited in the physical sciences (where it is widely accepted that "race" has no meaning in a biological sense) but continues to hang on in a revanchist branch of social science that attributes white supremacy to "cultural" rather than to biological differences. Baer thus seeks to draw a "[b]right yet very narrow line around a specific type of speech that undermines the equal participation in the university" (40). That line circumscribes, and proscribes, speech that proposes that some humans are innately inferior to others, and thus undermines the baseline assumption of human equality without which, for Baer, free speech degenerates into an exercise in domination. "There is no academic reason," Baer writes, "for discussing the once-popular idea of the benefits of slavery for the enslaved as a valid political notion, or that homosexuality is a curable disease as a scientific theory, or that women are less skilled in abstract thinking as a biological fact" (36).[13] Indeed, these are ideas

13. Baer does not address the question of intellectual disability anywhere in *What Snowflakes Get Right* and arguably leaves the door open for Peter Singer to read people with significant intellectual disabilities out of the category of "persons" altogether. But we think the principles Baer sets forth apply equally—in the name of equality—in the case of disability.

"that are not only obsolete, not only settled long ago, but also under-mine the university's functioning" (40). Thus,

> The idea of organizing society around the supremacy of the "white race," or subordinating women to secondary status, does not merit debate on campus. To debate the idea of racial superiority does not serve the university's fundamental mission, or what the law calls its "compelling interest," since it re-hashes a disproven theory which had once been popular but, based on expert consensus, is now no different from other obsolete ideas of junk science. In the context of higher education, such speech undermines the conditions for and legal requirement of equal participation on which a university is based. (41–42)[14]

The second reason for excluding the excluders goes back to our argument at the close of chapter 3, namely, the recognition that some forms of groundless, delusional, or corrosive speech are more dangerous than others, given the context in which they are uttered. To illustrate, let us return to the case of Amy Wax, with which we began this book.

This time, however, we do so with the caveat that while we see Wax's beliefs as disqualifying, this view is not shared widely. On the right, she is a hero and a victim, unfairly disciplined by her

---

14. Here, a nod to an apposite passage from the work of Matsuda would have been helpful, and so we will provide one: "we accept certain principles as the shared historical legacy of the world community. Racial supremacy is one of the ideas we have collectively and internationally considered and rejected" (37). Apparently we need to be reminded time and again that we have, in fact, internationally considered and rejected the idea of racial supremacy.

administration for bravely bucking the liberal orthodoxy on cultural differences; among libertarians, she is a cause célèbre for freedom of speech.[15] Writing on the AAUP's *Academe* blog, for instance, Keith Whittington, the William Nelson Cromwell Professor of Politics at Princeton University and the author of *Speak Freely: Why Universities Must Defend Free Speech*, claims that "the Wax case is not a hard case":

> She should be fully protected from employer sanction based on the content of the views that she has expressed in her public writings and speeches. This principle is foundational to the modern protection of academic freedom, and there is no exception for faculty speech that makes students uncomfortable or contradicts a dean's opinion about the values of the institution. Wax is being criticized not merely for how she says things, but for the very substance of her ideas, ideas that are close to her scholarly endeavors. If her speech is not well inside the protected sphere of academic freedom, then academic freedom has little to offer those who might hold controversial views. ("Academic Freedom, Even for Amy Wax")

Like most free speech absolutists, Whittington refuses the idea that objections to the content of Wax's statements are acceptable. But we

---

15. In 2018, Penn trustee emeritus and Penn Law school overseer Paul S. Levy actually resigned in protest over Penn's decision to remove Wax from required first-year courses, writing to President Amy Gutmann that the decision effectively suppresses "open, robust and critical debate over differing views of important social issues." Levy's resignation letter suggests that he was not familiar with the issues in Wax's case, one of which, surely, is the fact that academic freedom does not include the right to tell lies about the academic performance of one's Black students. (See Fortinsky.)

note that this characterization of Wax's remarks relies repeatedly on obfuscating language such as "speech that makes students uncomfortable or contradicts a dean's opinion about the values of the institution" and (that old standby) "controversial views." This seems to us an impressively anodyne way of describing statements like this:

> Perhaps the most important reason that the cultural case for limited immigration remains underexplored has to do with that bête noire—race. Let us be candid. Europe and the First World, to which the United States belongs, remain mostly white for now; and the Third World, although mixed, contains a lot of non-white people. Embracing cultural distance, cultural distance nationalism, means, in effect, taking the position that our country will be better off with more whites and fewer non-whites.

These remarks were made in Wax's speech to the National Conservatism Conference in July 2019 and later published online by *The Federalist*; the speech is peppered with citations of the beliefs of noted Islamophobe Daniel Pipes and notorious British xenophobe Enoch Powell (in Wax's words, "a prophet without honor in the last century"), as well as a shout-out to Lawrence Mead—to whom she refers as "Larry"—for his groundbreaking work in *The Burdens of Freedom*. (To be fair, the speech is not excessively dry and scholarly. It also contains critical anecdata about how "cultural transmission is importantly shaped by the small-bore interactions within families, or mother-child." "And if you doubt that," Wax said, "just go to the South of France where I was recently, and you watch three-year-olds sitting for two hours at the table, their mothers prodding them every step of the way. Somebody ought to study that." We await the full, peer-reviewed study.)

Whittington acknowledges the problem we discussed in chapter 2, namely, the question of the relation between a professor's extramural speech and his or her areas of scholarly expertise:

> Precisely because Wax's remarks about immigration policy are related to her scholarship, it might be possible to demonstrate that her remarks are evidence of professional incompetence and scholarly malpractice. If so, that might justify her being sanctioned by a university. In the context of legal scholarship, that is a very heavy lift. In the course of their scholarly activities, law professors say lots of wrongheaded things about which they have limited scholarly expertise. Any reasonable standard that would result in Wax being dismissed for professional incompetence would sweep fairly broadly through the ranks of the elite law schools.

We have no doubt that Whittington is right about this, and so much the worse for our elite law schools.[16] We are dismayed, then, that his

16. Just to take two egregious examples from 2020 alone, in which widely influential law professors at elite institutions descend into extramural crackpottery, we could point to Hoover Institution law professor Richard Epstein's assurance that the death toll from COVID-19 in the United States would level out at about 5,000 (he had originally claimed 500, then corrected himself, claiming that he had made a mistake with the math), and George Washington University law professor Jonathan Turley's postelection claim, to *Fox and Friends*, that Dominion voting machines may have fraudulently tipped the Michigan election to Joe Biden. ("In Michigan, you had thousands of votes that were given to Biden that belonged to Trump," Turley claimed. "Now, that doesn't mean it was a nefarious purpose. This is a new software that apparently is vulnerable to human error.") The latter claim is well beyond ordinary crackpottery and ventures into the alternate universe of

solution to this problem is to say, "[f]or academic purposes, far better to ignore her work or demonstrate its flaws than denounce it as repugnant." Let us just say once again—with feeling, in italics—that *demonstrating the flaws in this kind of work doesn't work*. It is impervious to rebuttal on all empirical and rational grounds. That is how it has survived to this day.

As for ignoring Wax's work, Whittington's own conclusion demonstrates why it is impossible to treat it as the mutterings of a random person on a street corner:

> I have little sympathy for Amy Wax's arguments about immigration. I suspect they are empirically dubious, and they certainly reflect values that are not my own. But they also reflect a set of positions that has substantial support in the political arena and that has often influenced American public policy. She offers actual arguments for her views, and generally does not engage in the kind of rhetorical excesses that, say, our current president and many of our university faculty regularly use on social media.

With regard to that last sentence, we suspect that Whittington may have passed over this passage from Wax's speech:

> This position requires forthrightly acknowledging the stark differences between the First and the Third Worlds, their deep roots, and being honest about the homegrown conditions and failures

---

QAnon conspiracy theories. See Jonathan Chait, "Richard Epstein Can't Stop Being Wrong about the Coronavirus," and Colby Hall, "'I Looked Into It': Steve Doocy Debunks Trump's Dominion Software Voter Fraud Conspiracy."

that hold countries back—kleptocracy, corruption, lawlessness, weak institutions, and the inability or unwillingness of leaders to provide for their citizens' basic needs, and also asking the very hard questions about why these conditions continue to persist. But these are toxic topics that lie outside the Overton window in polite society, as evidenced by the outraged reaction to Trump's profane and grating question, "Why are we having all these people from sh-thole countries come here?" That needs to be regarded as a serious question and not just a rhetorical one.

So much for Wax's distance from Trump's rhetorical excesses. But what's truly remarkable about Whittington's defense of Wax is his acknowledgment that her views "reflect a set of positions that has substantial support in the political arena and that has often influenced American public policy." Well, exactly. As we argued with regard to Mead, *that is precisely the problem. This is what makes these views dangerous.* They are operationalized, literally *realized*, in ways that shore up and enforce white supremacy in law and in policy.

In a follow-up post on the *Academe* blog, Henry Reichman concludes that "Wax most definitely is entitled to the protections of academic freedom" but that "she must not be protected from legitimate criticism." Again, this is an instance of the liberal faith that the best antidote to hate speech is more speech, a faith we can no longer profess in good conscience. But interestingly, Reichman ends by citing a blog post by University of Colorado law professor Paul Campos, which makes the point we want to underscore here:

If Amy Wax were, say, a Maoist, or a proponent of the divine right of kings, I wouldn't pay any attention to her. One of the costs of tenure is that sometimes people will use their academic positions to push intellectually bankrupt, morally noxious, off-the-grid points of view.

The problem of course is that Wax's views, while intellectually bankrupt and morally noxious, are the opposite of off the grid. White supremacy is at the center of the contemporary American right wing, which is why such desperate efforts are being made both to deny this, and to cover it up with the thinnest of pseudo-academic gloss. This is why Wax was given a starring role at the National Conservatism conference, despite the organizers' valiant attempts to try to ensure that the intellectual defense of contemporary American conservatism would get back to saying the loud parts quietly again.

Amy Wax's name is legion, although most of her fellow travelers do a better job of keeping their real views a bit more on the down-low. She is a symptom of how depraved American conservatism has become in the age of Trump, and the fact that she is such [a] florid symptom of the underlying disease should be acknowledged and studied by students of that disease. ("Amy Wax's Mexican Problem")

We share Campos's sense that the handful of American Maoists are not a serious threat to the egalitarian premises of the United States, whereas white supremacy has been in profound tension with those premises from the moment they were premised. But as for Whittington, we submit that one has to be determinedly cavalier about the re-emergence of open and sometimes murderous white supremacy in the United States to wave Wax's arguments away with the assurance that versions of such arguments enjoy substantial support in the political arena and have often influenced American public policy.

Ultimately, judgments about the place of white supremacy in the United States go far beyond any one racist professor or even one school of thought populated by legions of racist professors. They go to the very self-definition of America, and the degree to which many Americans remain unwilling to acknowledge the nation's imbrication in white supremacy—as evidenced, as we noted in the previous chapter, by the fierce backlash against the 1619 Project's claims that slavery was central to that self-definition. But the American legacy of white supremacism was, or should have been, undeniable all along; it is the motive force behind the ethnic cleansing of the Native populations, the creation of the system of chattel slavery, and the century-long maintenance of Jim Crow. We fail to understand how this proposition can legitimately be understood as controversial. Baer invokes this legacy in a response to one of the leading theorists of First Amendment jurisprudence:

> The constitutional expert Floyd Abrams . . . insists that the First Amendment has always helped minorities, even though it was not once cited or applied from the date of its ratification in 1791 until 1919. In *The Soul of the First Amendment*, Abrams further explains that the United States protects hate speech since it has no history of racially motivated state-sponsored violence or genocide, unlike democracies such as Germany and South Africa. "It is understandable that some nations have sometimes responded by limiting particularly hateful speech that may have contributed to past tragedies. The United States has been fortunate not to have suffered such horrific events, and I am unwilling to criticize nations that have responded to such calamities by urging them to change their policies. For this nation, though, strict constitutionally imposed limitations on such legislation have served us well." (87–88, quoting Abrams 49)

Abrams's is a pungent version of American exceptionalism, finely distilled. The fact that it was published in 2017 is alarming. Whittington was willing to underestimate the virulence of contemporary white nationalism and white supremacism in the case of Amy Wax; Abrams effectively makes a guiding historical principle out of what we might call white supremacism denial. *Thank goodness none of those horrific events happened here.*

To dissent from what some might believe is a baffling and profoundly mistaken assessment of American history, Baer discreetly notes, is not to equate slavery and Jim Crow with the Holocaust or apartheid:

> The point is not to create false and misleading equivalencies, and Abrams is correct to differentiate between the incommensurate and truly incomparable horrors of the Holocaust, apartheid, and crimes such as chattel slavery and the genocide of Native Americans. But has our varying legislation around hate speech, which Abrams defends by omitting a crucial part of our nation's history, really "served us well"? Differently put, who in America has benefitted from the protection of hate speech, which Abrams unequivocally champions especially for vile and incendiary speech? (87–88)

One persuasive answer has been offered by Brittney Cooper, in an essay titled "How Free Speech Works for White Academics." Commenting on the Gilley affair, Cooper takes her distance from the social-media outrage that followed the publication of "The Case for Colonialism": "eventually the publisher withdrew the article, after the editor had received death threats. That kind of violent trolling and harassment is absolutely unacceptable." But, Cooper argues, that does not mean that Gilley should enjoy the protection of academic freedom for explicitly, unambiguously racist work:

> It is also unacceptable to publish work that defends the right of any nation to violently colonize another group. Trying to make the case for colonialism, given what we know about the genocide of indigenous folks and the multigenerational trauma of the trans-Atlantic slave trade, is harmful. It is not merely a difference of opinion. But this is often how freedom of speech works for white academics—they are given a platform for their ideas, even when it is clear that the ideas don't meet academic standards.

We want to emphasize Cooper's final point—that the ideas that support a defense of colonialism don't meet academic standards. For, to return to Timothy Burke's response to Lawrence Mead, those ideas did meet academic standards for decades, standards set by an academy consisting almost exclusively of white men; the question now is how to raise those standards so that they exclude what is now obviously ignorant hackwork.

In the course of our discussions with colleagues, we have encountered the objection that Baer's conception of free speech relies heavily on a German intellectual tradition that is not in the mainstream of American thinking (this despite its continuities with the American countertradition of CRT). Our response is: so much the better. Perhaps we can learn something from an intellectual tradition that has been compelled to take genocide seriously; perhaps that tradition can help repair the lacunae in a tradition defined by a form of exceptionalism that, at an extreme, entails a systemic denial of the genocide of the Native inhabitants of the hemisphere and the enslavement and violent subordination of Africans. The German intellectual tradition has an urgent need to disavow its white supremacist past and refuse to countenance its neo- manifestations today; the American tradition has much to learn from that example. To say this is not—we repeat, not—to say that the United States is hopelessly or irredeemably racist. Quite the contrary: it is to say that a full and honest accounting of our history is necessary for the formation of a more perfect union. We still believe in that egalitarian promise. We do not want to see it betrayed by people who refuse to acknowledge that any such accounting is necessary.

But then that invites the obvious question: why haven't we Americans learned from our own history? Why have the Germans been able to institutionally internalize the lessons of the Holocaust while we haven't been able to internalize the lessons of slavery and settler colonialism?[17]

More accurately, some of us have and some of us haven't yet but may be ready to. We (here, we literally mean our two selves) are classic examples of the white left-liberal stunned by Trump's election and by wave upon wave of police and vigilante killings of Black men and women into thinking much more critically about what Jennifer Richeson, in her essay "Americans are Determined to Believe in Black Progress" (subtitled "Whether It's Happening or Not") has called the "uniquely American mythology." "When we think about the nation's racist history," she writes, "we often envision a linear path, one that, admittedly, begins in a shameful period but moves unerringly in a single direction—toward equality." "This redemptive narrative not only smooths over the past but it smooths over what is yet to come," she continues; "It holds out the promise of an almost predestined,

17. For one especially compelling answer, see Susan Neiman, *Learning from the Germans: Race and the Memory of Evil.*

naturally occurring future that will be even more just and egalitarian." If Obama seemed to affirm the inevitability of this narrative, Trump affirmed its opposite, that *it can happen here—and it has.* How to reconcile a version of history that moves steadily in the right direction (if sometimes two steps forward, one step back) with one in which a nation's history can be so easily hijacked? Neither versions of history (American progress, German aberration) fit the United States. Perhaps nothing demonstrates this as well as the post-Reconstruction project of Southern Redemption. In our experience, white Americans—including the white Americans we have known as students—have an especially difficult time understanding that after 1877, and for many decades thereafter, living conditions for many Black Americans became markedly *worse.* It is far easier to imagine that the Civil War ended slavery and then gradually, only about a hundred years later, the civil rights movement came along.

In *Red, White, and Black: Cinema and the Structure of U.S. Antagonisms*, Frank Wilderson III distinguishes between "gratuitous" and "contingent" violence. Contingent violence upon a person is contingent upon some act, some rule broken or some other transgression rightly or wrongly construed; gratuitous violence is that violence that can be enacted upon persons when they are not recognized as being fully persons. The German Jew was subject to contingent violence (break a law, get forcibly incarcerated) until they weren't, when they became people suffering gratuitous violence. The history of Black America, by contrast, begins with gratuitous violence. The Jew was a citizen and then they were not and then they were again. The Black American was not a citizen, and now is one formally but not substantively. Especially now that ubiquitous recording technology has revealed to white America the undeniable frequency with which gratuitous violence continues to be enacted upon Black persons, the claim that formal equality translates into substantive equality has become utterly specious. "Giorgio Agamben's meditations on the Muselmann," Wilderson writes, "allow him to claim Auschwitz as 'something so unprecedented that one tries to make it comprehensible by bringing it back to categories that are both extreme and absolutely familiar: life and death, dignity and indignity'" (35). To this, Wilderson responds, "Agamben is not wrong so much as he is late. Auschwitz is not 'so unprecedented' to one whose frame of reference is the Middle Passage, followed by Native American genocide" (36). But Wilderson does not then succumb to what he calls "the ruse of analogy," because easy equivalencies only paper over important differences. "The Muselmann," he writes, "can be seen as a provisional moment within existential Whiteness. . . . Jews went into Auschwitz and came out as Jews." "Africans went into the ships and came out as Blacks," Wilderson continues, "The former is a Human holocaust; the latter is a Human and a metaphysical holocaust" (38).[18]

In closing this chapter, we want to turn not to Germany but to South Africa—for a lesson about academic freedom and its relation to structural racism. Toward the end of the previous chapter we cited

18. Back in 1973, Joyce Ladner made a related point about the difference between Black Americans and other minorities in the United States in her introduction to *The Death of White Sociology*:

> One of the prevailing premises in mainstream sociology has been that Blacks are a minority group which would, in time, become part of the 'melting pot' in much the same manner as European ethnic groups have done. There has been an almost total negation of the different historical conditions that differentiate Blacks from European minorities. The salient factor that Africans came to America *involuntarily*, that they were enslaved and subsequently granted second-class citizenship which, for the most part, still exists means that they cannot be analyzed in the same way as Europeans who *voluntarily* came to the United States seeking better lives. (xx)

a passage from Adam Sitze's essay "Academic Unfreedom, Unacademic Freedom." We return to it now for Sitze's explanation of the backstory behind what is often considered the first victory for academic freedom in the US courts—*Sweezy v. New Hampshire* (1957). Sitze is particularly interested in Judge Felix Frankfurter's opinion in the decision, which sets out the "four essential freedoms of the university—to determine for itself on academic grounds who may teach, what may be taught, how it shall be taught, and who may be admitted to study." Sitze explains that when Frankfurter's opinion is cited today, it is usually used to support three arguments: "that academic freedom inheres in institutions and not professors; that university autonomy entails the right of universities to protect intellectual life from government intervention; *and that entailed in this autonomy is the responsibility of universities to remain neutral with respect to the great social and political controversies of their day*" (emphasis added, 772). Sitze unearths the fact that Frankfurter's opinion was itself largely based on another text—*The Open Universities in South Africa*, which was published the same year as the *Sweezy* decision. This text summarizes the proceedings of a conference held by the University of Cape Town and the University of the Witwatersrand (Johannesburg). "The occasion for this conference," Sitze explains, "was provided in March 1957, when the Nationalist Party—the South African political party responsible for the imposition of apartheid in South Africa in 1948—introduced into Parliament a bill that aimed to extend the policy of apartheid to the two South African universities that at that time admitted African students." *The Open Universities in South Africa* is a declaration of opposition to this bill.

"No reader who absorbs the text's opening chapter in full, particularly with an eye to the parliamentary debate that occasioned it," Sitze writes, "can have any doubt about the text's purpose" (772). Its purpose is to make clear that "academic apartheid and academic autonomy are mutually exclusive." According to Sitze, Frankfurter relies on this document in all respects *except* its contextual relation to the apartheid bill which is its very reason for existing. Frankfurter, Sitze writes, "quote[s] exclusively from the first three pages of the text's second chapter, which is a history of the idea of the university and which contains no objections to the policy of apartheid" (773). The effect of this subtraction of specifics is wildly paradoxical: namely, that Frankfurter's quotations from this text will lead many of his readers to conclude that the principle that academic institutions must remain politically neutral is central to academic freedom when, in fact, the South African universities' defense of academic freedom rests on defiant opposition to a political act, a Parliamentary bill. The state wants to impose apartheid, and the universities want to refuse. They do so by insisting on the universities' independence from the state. Ironically, in the American context, in a consequential game of telephone, this assertion of "independence" translated into the Frankfurter opinion and that, in turn, when paraphrased in histories of academic freedom, morphs into "neutrality." The university must remain neutral with regard to affairs of the state. "Independence" and "neutrality" are not the same thing. In the South African context, neutrality would have meant acceding to academic apartheid. Once the backstory is supplied (and history returned to theory, as in the work of Charles Mills), the lesson then is that the university must remain independent from the government but *cannot* remain neutral. Faculty must make judgment calls on the university's behalf that take into consideration the historical and political circumstances in which their universities find themselves. We make the case for a committee to render these judgments in our next chapter.

CHAPTER 6

THE FUTURE OF ACADEMIC FREEDOM

Let's begin the case for a new senate committee by revisiting the outrage with which another such proposal was met. Faculty seem to be operating under the delusion that academic freedom and discrimination issues can be neatly separated, the former handled by faculty within the discipline-specific processes already established and the latter by human resources or Department of Equity and Inclusion offices. This half-conscious presumption is surely behind the hyperbolic response to the Princeton Faculty Letter's proposal for an antiracism committee that we discussed in our introduction. When the Princeton Faculty letter signatories suggested a committee to evaluate alleged racism among faculty, the reaction was swift and definitive: *this is utterly unacceptable.* The strong reaction to an antiracism committee suggested that many faculty believe either that racism *isn't* already being adjudicated with punitive consequences on campuses across the nation, or that if it is, such adjudication occurs only with regard to clearly circumscribed incidents handled by nonacademic officers conversant with workplace discrimination laws.

The Princeton Faculty Letter was one of many campus documents issued in summer 2020 as the nation reckoned with the aftermath of George Floyd's murder, but it received disproportionate attention from the media. On July 4, over four hundred Princeton faculty and staff sent an open letter to President Christopher Eisgruber and other top administrators calling for antiracist reforms. The letter makes numerous demands that will be familiar to faculty at campuses across the country, such as "Implement administration- and faculty-wide training that is specifically anti-racist in emphasis with the goal of making our campus truly safe, welcoming, and nurturing for every person of color on campus—students, postdocs, preceptors, staff, and faculty alike" and "Reward the invisible work done by faculty of color with course relief and summer salary." (You will recall critical race theorists' account of faculty of color "struggling to carry the multiple burdens of token representative, role model, and change agent in increasingly hostile environments" [*Words That Wound* 7].) The twenty-seventh demand is for Princeton "to constitute a committee composed entirely of faculty that would oversee the investigation and discipline of racist behaviors, incidents, research, and publication on the part of faculty, following a protocol for grievance and appeal to be spelled out in Rules and Procedures of the Faculty. Guidelines on what counts as racist behavior, incidents, research, and publication will be authored by a faculty committee for incorporation into the same set of rules and procedures." Throughout summer and then fall 2020, these 72 words were plucked out of the 4,172-word letter and denounced with apparently universal rage.

It will surprise no one that Bruce Gilley tweeted that the idea was an "Astonishing act of totalitarianism. . . . Every signatory should be fired." But the categorical rejection of it by liberal academics, often in similarly exaggerated terms invoking the Red Guards' struggle sessions or the Jacobins' guillotine, *is* a bit of a surprise. When signatories to that statement were contacted by *Atlantic* writer Conor

Freidersdorf, a few of them walked back or withdrew their support for that specific proposal. Others, cognizant of Friedersdorf's angle and the already-formed consensus, refused to comment. Undoubtedly, it was hard to defend the idea in the face of attacks that presumed to know the exact nature of such a committee before it had been created. Indeed, it *is* hard—and it *should* be hard—to make the case for disciplining faculty for what might be understood by some as political expression. But that it is hard does not mean that a case cannot or should not be made.

In "The Problem with Princeton's Racism Committee Proposal" on the AAUP *Academe* blog, John K. Wilson wrote that "a separate system to punish faculty for racism is an awful idea that threatens academic freedom." When Jennifer commented in support of what she called a committee "to look at racist research and design guidelines for how to think about what such research might be," Henry Reichman answered:

> Unfortunately, the letter does NOT propose a committee "to look at racist research and design guidelines for how to think about" that research. It proposes a committee to "oversee the investigation and discipline" of racist behaviors, incidents, research, and publication. In short, a committee that could discipline (i.e., punish) a faculty member if it deemed her publications unacceptable. Not a tenure and promotion committee, making legitimate assessments on the basis of clear criteria, but a special committee designed to sniff out (investigate) and punish (discipline) whatever it deems "racist."

Reichman suggests that faculty bodies like promotion and tenure committees are acceptable but a "special committee designed to sniff out (investigate) and punish (discipline) whatever it deems 'racist' is not." Fair enough. The overwhelming majority of commentators—not just on the blog, but everywhere—took this tack: a special committee (read: mob) subjecting faculty to struggle sessions over racism is unacceptable. But did we all somehow forget—or simply not know—that these special committees already exist on every campus across the country? They are called offices of diversity, equity, and inclusion. (Or, on some campuses, they are creatures of human resources.) If someone has not been personally under investigation for discrimination at their university, it is possible that they don't know or didn't quite realize the full extent of these offices' power to investigate and recommend punishment. It is also possible that because these investigations all happen out of faculty view (other than that of the faculty respondent's, of course) and outside faculty governance, with no guarantees of transparency or due process, we vaguely know of and fear them but tend to repress their existence when debating issues in the faculty-dominated arenas with which we are more familiar.

But yes, faculty are already routinely punished for speech found to be discriminatory. Human resource departments, offices of diversity, equity and inclusion, and other bureaucracies of the university pursue these investigations, and with steadily increasing frequency and severity of consequence over the last decade. When faculty and staff are investigated for discrimination at Portland State University, the Office of Global Diversity and Inclusion produces a report and recommends discipline if it has "findings" (that is, it determines that discrimination occurred). It is then up to the administrator (typically, dean, provost, or president) to decide on disciplinary sanctions, which can range from an oral reprimand to termination. At most places, all of this happens without a scintilla of shared governance: there is no faculty input whatsoever. At a few institutions, typically those with exceptionally strong faculty senates or strong collective bargaining chapters, a mechanism has been created to ensure that a faculty member or academic professional who is subject to any consequences more severe than a written reprimand can request a panel of peers to weigh in before discipline is imposed. In effect, the committee proposed by the Princeton letter would make this option *the* default process—not something that might kick in as a last resort after a faculty member has already been subjected to what is usually an extremely protracted investigation. In Jennifer's three years of experience as her union's representative for respondents accused of discrimination, investigations have taken from three months to nearly two years to conclude and entail a great deal of limbo punctuated by sessions when the respondent is interviewed. (A respondent might be interviewed one to four times before an investigator finishes their report.)

One response to Wilson's post came from someone who was punished in one of these types of investigations and, as a consequence, sees the merits of a faculty committee. "At least," Frank P. Tomasulo wrote, "there would be a 'rule book' by which professors would know what was verboten and what was acceptable. In theory, such a list of 'deplorable' acts might also be able to spell out the penalties for violating the 'laws' and might make distinctions between egregious behavior and an inadvertent MICRO-aggression." Not only might there be some clarity under a model in which a faculty committee was under an obligation to offer clearer guidelines than any faculty currently receive; more important, it would not be lawyers or HR personnel alone judging events that unfolded in places most of them rarely inhabit—like classrooms. The diversity officers' expertise notwithstanding (and that expertise is considerable, we know), are not faculty better positioned to understand the nuances and complexities involved in teaching and research? As the person who accompanies faculty respondents, Jennifer has witnessed a number of investigations in which the diversity officer's lack of experience in the classroom was a problem for a fair investigation. To give you one example: a student cites as one piece of evidence of disrespect—and, thus, discrimination—that the professor interrupted them during a class presentation. The diversity officer takes this at face value and is skeptical when the respondent explains that the class was on a tight schedule and the complainant had exceeded their allotted time. The investigator has not experienced the pressures of time management in the classroom and imagines that the student could easily have been allowed to finish. Ordinarily we would not have to emphasize so basic a point, but it is routine to stop a student who has gone over time in order to make sure others have a chance to do their presentations and the class stays on schedule. This situation will sound hard to believe to those of you who have not been investigated, but we assure you this kind of disconnect occurs.

More to the point perhaps is that investigations can and do stray into academic freedom territory—particularly with regard to academic and professional judgment. Because investigators are looking for evidence that a student has been treated differently than other students, they ask to look at grades given to other students, emails exchanged with students in the same class or similar classes as the complainant, and anything else that they think might help them determine differential treatment. There are no restrictions, in Jennifer's experience, on what information an investigator may request. In the hands of someone looking for evidence that a student was treated unfairly, emails lose the rich context within which the instructor operates, and a permissive email to a student with a long record of conscientious effort looks sinister next to the stern email to a student with a history of avoidance. Investigators *are* second-guessing faculty judgment at times in these investigations, which is precisely what they are not supposed to do. There is no easy solution to this reality, given the messiness and degree of subjectivity necessarily involved in even the best-run investigations, but clearer limits about what documents investigators may demand combined with actual faculty governance involvement in the process could considerably reduce the potential for arbitrary outcomes.

We want to underline our belief that all members of a university must have the right to file discrimination complaints and have them investigated. Real harm is done by unwitting and sometimes witting professionals who use disparaging language, or in any number of other ways demonstrate bias, when performing their roles in the university community. Indeed, we've named a few of these people in this book. It is undeniable that some respondents deserve the sanctions and trainings meted out to them. In this book, we've been emphasizing the academic illegitimacy of white supremacist and colonialist arguments rather than their potential for harm for two reasons, both of which stem from conversations with some of our colleagues of color. The first is that reliance on the term "harm" can invite what one colleague of color calls "trauma porn," in which students or faculty of color are compelled to testify to the harm they have suffered as a result of racist utterances or displays (ranging from scholarly articles on the inferiority of nonwhite peoples to the annual appearance of Halloween blackface), on a scale from microaggressions to macroaggressions. The second, even more disturbing reason is that the invocation of harm often provokes the response that the source of the harm derives not from the falseness of the statements but from their truth. This is, as we have noted above, how racists and assorted trolls ply their trade: they say outrageous and unfounded things, and in response to criticism, cast themselves as brave truth-tellers fighting the good fight against feel-good liberal group-think. Take for example the *Wall Street Journal* op-ed in which Amy Wax replied to her critics: "The mindset that values openness understands that the truth can be inconvenient and uncomfortable, doesn't always respect our wishes, and sometimes hurts. Good feelings and reality don't always mix" ("The University of Denial"). The reason nonwhite people are hurt by statements about their inferiority, in other words, is that those statements are true. That trollish response is an insult to intelligence—literally an insult upon injury.

Our earlier point is simply that investigations run by one diversity officer risk outcomes that directly infringe on academic and professional judgment. Once an investigation has concluded, faculty are punished behind the scenes in ways that the rest of us might or might not agree with but will never know about. It's bad enough that our current reality is one that subjects our community members to a largely invisible and intimidatingly mysterious process that was designed without any faculty input, but for our purposes in this book, here's what is perhaps even worse: we—and our students—are *still* forced to live in perpetuity with that faculty member whose discriminatory actions are *not* unintentional. The rare but recognizable faculty member who *is* an ideologue who opposes efforts related to diversity and inclusion and trumpets his contempt for racial-justice work or the dignity of transgender people: this person is rarely disciplined. And if he is, he is disciplined with significantly less severe consequences than are others. This is because he implicitly or explicitly threatens lawsuits and engages right-wing organizations with deep pockets to back him—all with the leverage of his claim that his academic freedom is being violated. This claim effectively derails the case precisely because diversity officers, human resource professionals, and/or a few administrators do not possess enough credibility to adjudicate academic matters on their own. They need faculty for that. A claim at this point of a violation of academic freedom brings the bureaucratic machinery to a full stop. Diversity officers might want to see these actors disciplined, but they are overridden by university administrators who consider the risks of public warfare too great.

And here's where even the most libertarian faculty member should have sympathy for the people working in these offices. The burnout rate for diversity officers is unusually high, because demoralization inevitably sets in when diversity officers repeatedly find that their recommended sanctions are enforced for the relatively disempowered members of the academic community but not for the powerful ones with tenure, money, and/or significant public visibility. It does not feel good to see your recommendation for the adjunct or academic professional readily adopted but not the recommendation for the full professor. It feels even worse to be asked to modify (that is, soften) reports on powerful university figures but rarely, if ever, on others all the while still being expected to tell complainants and respondents alike that you do not represent the university's interests and are completely impartial. In consultation with the office of general counsel, the office of the provost or president makes the final decision, and this often means that, even though less litigious or less protected faculty and staff have received severe sanctions in comparable circumstances, the litigious and well-connected professor will not. In these cases, it is clear to us that a faculty-led committee (which could, and should, include professionals with expertise in diversity, equity, and inclusion) could pressure the university to uphold its values more powerfully than can the diversity officer alone.

In sum, racist (and other discriminatory) behavior and incidents are routinely investigated but unevenly disciplined. To repeat, the variation in punishment is not the fault of the diversity and inclusion (or equity and compliance) officers but that of the administrators to whom they report. The investigators in these offices, we believe, strive to be impartial and they have needed expertise in their areas, but they are not eligible for tenure and do not enjoy the protections of academic freedom. They work directly for provosts and presidents. They are hired by them, promoted by them, and fired by them. They may or may not do their (very demanding) jobs fairly and professionally, but they cannot be accused of hypocrisy. That accusation must be reserved for the provost or president who, usually after consultation with the office of general counsel, decides against risking a lawsuit.

IN A BLISTERING indictment of these offices in *Inside Higher Education*, "Farewell to DEI Work," Tatiana McInnis explains what she calls the "ever-expanding acronym" of these offices: "While once campuses focused only on diversity, many institutions have broadened that focus to include equity and inclusion, so it now commonly refers to all three, as in the Office of Diversity, Equity and Inclusion, or DEI." Having recently quit her job in one of these offices, the disillusioned McInnis continues, "These words, and the intentions they seek to express, are well and good, yet they fall flat as offices fail and refuse to address systemic white domination, anti-Blackness, misogyny or any group-specific violence in their mission statements." These offices are what she later calls "spaces of impossibility" because "they are not empowered to hold community members accountable when they fail to uphold stated investments in equity."[1]

1. See also Brown, "College Diversity Officers Face a Demanding Job and Scarce Resources" and Mangan, "The U. of Iowa Keeps Losing Diversity Officers."

Most faculty, we believe, want to see discrimination laws enforced. They do not want to see anyone—student, staff, or faculty—discriminated against on the basis of disability, race, sex or gender identity, country of national origin, religion, or marital status. They want bad actors held accountable. At the same time, most faculty have a reasonable mistrust of these offices and a reasonable mistrust of the administrators who oversee them. Some of the mistrust of these offices stems from the sense that the personnel in them do not understand our jobs and have too low a bar for launching investigations. Some mistrust stems from the sense that BIPOC and white women are investigated in disproportionate numbers because students' own biases can mean they are both more critical of these faculty and more confident in their power to lodge complaints against them. And some mistrust comes from the impression that these offices are institutional window-dressing that advertise diversity on behalf of the administration without truly supporting the BIPOC people working in the university.[2] Faculty need to get involved in holding one another accountable for both disinterested and self-interested reasons. If review procedures can be incorporated in some form in faculty handbooks or bargaining contracts, faculty can have some role in making

2. In "Why Was it So Easy for Jessica Krug to Fool Everyone?", Jason England writes: "The DEI sector becomes a hothouse of symbolic progressivism, where progressive and radical (and sometimes inane) ideas can be given lip service while institutions and systemic racism remains largely unchanged. Cliché programming, focus groups, town halls, anti-racism reading lists, testimonials of hurt, and confessions of guilt touch deep nerves and emotional wells in each of us as individuals, summoning up sadness, self-righteousness, love, and hate. But there is no measurable progress to be found as a result of these undertakings." See also Cathryn Bailey, "How Diversity Rhetoric Obscures Structural Inequities in Higher Education."

sure that the diversity rhetoric of brochures bears some relationship to reality and that administrators do not shrink from the professed values of the university when faced with litigious actors or angry politicians. And, for self-interested reasons, faculty need to get involved to protect ourselves from the potential for misunderstandings of diversity officers regarding the nature of our jobs or simply the dangers of having one person—one attorney, often—make a recommendation to administrators that can have serious consequences.[3]

We'll return to this question of hypocrisy in the office of the president, but first let's circle back to Wilson's post and the question of faculty governance over charges of racism. Arguing with one commentator, Wilson poses a simplified and simplifying opposition between what he calls "my idea of freedom" and "your embrace of censorship for the university." A commentator going by the handle of "Not John Deane or Doane" gets closer to the stakes of the Princeton Faculty Letter when they write:

> I disagree with Wilson on the overlap between free speech and
> academic freedom. As I read the AAUP documents on academic

3. We highly recommend the *New York Times Magazine* feature, "The Accusations Were Lies. But Could We Prove It?", detailing the ordeal experienced by Marta Trecodor and her partner Sarah Viren (the article's author) when Marta became the respondent of a malicious sexual discrimination complaint. The degree to which everything for this couple rested on one lawyer's ability to grasp a bewildering culturescape in which social media intersected with tenure-track job scarcity is terrifying. Such complex situations cannot be left to one lawyer and then the sometimes arbitrary decision-making of administrators who apply policies unevenly (and thus unfairly) and may be ignorant of the complexities of an issue when it touches on elements outside their own particular fields.

freedom, the goal is to assure that faculty have total freedom to pursue research, and that freedom attaches to many different parties: to the individual first and foremost, but also to departments, institutions, and professional associations. right now, for example, many fields close to biology consider eugenics, very broadly speaking, to be unacceptable. here, academic freedom rightly attaches to disciplines and departments. disciplines are doing their jobs when they say that eugenics is racist pseudoscience. there are still problems: there are subdisciplines ("evolutionary psychology" is one such now) that develop specifically to advance racist ideas that are unacceptable in the main disciplines they are part of. this remains a real problem, though institutions have, in my opinion, the academic freedom and governance responsibility to decide whether or not to allow programs in those fields to flourish. that is *already* a kind of "star chamber" that exists well distributed in the administration of universities. historic racism is one of the areas that it does address, and should.

For this commentator who, like us, finds terms like "star chamber" hyperbolic distractions, there is no need for such a committee as far as academic research is concerned because the necessary oversight it would provide is already embedded within the university, in offices devoted to research integrity (and its opposite, research fraud). His rejoinder to Wilson makes a great deal of sense to us; we know such review committees exist, and Michael has chaired one, involving an academic integrity case. But there is ample evidence, accumulating over the course of the past few decades, that our existing infrastructure for internal review is not enough.

When universities respected the integral relationship between job security and academic freedom, and the majority of faculty were tenure-line, these processes worked for the most part. Before fundamental changes to American news outlets, social media, and democracy in the first two decades of the twenty-first century, changes that led to the profound polarization of the electorate and the proliferation of phrases like "alternative facts," these processes were adequate. When there was a more or less shared reality (rather than one in which the Sandy Hook massacre occurred and one in which it didn't), these processes sufficed and, indeed, were great accomplishments of the twentieth century (thanks to the AAUP). With fundamental changes to the environment both inside (with the erosion of tenure) and outside (with the erosion of a shared reality) of the university, they no longer appear to.

The most obvious examples of how the current infrastructure no longer suffices to regulate the integrity of faculty expression and ensure its protection–that is, academic freedom—are not necessarily the Lawrence Meads and Bruce Gilleys who earned tenure before anybody could stop them from, respectively, recycling debunked racist stereotypes and calling for Western European countries to recolonize African ones. They are the Jeff Klinzmans.[4] Klinzman had been an adjunct English professor at Kirkwood Community College for over 16 years when a comment he made on an Iowa Antifa Facebook page was picked up by a local news outlet. When someone on the Facebook page shared a barely coherent Trump tweet calling Antifa protesters "gutless Radical Left Wack Jobs who go around hitting (only non-fighters) people over the heads with baseball bats," English professor Klinzman responded in more coherent syntax, "Yeah, I know who I'd clock with a bat." *Inside Higher Education* quoted

4. See Reichman, "Do Adjuncts Have Academic Freedom? Or Why Tenure Matters" for more cases.

Kirkwood President Lori Sundberg, who said that Klinzman's opinions have "drawn considerable attention from many inside and outside of the Kirkwood community just as we embark on a new school year" (Flaherty, "Pro-Antifa Professor Out"). Under pressure to fire Klinzman, Sundberg succeeded in forcing his resignation. After first claiming that Klinzman's comments conflicted with the community college's mission, Sundberg later professed that Klinzman's removal from the classroom was not punishment for his speech but an attempt to ensure the campus's and his own safety. After the case was publicized, and FIRE and others got involved, a settlement was reached through a mediator. According to FIRE's website, "Although Klinzman will not return to work at Kirkwood, the school agreed to pay $25,000, which is approximately the amount it would have paid Klinzman to continue teaching for over three and a half years" ("Victory").

Would the situation have played out differently had Klinzman been tenured? Undoubtedly so. Either Klinzman's job would be safe or, if administrators were doggedly determined to appease external forces, the "settlement" reached would have been to the tune of six or seven figures rather than $25,000. And this strikes us as deeply hypocritical. The very same speech act will lead to two fundamentally different judgment calls by the office of the president depending on the job status of the person making it. Klinzman's case is but one of hundreds of reminders that the professoriate writ large has a very serious academic freedom problem *when adjunct instructors make up 70 percent of the college workforce* and it is this easy to get rid of them when they create a headache—more accurately, when partisan news outlets turn them into a headache—for administrators.

Had there been a previously agreed-upon mechanism by which Kirkwood faculty might turn to an academic freedom committee, they might have redirected some degree of authority over the handling of Klinzman's case from the panicked president to themselves and ensured due process.[5] Would terminating Klinzman over extramural political speech violate his academic freedom? Did that speech shed light in any way on his fitness to teach his subject? "Yes" and "no" might well have been such a committee's considered conclusion. Next time around, when an adjunct instructor becomes a public headache and a pusillanimous administration encourages a chair to claim simply that the courses that person teaches are no longer needed, that same committee might at the request of the concerned adjunct instructor convene to determine whether the chair's reason for nonrenewal is plausible or if the issue at heart is, again, academic freedom. All else being unequal, in this polarized climate in which administrators cannot be trusted to ensure due process, such a committee would be a welcome addition to the cause of academic freedom.

THE PRINCETON LETTER calls for a racism committee, not an academic freedom committee. But might the latter fulfill much the same purpose in addition to the others we've just outlined? Oberlin has already demonstrated this, after all, with the committee it convened to adjudicate the question of fitness raised by the anti-Semitism and sheer irrationality of Joy Karega's claims. How many times have universities and colleges instead been reduced to either tolerating

---

5. A more recent case at Cypress Community College involving an adjunct instructor removed from her class by administrators is also an excellent example of one that needed to be handled by a faculty committee, not by anxious administrators. See Jaschik, "Cypress Suspends Adjunct over Her Comments on Police."

professorial unfitness out of apparent helplessness (think Gregory Christainsen) or reaching a settlement with the offending faculty member, thereby facilitating the flow of millions of dollars from higher education to conspiracy theorists, racists, serial harassers, and other varieties of the academic opportunist? A faculty committee that respects due process by constituting a panel of experts in the area in question would carry a lot of weight in a courtroom and might protect higher education's coffers (tuition-paying students, and, in the case of public institutions, taxpayers as well). Such a committee's judgment would wield influence because it would establish a context that precludes the "both sidesism" to which a judge or jury might otherwise be likely to default.

After Charlottesville, Trump famously commented that there were "very fine people on both sides." "Both sidesism" has come to refer to the tendency to treat two opposing groups or ideas as if they were equivalent when they patently are not. Trump attempted to do this with Antifa, of course, redirecting the public's attention from the ongoing violence of white supremacist organizations to antifascist groups by suggesting that the latter are just as dangerous, if not more so. This flies in the face of ample research showing that white supremacist organizations are historically and currently responsible for far more violence and exponentially many more deaths than are left-wing organizations.[6] Yet because the common sense of "impartiality" or "neutrality" still has considerable hold on the American public (thankfully, in certain respects, but annoyingly when political commentators pretend that Democrats and Republicans are both to

6. See, for example, the description of a report by the Center for Strategic and International Studies in the *New York Times* article by Jenny Gross, "Far Right Groups Are Behind Most Terrorist Attacks, Report Finds."

blame for dysfunction in Washington), the temptation is always to believe that both sides of an argument need to be heard. This principle sometimes then slides into the presumption that both sides also need to be understood to possess equal value. We've gotten past this trap on precious few topics: flat-earthers' arguments do not carry the same value as round-earthers; Holocaust denial no longer gains a hearing; creationists do not deserve equal airtime with evolutionists. But is that it? Is that all we've managed to establish?

In chapter 4, we looked to Mark S. James, a Black professor in the English department at Molloy College, for an analysis of what "both sidesism" meant for BIPOC faculty and students in the classroom during the Trump years, but even some white, conservative professors found themselves unable to participate in the bad faith of alleged neutrality. For example: Mark Rupert in the political science department at Syracuse University wrote a powerful letter to his administration titled "Teaching in the Time of Trump" because he anticipated "that Syracuse University administrators will hear complaints of partisanship about my teaching."[7] Rupert's letter was prompted by Chancellor Kent Syverud's remarks before the Faculty Senate, remarks that in Rupert's opinion encouraged precisely the kind of "institutionalized affect" of neutrality that James identified in his essay. Rupert wrote:

7. It should have been an open letter, in our opinion, because many faculty across the nation would have recognized in it a helpful framing of their own cognitive dissonance. It's worth noting here the way open letters have played such an outsized role in academe during the Trump era. To our minds, this is implicit confirmation that the academic infrastructure has proved inadequate or, more precisely, incomplete. It must be overhauled, prompted to undertake internal reforms that will become a permanent part of shared governance in American universities.

I agree with Chancellor Syverud that [teaching in a deeply polarized national environment] is an extremely important professional challenge that faces each of us individually, and all of us collectively. . . . My own approach to these challenges starts from the notion that my most basic commitment to my students is honesty. I must tell them what I believe to be true about our political and social lives. My interpretations are of course fallible, but they are not simply personal opinions insofar as they are based on decades of study and professional experience as a professor of political science. . . .

I understand the modern conservative movement to be a confluence of libertarian tendencies emphasizing individuals' rights to make choices regarding their lives, and social or religious conservatives emphasizing the importance of traditional values and faith traditions in helping us to distinguish right from wrong and to use our freedom to make morally reflective decisions. These I believe are both intellectually respectable positions and historically significant in the foundation of the contemporary conservative movement . . . [and] deserve to be critically examined and their strengths as well as their weaknesses explored with students. . . . But this is not the same as assuming that the contemporary Republican party is acting in good faith in its political practices. It has been well documented by historians and scholars of politics that the GOP has systematically used coded racial appeals to mobilize white voters since the era of the Civil Rights and Voting Rights Acts. President Trump's politics and policies are the culmination of a decades-long process of embracing racial divisiveness, hatred and fear as a partisan political tool. . . . This pedagogical challenge is now compounded by a President, and the political party supporting him, who have openly embraced racism and mendacity as the core of their politics. From the moment he stepped off the escalator to announce his candidacy, Mr. Trump has deployed racial stereotypes and scapegoating as political tools. . . . To pretend that this form of politics is as respectable, or no more reprehensible, than that practiced by others would not be objectivity but a distortion of the truth in order to avoid controversy, a cowardly abdication of my most basic professional responsibility for which I don't think I could forgive myself.

Having distinguished what he does in the classroom from the kind of classroom experience invoked by the phrase "marketplace of ideas," Rupert concluded his letter by saying that he hoped his administration would not mistake his well-considered speech in the classroom "for unreflective partisanship or personal opinion."

Rupert differentiates between the exercise of free speech (which makes room for "unreflective partisanship" and "personal opinion") and that of academic freedom (which takes evidence and reason into account). In an ironic twist that is now familiar to many of us, Rupert expected to be accused of some kind of bias or discrimination because he was prepared to name this difference and its implications in the classroom. He feared that students who favored Trump would accuse him of some form of intolerance. Did this happen during the Trump years? It most definitely did but not very often, we suspect, to white conservative-identified professors like Rupert. It happened more often to BIPOC faculty who, like Rupert, insisted on teaching honestly, come what may. It would be incredibly useful to get solid nationwide demographic data on this so as to discern patterns: what category of complaint is most often filed? What are the demographics of the complainant and the respondents? What are the ranks and employment categories of respondents?

Faculty senates need to get involved. In its many statements and policies regarding academic freedom, due process, and discrimination, the AAUP has for decades recommended faculty review processes overseen by senates or other duly elected bodies. But with the rise of DEI and HR offices, investigations around discrimination have largely proceeded without faculty involvement. As we mentioned earlier, some exceptionally strong senates and collective bargaining chapters have language that can be mobilized to demand some degree of faculty review. But they are often tethered to specific issues, such as conflicts with regard to the promotion and tenure process, academic integrity, or termination for cause (such as dereliction of duties), and have not been framed so as to capture the array of issues that have arisen with increasing frequency over the last decade. An academic freedom committee that included and/or consulted relevant experts and provided a university-wide layer of review would redirect some authority over the cases from administrators.

Administrators would be wise to embrace this idea. Deferring to the recommendations of such a committee might just save them from, or in, potentially crushing lawsuits. Administrators in possession of a senate committee recommendation accompanied by an informed report that preempted the false equivalencies to which a judge or jury might otherwise resort would be in a stronger position to defend the university's decisions than those without. Take the case of the late Michael Adams, who was a tenured professor of criminology, at the University of North Carolina–Wilmington (UNCW). In 2004, after Adams was denied promotion from associate to full professor, he sued the university, naming his department chair and others in the suit. The department had recommended against promotion on the basis that his research was thin, but he alleged that this was a pretext for retaliation over his Baptist religion and his right-wing political positions. In his dossier for promotion, Adams included nonrefereed work—essays, op-eds, and appearances he'd made promoting various conservative viewpoints on abortion, free speech, diversity, etc. He also included *Welcome to the Ivory Tower of Babel*, a book he'd published with the far-right Regnery Press, and another book he had coauthored that was under consideration—*IndoctriNation: How Universities Are Destroying America*. The UNCW legal team argued that these public-facing works outside the field of criminology were nonrefereed and so could not be counted toward scholarship. Had they kept it at that, they may have kept some of the issues raised in the case separate and managed to prevail.

In rebutting Adams' claim of retaliation, however, legal counsel felt they needed to bolster their arguments by invoking *Garcetti v. Ceballos* (2006) so as to invalidate these external writings as unprotected employee speech when considered in the context of promotion.[8] Adams's political opining, they argued, may be protected under the First Amendment when expressed in public forums, but it converted to unprotected speech when submitted as part of a dossier for promotion. This was not an entirely unreasonable way to signal that the work was thus subject to rigorous academic evaluation rather than to the much less exacting standards of the First Amendment. The judge ruled for UNCW but he fastened on *Garcetti* in his judgment, and by doing so, sparked another round of litigation. The AAUP, FIRE, and the Thomas Jefferson Center for the Freedom of Expression jointly

8. *Garcetti* held that public employees do not enjoy First Amendment protection for statements they make in the course of their duties *as* employees, and the Court did not exempt professors at public universities from this decision.

filed an amicus brief agreeing with the judge that Adams had not proven discrimination on the basis of religion but arguing that the issue of viewpoint discrimination was not yet decided because the ruling had tripped up when it invoked *Garcetti*. Protected speech cannot morph into unprotected speech, these organizations argued. The Fourth Circuit demanded the case be remanded and retried. The judge punted the retrial to a jury with no patience for questions of disciplinary procedures, refereed versus nonrefereed publications, etc. They found Adams's colleagues' emails expressing disgust with his various offensive op-eds evidence that they may have retaliated against him for his viewpoints.[9] The court demanded that UNCW promote Adams to full professor, award him back pay for the years

9. As suggested by the following passage in the joint amicus brief, this outcome is likely not the one hoped for by the groups involved in filing it, least of all the AAUP:

> *Amici* also take no position on whether or not Adams actually suffered retaliation for his speech; that is a fact-oriented inquiry best entrusted to the district court, undertaken by appropriately considering the complex issues and implications of the case. This requires application of the correct analytic framework and proper consideration of all of the special issues in academia—a consideration that cannot be made properly through summary judgment or reliance upon the inapposite "official duties" framework articulated for most public employee speech in *Garcetti*.
>
> Therefore, *amici* respectfully urge this court to recognize the Supreme Court's exception for academic speech, and to remand this case to the court below for a proper analysis of the unusually complicated facts in light of precedent, the longstanding principles of academic freedom, and the reservation for academic speech articulated in the majority's opinion in *Garcetti*. (*Adams v. Trustees* 24)

of the suit during which he'd been paid as an associate, and pay his hefty legal fees.

After another handful of painful and contentious years during which Adams subjected the community to what the university rightly called "vile" and "hateful" tweets and writings, the university paid him to retire, offering to continue his salary for five years so long as he did not earn it through teaching and service (see Li). UNCW chancellor Jose V. Sartarelli said that under the circumstances he (the chancellor) had had only three options:

1) Have him continue as a faculty member and accept the ongoing disruption to our educational mission, the hurt and anger in the UNCW community, and the damage to the institution. 2) Attempt to terminate him, and face drawn out, very costly litigation, that we might not win, which was the case when Dr. Adams sued UNCW and won a First Amendment retaliation lawsuit in 2014. That legal process lasted 7 years and cost the university roughly $700,000, $615,000 of which was for Dr. Adams' attorneys' fees. Losing a similar lawsuit today could cost even more. 3) Negotiate a settlement when, as part of a conversation with me about his conduct and future at UNCW, I learned Dr. Adams was interested in retiring. This approach allows us to resolve the situation quickly, with certainty, and in the most fiscally responsible way. This is the best option for our university and our community. (Jaschik)

We applaud UNCW for rejecting option one, which would have meant continuing, however reluctantly, to give Adams a comfortable perch from which to spew bigotry. We just wish it had not come at such a steep cost to a cash-strapped public institution. We also worry that the precedent set here has generated the perverse but distinct possibility that some faculty may calculate that persisting in, and even escalating, attacks on their own university communities may result in their own golden parachutes. It would be nice to receive a handsome retirement and then, by virtue of the publicity generated by the conflicts over the years, land a gig with a conservative think tank for the remainder of one's work years.[10]

IN A POLARIZED America, there is no foolproof way to protect universities from such calculations. But if UNCW had developed its own internal university-wide academic freedom committee to which Adams had been obliged to turn *before* turning to the courts, might the outcome have been different? Academic freedom is a concept intended to shield faculty and their institutions from external coercion, and this means protecting not only the individual professor's speech but also the collective speech professors necessarily undertake in the course of their jobs when they evaluate one another. The situation to be most avoided is one in which this collective speech—the speech involved in discriminating high-value from low-value work—finds itself at the mercy of a judge or jury with no experience distinguishing between free speech and academic freedom. A judge or jury is very likely to fall back on free speech's premise of viewpoint neutrality and find it difficult to admit claims regarding high- and low-value speech. Making distinctions between the democracy-legitimating principle of free speech and the principle of academic freedom can be hard enough after all even for faculty members who, unlike the public, are intimately familiar with the disciplinary procedures organ-

10. This was not Adams's path, though. His took a much sadder turn. Tragically, after settling with the university to retire, Adams committed suicide in the summer of 2020.

izing their careers. Surely, though, faculty members are better prepared to grasp the complexities. And just to make sure they are, we'd want any academic freedom committee to undertake its work equipped with Robert Post's 2012 book, *Democracy, Expertise, and Academic Freedom: A First Amendment Jurisprudence for the Modern State.* In fact, we'll personally buy a copy of the book for the first five academic freedom committees to notify us of their existence. It is an indispensable primer for understanding why academic freedom might well be a special concern of the First Amendment, in the oft-quoted words of the Supreme Court, but for that very reason cannot be considered identical to it. We have insisted throughout this book on the difference between free speech and academic freedom, and we want to close the deal by returning to Post's definitive grounds for the distinction.

Post distinguishes "democratic legitimation," which is why we have the First Amendment, from "democratic competence," which is why we have universities. He developed these terms, as he explained in a 2012 interview, after "notic[ing] that First Amendment protections can function to debase knowledge into mere opinion and thereby to undercut the very political conversation that the First Amendment otherwise fosters."[11] "The continuous discipline of peer judgment, which virtually defines expert knowledge, is quite incompatible with deep and fundamental First Amendment doctrines that impose a 'requirement of viewpoint neutrality' on regulations of speech," he writes (9). Indeed, he says, "Expert knowledge requires exactly what normal First Amendment doctrine prohibits" (9). He writes:

11. Kip M. Hustace, "Elevating the Discourse: An Interview with Robert C. Post."

To theorize the value of democratic competence is to confront a seeming paradox. Democratic legitimation requires that the speech of all persons be treated with toleration and equality. Democratic competence, by contrast, requires that speech be subject to a disciplinary authority that distinguishes good ideas from bad ones. Yet democratic competence is necessary for democratic legitimation. Democratic competence is thus both incompatible with democratic legitimation and required by it. This is an awkward conclusion that should prompt us to think hard about how democratic competence can be reconciled with democratic legitimation. (34)

The two can be reconciled if we understand the relationship between academic freedom and the value of democratic competence. Democratic competence—the knowledge and insight made available to society through its universities—can be ensured when academic freedom, not free speech, is the ruling principle:

> Academic freedom protects scholarly speech only when it complies with "professional norms." It is for this reason that universities are free to evaluate scholarly speech based upon its content—to reward or regulate scholarly speech based upon its professional quality. Universities make these judgments whenever they hire professors, promote them, tenure them, or award them grants. (67)

And now we're back to where we started in this chapter—with our contention that these academic judgments, as they are already routinely made at most institutions, *would* be infrastructure strong enough to uphold academic freedom if we were living in the university as it existed forty or fifty years ago. But in a changed context involving social media, tenure erosion, and political polarization emboldening white supremacism, they patently are not. Court cases like Adams's prove as much. A state of affairs in which academic freedom is conflated with free speech "virtually invites the state to suppress knowledge practices to short-term political and ideological interests," Post writes, since "standard First Amendment jurisprudence . . . tends to reduce complex speech to opinions that can neither be true nor false" (98).

Universities are critical institutions in democratic countries because the work they perform—discriminating between opinion, on the one hand, and reasoned argument, on the other—inhibits the development of alternate realities rooted in power, special interests, and conspiratorial delusions. Post claims that the guarantee of "competence" provided by universities is poorly understood because democratic legitimation is so central to our identities as freedom-loving Americans—the idea that everyone has a right to speak their mind. Post goes on to argue that while "it is not intelligible to believe that all ideas are equal," Americans gravitate to free speech over the cognitive ideal embedded in academic freedom because "Americans are committed to the equality of persons" (10) and "the deep egalitarian dimension of the First Amendment resonates far more with this ethical value than with any cognitive ideal" (10). He's undoubtedly right in one sense, but in another, we suspect that this one of those moments when white faculty pay homage to American ideals not borne out by reality: *Americans are committed to the equality of persons? All persons?* We have to wonder whether this part of Post's argument has aged well in the eight years since it was published. It seems more plausible to say, after witnessing the Trump years and surveying the terrain we have covered in the previous two chapters, that *some* Americans are committed to the equality of persons. To return to the words of Mark James from chapter 4, the fiction that everyone is making a good-faith effort to find a way to share this country has become impossible to sustain. Acknowledging this reality and ensuring that white supremacy or white nationalism in any form does not gain legitimacy in the academy is work white faculty must do if they want the university to commit to the ideal Post imagines all Americans do.

A democratic government has legitimacy if it is accountable to all its citizens, not only to one group or a powerful few. Post's project takes for granted the concept of "democratic legitimation" so that his book can illuminate the dimly understood but fundamental role of democratic *competence*. Our project in this book has been to argue that the *democratic* element in the conception of academic freedom that underwrites democratic competence needs to be better understood as well. A robust theory of academic freedom must be grounded in the common good. The common good is an intelligible concept only if what Charles Mills calls non-ideal (that is, not colorblind and abstract but historically and reality-based) forms of equality and justice are as highly valued as is freedom. If we do not presume the equal dignity and value of all humans, we will inevitably create regimes of abstract "freedom" that privilege some groups over others in the name of a specious universalism. Academic freedom committees would operate with a high degree of clarity around the distinction Post makes between democratic legitimation, for which the First Amendment is necessary, and democratic competence, for which faculty review processes are necessary. They would also, we hope, understand that academic freedom's justification is to serve the common good, which is not one and the same as the abstract pursuit of an ever-contested truth.[12] If universities are to offer their societies *democratic* compe-

12. See also Tracy Fitzsimmons's appeal to "a commitment to bettering humanity" (rather than the usual "the pursuit of truth") in this passage from her

tence, which is their *raison d'être* according to Post, they must consider whether the competence they cultivate serves all citizens not just one subset of them.

The report of a new faculty senate committee that understood its charge in these terms—around evaluating competence in standard disciplinary terms and also in its democratic valence—could be presented as evidence in the event that a case is taken to trial. Judith C. Areen, Georgetown law professor and executive director and CEO of the Association of American Law Schools, makes an argument very similar to Post's. Areen writes:

> The governance dimension of academic freedom has been overlooked by most legal scholars who have written on the First Amendment's application to academic freedom, or reduced to a right that belongs only to the governing board or administration of a college or university. Debate over whether academic freedom is an individual or an institutional right has claimed a disproportionate share of the scholarly literature, yet for the most part that literature has failed to consider whether faculty involvement in an academic governance decision should affect the level of constitutional protection provided for that decision. (947–48)

---

essay "Enough!": "Finally, we should abandon any pretense that all ideas are equal. They are not. We should demand that ideas are articulated and defended in meaningful ways that are grounded in science, data, knowledge of history and a commitment to bettering humanity." We would replace "bettering humanity" with "furthering democracy." No terms are, of course, immune to conflicting interpretations but the different emphases terms carry are significant, and we want specifically to emphasize the relation between academic freedom and democracy. Professor Fitzsimmons is the president of Shenandoah University. We hope more university presidents join her in issuing such statements.

Areen sketches what she calls "the government-as-educator doctrine" in which "if a university shows that its disciplinary decision was supported by the faculty (or by an authorized committee of the faculty), a court should presume that the decision was made on academic grounds and defer to it" (995). In situations in which the existing disciplinary procedures are contested (such as in Adams's case) or are inadequate when a conflict arises (such as in Klinzman's case), an academic freedom committee under the auspices of faculty senate might provide a needed and valuable level of governance to which the courts would be predisposed to defer. "Following *Ewing*," Areen writes, "courts should defer to an academic decision made by the faculty as a body (or a standing committee of the faculty) unless the plaintiff is able to show that the decision was 'such a substantial departure from accepted academic norms as to demonstrate that the faculty did not exercise its professional judgment'" (995).

In some cases, such as that of Scott Atlas and Stanford's Hoover Institution, faculty senates are already getting involved. In the latter half of 2020, Atlas achieved fame as Trump's anti-Fauci, appearing frequently on Fox News to urge Americans not to wear masks or practice social distancing. On October 20, 2020, *Stanford News* reported that "differences of opinion about the best approaches to fighting COVID-19 have prompted concerns among faculty members about how policies regarding academic freedom at the university should be applied and about Stanford's relationship to the Hoover Institution" (Chesley). What happens—or should happen—when Atlas parades his Stanford credentials while promoting as a scientific position an opinion that has been proven false by his academic peers? And does so while commanding the attention of the entire country? In the last chapter, we made the point that one major reason to hold people like Amy Wax accountable is precisely because her bad ideas are catnip to some groups of policymakers and government officials. Atlas makes that point incontrovertible.

On September 9, 2020, on "Stanford Medicine" letterhead, ninety-eight physicians and researchers, microbiologists and immunologists, epidemiologists and health policy leaders declared they had a "moral and an ethical responsibility to call attention to the falsehoods and misrepresentations of science recently fostered by Dr. Scott Atlas, a former Stanford Medical School colleague and current senior fellow at the Hoover Institute at Stanford University" ("Open Letter"). The signatories gave not only their names but also all of their degrees and all of their current and former academic titles. This was not a display of elitism but a shorthand for the credibility conferred upon them by the very academic infrastructure whose legitimacy is called into question by opportunists like Atlas. An impressive number of impressively vetted academics were contesting the views of one individual. To be sure, Atlas has degrees and titles (not in epidemiology, we note), but the point is that a significant number of his equally vetted peers were passing judgment. Again, this is what differentiates academic freedom from free speech: this horizontal work of peers policing one another. It is what justifies the professoriate's refusal to let that policing be pursued by the state or by moneyed interests (two forces that too often are one and the same).

At Stanford's October 22 faculty senate meeting, professor and associate chair of the Department of Psychiatry and Behavior Sciences David Spiegel asked the president and provost whether Atlas's words and actions merited university sanctions. "Atlas's conduct," he said, "is not merely a matter of expressing an opinion—it is a violation of the American Medical Association's Code of Ethics," and, he continued, a probable violation of the Stanford Code of Conduct.

Stanford's president deflected the challenge by invoking Atlas's academic freedom, citing the university's statement on academic freedom, which includes strong language about the desirability that "viewpoints" be "free from institutional orthodoxy and from internal or external coercion." When asked to comment by *Stanford News* on the president's response, David Spiegel expressed his dissatisfaction this way: "There are limitations to academic freedom. What you express has to be honest, data-based, and reflect what is known in the field. If you are going to claim academic freedom, you better be academic, as well as free" (Chesley).

Atlas responded to his peers' open letter by threatening to sue the signatories. He engaged an attorney who sent a letter to each of them, demanding that they "immediately issue a press release withdrawing your letter and that you contact every media outlet worldwide that has reported on it to request an immediate correction of the record." The letter required, according to *Inside Higher Education*, "satisfactory written proof" that the professors comply, or Atlas and his attorney would take "necessary and appropriate actions to enforce our client's rights, seek compensatory and punitive damages for the harm you have caused, and vindicate his reputation in court" (Flaherty, "Not Shrugging Off Criticism"). The signatories did not comply, yet some of them did apparently feel the need to engage an attorney of their own in response. This bears emphasizing. Quite apart from the time, money, and psychological duress involved in lawyering up, the faculty facing counterattacks like Atlas's testify to how difficult and dangerous it can be to call out a colleague by name. There are very good and obvious reasons why an individual faculty member cannot casually name the people whose work and actions seem to them to violate basic academic and/or ethical standards: these are the people who will instantaneously alert Campus Reform and other organizations, launching a campaign of harassment. Additionally, they are likely to demand that administrators discipline the whistleblower under the professional code of conduct, and/or sue them personally for libel. Many of us have been aggressively discouraged from addressing concerns that cry out to be discussed on our campuses and in the public sphere, precisely because of the near certainty that doing so will backfire in some way when we're dealing with actors with deep pockets (or access to them) and large appetites for using media outlets to proclaim their martyrdom and further their cause. Private individual faculty members cannot raise the alarm (or when they do, they can do so only in the questionable protection of a collective, as with the open letters); this is one of the reasons why there needs to be shared governance mechanisms for doing so.

Yet another open letter, "COVID-19 and the Hoover Institution: Time for a Re-Appraisal," initiated by Stanford professor of comparative literature David Palumbo-Liu and signed by over a hundred Stanford colleagues in a wide range of disciplines, redirected Stanford's conversation about Atlas from one in which administrators are asked about disciplinary sanctions to one over which the faculty senate itself presided. This, we think, is an excellent intervention: the senate, not the office of the president, is where conversations like these need to reside. The signatories of this letter assert:

> The production of unbiased scientific facts is one of the most important roles of a university, and one in which Stanford has excelled— we are regarded as a trusted source of knowledge worldwide. Thus, we are profoundly troubled by this distortion of our role, and by the university's name being used to validate such problematic information. We find this antithetical to Stanford's commitment to serving the public good through responsible scholarship and teaching. Let us be clear—this is not a partisan issue—it is a matter of science and facts.

No "both sidesism" allowed, in other words. Faculty Senate Chair Linda Goldstein welcomed the open letter's intervention, believing that "Faculty Senate is the right place for the issue of academic freedom to continue to be discussed." "Our work," she told *Stanford News,* "is subject to oversight by the professional organizations in our disciplines. When published, we have confidence in our research. But when you are doing public policy, I don't know that the university has established any guardrails akin to the oversight of professional organizations" (Chesley).

The implication of the Atlas case, for us (and quite possibly for people like Goldstein), is that it is time to establish one such guardrail in the form of faculty senate standing committees on academic freedom that design review procedures that include consulting the relevant professional organization, and its standards of professional ethics, when appropriate. Such a committee would not only provide the stopgap now needed to prevent what might be called the abuse of academic freedom in cases like Atlas's; it would also offer a degree of due process lacking now for others deserving of academic freedom protections (namely, non-tenure-track faculty). That such a committee would meet with the American Association of University Professors' approval is likely, since this principle is central to the 1994 AAUP statement, "On the Relation of Faculty Governance to Academic Freedom":

> It is the faculty—not trustees or administrators—who have the experience needed for assessing whether an instance of faculty speech constitutes a breach of a central principle of academic morality, and who have the expertise to form judgments of faculty competence or incompetence. As AAUP case reports have shown, to the extent that decisions on such matters are not in

the hands of the faculty, there is a potential for, and at times the actuality of, administrative imposition of penalties on improper grounds. (125)

What would such a guardrail look like and how might it be designed to consider the sometimes very disparate cases involving academic freedom? Here, we've discussed cases involving adjunct nonrenewal, tenured faculty accused of intolerance for speech likely deserving protection, and faculty members using their credentials to promote specious information in the public sphere. There are a number of other possibilities, and the very range of possible issues makes it difficult to imagine an appropriate body for their adjudication for all campuses—as the examples we've offered here clearly demonstrate.

Nevertheless, we can report that on Jennifer's campus, the Portland State AAUP chapter has begun work in conjunction with the Portland State faculty senate to imagine such a committee and how it might be written into senate bylaws and into bargaining contracts. The concept paper for the committee reads:

> In the last few years, there have been growing concerns about the disproportionate responsibility placed on Administration to adjudicate academic freedom issues and determine actions. There is a need for a more robust process of shared governance to engage appropriate expertise and responsibility. For example, although the CBA [collective bargaining agreement] commits the institution to uphold academic freedom, disputes that may implicate academic freedom will often be matters of "academic judgment" and thereby excluded from the dispute resolution process that operates for other guarantees in the contract.

The proposal to design a committee names the ways in which a committee might require engagement with other groups or individuals on campus. "When disputes arise in relations to academic freedom, the remit of an academic freedom committee would probably require some engagement with promotion and tenure and continuous appointment reviews, disciplinary processes (e.g., concerning the faculty code of conduct or matters handled by the Office of Diversity and Inclusion or Equity and Compliance), and contract (non)renewals." Senates may well develop an academic freedom committee along different lines—a standing committee or one convened by senators on an ad hoc basis, one with permanent members or one that assembles a new panel tailored for each specific case, etc.—but however it is ultimately comprised and defined, such a committee should be written into handbooks, constitutions, bylaws, and bargaining contracts (where applicable). For faculty at institutions with a historically inactive senate or one that is overly deferential to administrators, then AAUP chapters committed to racial justice and adjunct protections, whether they be collective bargaining or advocacy chapters, are sites where organizing to create such a committee could occur. More and more, unions are taking a lead in pushing their universities towards greater racial and social justice—but we are aware that many faculty work in institutions where, because of so-called right-to-work laws, unionization is not an option. For that reason, we are proposing something that can be created on any campus in the United States and that would help to strengthen shared governance after decades of erosion as a result of what is commonly referred to as the corporatization of the university.

Faculty at institutions with strong traditions of shared governance understand the power of university-wide faculty committees, but they may harbor doubts about our proposal nonetheless.

They do not labor under the illusion that some *other* body, one not made up of peers, is gifted with a degree of clarity and insight that eludes faculty, but they still have reason to wonder if we can trust each other. We, the faculty, lose academic freedom the moment we search for recourse in any authority but our own but, then again, who are *we*? *We* exist in the same typically predominantly white institutions that have housed Christainsens and Gilleys for years. *We* are the people who have been unable or unwilling to integrate what Mills and other colleagues of color have pointed out repeatedly. *We* are also the people who jealously guard any apparent infringement on absolute autonomy, willing to protect those we abhor if we think it makes our own protection more invincible.

The faculty are still dominated by a "we" for whom the traditional and largely libertarian defense of academic freedom remains persuasive. *But only by a slight margin.* These traditional defenders have grown increasingly alarmed by what they interpret to be the younger generation's ignorance regarding academic freedom's purpose and importance. Surveys have been piling up over the last five years that purport to document that senior faculty understand academic freedom while junior faculty do not. Their evidence is, for example, that graduate students and junior faculty appear to support human subjects review boards while senior faculty see them as intrusive.[13] These surveys give us hope. This is not nearly as paradoxical

---

13. For one example, see "Academic Freedom: A Pilot Study of Faculty Views" by Jonathan R. Cole, Stephen Cole, and Christopher C. Weiss. They found that faculty in earlier stages of their careers tended to approve more of disciplinary actions and/or interference in the complete autonomy of researchers and instructors than did faculty in the later stages of their careers. This tendency appeared to be unrelated to tenure status, as senior faculty

as it sounds. We have suggested throughout the book that traditionalist defenses of academic freedom are failing to grasp how insights from the last eighty years of American history should prompt us to rethink what academic freedom should and should not mean. "Colorblindness" has not cured America of white supremacism; social media, as Sarah Repucci has noted, "give far-right parties and authoritarians an advantage"; and the gig economy (and academy) has not been a boon to laborers but has undermined collective security and rights.[14] An academic freedom worth championing protects and promotes *democratic competence,* with an emphasis on both the terms of this phrase. It does not traffic in theory of the kind that prescribes what should be in an ideal world, but rather takes into account existing reality and its history, its power and economic asymmetries, its ongoing and compounding injustices and inequities.

Shaken out of their—our—complacency by the Trump years, no small portion of older white liberal faculty are also ready to consider a conception of academic freedom based on democratic competence. More and more of us recognize that American structural racism is a home-grown form of fascism, and that the historical and ongoing abuse of knowledge to rationalize that racism destroys democracy.[15] The academic freedom we champion, therefore, pre-

---

without tenure responded similarly to senior faculty with tenure. They interpret this to mean that junior faculty don't understand academic freedom when it is just as likely (more likely, in our opinion) that these faculty understand better than senior faculty academic freedom's role in ensuring democratic competence.

14. See Repucci, "Media Freedom: A Downward Spiral."

15. The work of Sarah Churchwell is exemplary in this regard. See, e.g., "American Fascism: It Has Happened Here" and "The Return of American Fascism." See also Alberto Toscano's "The Long Shadow of Racial Fascism,"

sumes the equality of persons, not the equality of ideas. Accordingly, we see democracy—and we encourage you to see democracy—not as an unfortunate obstacle to academic freedom but as its very reason for being. As Judith Butler wrote, the struggle for academic freedom is the struggle for democracy; but that struggle must be predicated on the belief that academic freedom is a matter of democratic competence, not a license to say and believe anything and everything imaginable. We hope that someday, someday soon, academe will hold that truth to be self-evident.

where Toscano credits the generations of Black activists and scholars who have long recognized the persistent form of fascism native to America.

WORKS CITED

Abrams, Floyd. *The Soul of the First Amendment*. Yale UP, 2017.

Abrams, Samuel J. "Young Americans Are Too Sensitive about Speech." *Minding the Campus*, November 23, 2020. https://www.minding thecampus.org/2020/11/23/young-americans-are-too-sensitive -about-speech/

Ackerman, Spencer. "DHS Crushed This Analyst for Warning about Far-Right Terror." *Wired*, August 7, 2012. https://www.wired.com/2012/08/dhs/

Adams v. Trustees of the University of North Carolina–Wilmington et al. Brief amicus curiae of the American Association of University Professors, Foundation for Individual Rights in Education, and the Thomas Jefferson Center for the Protection of Free Expression. July 2, 2010. https:// www.aaup.org/NR/rdonlyres/58506EE0-4E81-4AA9-9616-3768FFA 8643A/0/Adamsamicusbrief7210.pdf

American Association of University Professors. "1940 Statement of Principles on AcademicFreedom and Tenure." https://www.aaup.org/report /1940-statement-principles-academic-freedom-and-tenure

———. "Academic Freedom and Electronic Communications." *Policy Documents and Reports*, 11th ed. Johns Hopkins UP, 2015. 42–57.

———. "Academic Freedom and Tenure: A Preliminary Report on Freedom of Expression and Campus Harassment Codes." *Academe* 77.3 (1991): 23–26.

———. "Committee A Statement on Extramural Utterances." *Policy Documents and Reports*, 11th ed. Johns Hopkins UP, 2015. 31.

———. "Controversy: More on Campus Harassment Codes." *Academe* 77.6 (1991): 32–41.

———. "On Freedom of Expression and Campus Speech Codes." *Policy Documents and Reports*, 11th ed., 361–62. Johns Hopkins UP, 2015.

———. "On the Relation of Faculty Governance to Academic Freedom." *Policy Documents andReports*, 11th ed., 123–25. Johns Hopkins UP, 2015.

Ahmed, Sara. "Whiteness and the General Will: Diversity Work as Willful Work." *philoSOPHIA* 2.1 (2012): 1–20.

Anderson, Carol. *White Rage: The Unspoken Truth of Our Racial Divide*. Bloomsbury, 2016.

Apollo 18. Directed by Gonzalo López-Gallego. Dimension Films, 2011.

Areen, Judith. "Government as Educator: A New Understanding of First Amendment Protection of Academic Freedom and Governance." *Georgetown University Law Journal*. 97 (2009): 945–1000. https://scholarship.law.georgetown.edu/facpub/443/

Baer, Ulrich. *What Snowflakes Get Right: Free Speech, Truth, and Equality on Campus*. Oxford UP, 2019.

Bailey, Cathryn. "How Diversity Rhetoric Obscures Structural Inequities in Higher Education." *Academe*, Fall 2020. https://www.aaup.org/article/how-diversity-rhetoric-obscures-structural-inequities-higher-education#.X_pmxulKg6g

Barchi, Robert L. Letter to Dr. Peter March, August 29, 2018. Rpt. by TheFire.org, August 31, 2018. https://www.thefire.org/8-29-18-letter-from-r-barchi/

Bauerlein, Monica, and Clara Jeffery. "Facebook Manipulated the News You See to Appease Republicans, Insiders Say." *Mother Jones*, October 21, 2020. https://www.motherjones.com/media/2020/10/facebook-mother-jones/

Bazelon, Emily. "The Problem of Free Speech in an Age of Disinformation." *New York Times Magazine*, October 13, 2020. https://www.nytimes.com/2020/10/13/magazine/free-speech.html

@BazziNYU (Mohamad Bazzi). "This stunning article by Lawrence Mead, an NYU professor, argues that Blacks and Hispanics, because they are not European, are 'unprepared' for 'individualist culture' in America.

A few highlights:" *Twitter*, July 24, 2020. https://threadreaderapp.com
/thread/1286740934466719744.html

Beinart, Peter. "A Violent Attack on Free Speech at Middlebury." *The Atlantic*,
March 6, 2017. https://www.theatlantic.com/politics/archive/2017/03
/middlebury-free-speech-violence/518667/

Bell, Derrick. "*Brown v. Board of Education* and the Interest Convergence
Dilemma." In *Critical Race Theory: The Key Writings That Formed the
Movement*, 20–28. New Press, 2005.

———. "Who's Afraid of Critical Race Theory?" *University of Illinois Law
Review* 1995.4 (1995): 893–910.

Bernstein, Mark F. "The University, Social Justice, and Free Inquiry." With
Randall L. Kennedy, Carolyn M. Rouse, and Paul Starr. *Princeton Alumni
Weekly*, September 2020. https://paw.princeton.edu/article/university
-social-justice-and-free-inquiry

Bérubé, Michael. "Editor's Introduction." *AAUP Journal of Academic Freedom*
6 (2015). https://www.aaup.org/JAF6/editors-introduction#.X-uSm
-lKi3J

———. "Equality, Freedom, and/or Justice for All: A Response to Martha
Nussbaum." *Metaphilosophy* 40.3–4 (2009): 352–65.

———. *Life as Jamie Knows It: An Exceptional Child Grows Up*. Beacon, 2016.

———and Jennifer Ruth. *The Humanities, Higher Education, and Academic
Freedom: Three Necessary Arguments*. Palgrave, 2015.

Bilgrami, Akeel, and Jonathan R. Cole, eds. *Who's Afraid of Academic Freedom?*
Columbia UP, 2016.

Bollinger, Lee. *The Tolerant Society: Freedom of Speech and Extremist Speech in
America*. Oxford UP, 1986.

Booshi. "Yale Students Berating Professor Highlights." September 21, 2016.
YouTube, https://www.youtube.com/watch?v=kMc8pczn-hs&t=281s

@jbouie (Jamelle Bouie). "it is still strange to me how 'critical race theory'
became this bogeyman to the right. it is not that i think it's weird they
conjured up a fake crisis to justify their desire to repress, but that of all
the targets, a somewhat obscure set of ideas from the legal academy?"
Twitter, October 30, 2020, 2:32 pm. https://twitter.com/jbouie/status
/1322245096398561280

Bouie, Jamelle. "It Started with Birtherism." *New York Times*, November 24, 2020. https://www.nytimes.com/2020/11/24/opinion/trump-voter -fraud-birtherism.html

Blatt, Jessica. "John W. Burgess, the Racial State and the Making of the American Science of Politics." *Ethnic and Racial Studies* 37.6 (2014): 1062–79.

Brown, Sarah. "College Diversity Officers Face a Demanding Job and Scarce Resources." *Chronicle of Higher Education*, August 8, 2017. https://www .chronicle.com/article/ college-diversity-officers-face-a-demanding -job-and-scarce-resources/

Buckley, Cara. "New York Review of Books Editor Is Out Amid Uproar Over #MeToo Essay." *New York Times*, September 19, 2018. https://www .nytimes.com/2018/09/19/arts/ian-buruma-out-jian-ghomeshi.html

Burfeind, Peter. "Why Black Lives Matter Only Empowers Racist White Leftists." *The Federalist*, September 24, 2020. https://thefederalist.com /2020/09/24/why-black-lives-matter-only-empowers-racist-white -leftists/

Burke, Timothy. "Mucking Out Mead." *Easily Distracted*, July 28, 2020. https:// blogs.swarthmore.edu/burke/blog/2020/07/28/mucking-out-mead/

Butler, Judith. "The Criminalization of Knowledge: Why the Struggle for Academic Freedom Is the Struggle for Democracy." *Chronicle of Higher Education*, May 27, 2018. https://www.chronicle.com/article/The -Criminalization-of/243501

Campos, Paul. "Amy Wax's Mexican Problem." *Lawyers, Guns, and Money* (blog), July 25, 2019. https://www.lawyersgunsmoneyblog.com/2019 /07/amy-waxs-mexican-problem

"Caper Chase." *The Simpsons*. Fox, WNYW, New York, April 2, 2017.

Carlson, Licia. *The Faces of Intellectual Disability: Philosophical Reflections*. Indiana UP, 2010.

Chait, Jonathan. "Richard Epstein Can't Stop Being Wrong about the Coronavirus." *New York Magazine*, April 21, 2020. https://nymag.com /intelligencer/2020/04/richard-epstein-coronavirus-500-5000-deaths .html

Chakrabarty, Dipesh. *Provincializing Europe: Postcolonial Thought and Historical Difference*. Princeton UP, 2000.

Chatterjee, Piya and Sunaina Maira. *The Imperial University: Academic Repression and Scholarly Dissent.* U of Minnesota P, 2014.

Chesley, Kate. "Academic Freedom Questions Arise on Campus over COVID-19 Strategy Conflicts." *Stanford News*, October 30, 2020. https://news.stanford.edu/2020/10/30/academic-freedom-questions-arise-campus-covid-19-strategy-conflicts/

Chotiner, Isaac. "Why Did the New York Review of Books Publish That Jian Ghomeshi Essay?" *Slate*, September 14, 2018. https://slate.com/news-and-politics/2018/09/jian-ghomeshi-new-york-review-of-books-essay.html

Christakis, Erika. "Dressing Yourselves." Email to students of Silliman College, Yale University, October 30, 2015. Rpt. by the Foundation for Individual Rights in Education, https://www.thefire.org/email-from-erika-christakis-dressing-yourselves-email-to-silliman-college-yale-students-on-halloween-costumes/

———and Nicholas A. Christakis. "Whither Goes Free Speech at Harvard?" *Time*, December 4, 2012. https://ideas.time.com/2012/12/04/wither-goes-free-speech-at-harvard/

Churchwell, Sarah. "American Fascism: It Has Happened Here." *New York Review of Books.* June 22, 2020. https://www.nybooks.com/daily/2020/06/22/american-fascism-it-has-happened-here/

———. "The Return of American Fascism." *The New Statesman*, September 2, 2020. https://www.newstatesman.com/international/places/2020/09/return-american-fascism

Cobb, Jelani. "The Republican Party, Racial Hypocrisy, and the 1619 Project." *The New Yorker*, May 29, 2021. https://www.newyorker.com/news/daily-comment/the-republican-party-racial-hypocrisy-and-the-1619-project

Cole, Andrew. "What Is Academic? What Is Freedom?" *Daily Princetonian*, July 15, 2020. https://www.dailyprincetonian.com/article/2020/07/princeton-academic-freedom-white-surpremacy-racism-woodrow-wilson-free-speech

Cole, David. "Yale: The Power of Speech." *New York Review of Books*, November 18, 2015. https://www.nybooks.com/daily/2015/11/18/yale-power-of-speech/

Cole, Jonathan R., Stephen Cole, and Christopher C. Weiss. "Academic Freedom: A Pilot Study of Faculty Views." In *Who's Afraid of Academic Freedom?* ed. Akeel Bilgrami and Jonathan R. Cole. Columbia UP, 2016.

Colorado Conference of the American Association of University Professors. *Report on the Termination of Ward Churchill. AAUP Journal of Academic Freedom* 3 (2012). https://www.aaup.org/JAF3/report-termination-ward -churchill#.X-yNfulKi3I

Cooper, Brittany. "How Free Speech Works for White Academics." *Chronicle of Higher Education*, November 16, 2017. https://www.chronicle.com /article/how-free-speech-works-for-white-academics/

Cotton, Tom. "Tom Cotton: Send in the Troops." *New York Times*, June 3, 2020. https://www.nytimes.com/2020/06/03/opinion/tom-cotton -protests-military.html

COVID-19 and the Hoover Institution: Time for a Reappraisal. Stanford faculty open letter. 2020. https://docs.google.com/forms/d/e/1FAIpQL Sd8KotZQ83WM27ysRAbBZmsiTgfCctTULCo53EVgjQ5bv6uRA /viewform

Craven, Julia. "The Newspaper Baron Who Lobbied against Nikole Hannah-Jones," *Slate*, June 4, 2021. https://slate.com/news-and-politics/2021 /06/the-newspaper-baron-who-lobbied-against-nikole-hannah-jones .html

Crenshaw, Kimberlé, Neil Gotanda, Gary Peller, and Kendall Thomas, eds. *Critical Race Theory: The Key Writings That Formed the Movement*. New Press, 1995.

———. "Race, Reform, and Retrenchment: Transformation and Legitimation in Antidiscrimination Law." *Harvard Law Review* 101.7 (1988): 1331–87. Rpt. in *Critical Race Theory: The Key Writings That Formed the Movement*, 103–26. https://harvardlawreview.org/wp-content/uploads /2020/09/Crenshaw-Race-Reform-and-Retrenchment-pdf.

———. "The Capitol Riots and the Eternal Fantasy of a Racially Virtuous America." *The New Republic*, March 22, 2021. https://newrepublic.com /article/161568/white-supremacy racism-in-america-kimberle-crenshaw

Cruz, Emily. "The Termination of UW–Milwaukee Professor Betsy Schoeller." Change.org petition. https://www.change.org/p/university

-of-wisconsin-milwaukee-the-termination-of-uw-milwaukee-professor
-betsy-schoeller?recruiter=1020258215 &recruited_by_id= 4c4a50e0
-0b41-11ea-91b9-7d182ef84c7f

Culler, Jonathan. *On Deconstruction: Theory and Criticism after Structuralism.*
Cornell UP, 1982.

DeParle, Jason. "Daring Research or 'Social Science Pornography'?: Charles
Murray." *New York Times Magazine*, October 9, 1994. https://www
.nytimes.com/1994/10/09/ magazine/daring-research-or-social
-science-pornography-charles-murray.html

Dabhoiwala, Fara. "Imperial Delusions." *New York Review of Books*, July 1,
2021. https://www.nybooks.com/articles/2021/07/01/imperial
-delusions/

Dery, Mark. "The Professor of Paranoia." *Chronicle of Higher Education*,
May 21, 2021. https://www.chronicle.com/article/the-professor
-of-paranoia

Dooling Doug, Jr.,. "Blackface: A Halloween That Ripped a University."
Onward State, October 31, 2014. https://onwardstate.com/2014/10/31
/blackface-a-halloween-that-ripped-a-university/

Ebert, Roger. "Making Out Is Its Own Reward." *RogerEbert.com*, January 12,
2010. https://www.rogerebert.com/roger-ebert/making-out-is-its-own
-reward

Eden, Max. "Critical Race Theory in American Classrooms." *City Journal*,
September 18, 2020. https://www.city-journal.org/critical-race-theory
-in-american-classrooms

Edsall, Thomas. "Have Trump's Lies Wrecked Free Speech?" *New York Times*,
January 6, 2021. https://www.nytimes.com/2021/01/06/opinion
/trump-lies-free-speech.html

Ellison, Sarah. "How the 1619 Project Took Over 2020." *Washington Post*,
October 13, 2020. https://www.washingtonpost.com/lifestyle/style
/1619-project-took-over-2020-inside-story/2020/10/13/af537092-00df
-11eb-897d-3a6201d6643f_story.html

England, Jason. "Why Was It So Easy for Jessica Krug to Fool Everyone?"
Chronicle of Higher Education, October 2, 2020. https://www.chronicle
.com/article/why-was-it-so-easy-for-jessica-krug-to-fool-everyone?

Espinosa, Lorelle L., Jonathan M. Turk, Morgan Taylor, and Hollie M. Chessman. *Race and Ethnicity in Higher Education: A Status Report.* American Council on Education, 2019.

"Faculty Letter." Open letter from Princeton faculty, students, and staff to President Eisgruber, Provost Prentice, Deans Kulkarni and Dolan, Vice President for Campus Life Calhoun, and members of the Princeton Cabinet. July 4, 2020. https://docs.google.com/forms/d/e/1FAI pQLSfPmfeDKBi25_7rUTKkhZ3cyMICQicpo5ReVaeBpEdYUCkyIA /viewform

Fagone, Jason. "The 'Race Realist' on Campus." *San Francisco Chronicle*, June 24, 2021. https://www.sfchronicle.com/projects/2021/race-realist -cal-state-east-bay/

Feldman, Josh. "Colbert Tweet Triggers Firestorm, #CancelColbert Twitter Trend." *Mediaite*, March 27, 2014. https://www.mediaite.com/online /colbert-tweet-triggers-firestorm-cancelcolbert-twitter-trend/

Field, Laura K. "A Reply to the Claremont Institute's Claim that 'America is Not Racist.'" *Niskanen Center*, June 26, 2020. https://www.niskanen center.org/a-reply-to-the-claremont-institutes-claim-that-america-is -not-racist/

Finkin, Matthew, and Robert Post. *For the Common Good: Principles of Academic Freedom.* Yale UP, 2009.

Fish, Stanley. "Free Speech Is Not an Academic Value." *Chronicle of Higher Education*, March 20, 2017. https://www.chronicle.com/article/free-spe ech-is-not-an-academic-value/

———. *Save the World on Your Own Time.* Oxford UP, 2012.

Fitzsimmons, Tracy. "Enough!" *Inside Higher Ed*, January 8, 2021. https:// www.insidehighered.com/views/2021/01/08/call-action-behalf -democracy-those-who-work-higher-ed-opinion

Flaherty, Colleen. "Failure to Communicate." *Inside Higher Ed*, September 8, 2020. https://www.insidehighered.com/news/2020/09/08/professor -suspended-saying-chinese-word-sounds-english-slur

———. "Journal Editor Regrets Publishing Racist Article." *Inside Higher Ed*, July 31, 2020. https://www.insidehighered.com/quicktakes/2020/07 /31/journal-editor-regrets-publishing-racist-article

———. "Not Shrugging Off Criticism." *Inside Higher Ed*, September 23, 2020. https://www.insidehighered.com/news/2020/09/23/scott-atlas-white -house-adviser-coronavirus-threatens-sue-colleagues-back-stanford

———. "Pro-Antifa Professor Out at Iowa." *Inside Higher Ed*, August 26, 2019. https://www.insidehighered.com/news/2019/08/26/kirkwood -cc-announces-professor-sympathetic-antifa-wont-be-teaching-due -safety

———. "Resignations at 'Third World Quarterly.'" *Inside Higher Ed*, September 20, 2017. https://www.insidehighered.com/news/2017/09/20 /much-third-world-quarterlys-editorial-board-resigns-saying -controversial-article

———. "Unacademic Freedom?" *Inside Higher Ed*, March 1, 2016. https:// www.insidehighered. com/news/2016/03/01/does-academic-freedom -protect-falsehoods

Fortinsky, Sarah. "Penn Trustee Emeritus Resigns over University 'Treatment of Amy Wax.'"*Daily Pennsylvanian*, April 9, 2018. https://www .thedp.com/article/2018/04/amy-wax-board-of-trustees-paul-levy -penn-law-upenn-pennsylvania-upenn-gutmann-resignation

Foundation for Individual Rights in Education. "Halloween Costume Controversy." https://www.thefire.org/resources/spotlight/yale -university-school-feature/halloween-costume-controversy/

———. "VICTORY: College Settles with 'Antifa' Professor Fired for Criticizing President Trump on Facebook, Avoids First Amendment Lawsuit from FIRE." April 27, 2020. https://www.thefire.org/victory-college -settles-with-antifa-professor-fired-for-criticizing-president-trump-on -facebook-avoids-first-amendment-lawsuit-from-fire/

Friedersdorf, Conor. "The New Intolerance of Student Activism." *The Atlantic*, November 9, 2015. https://www.theatlantic.com/politics /archive/2015/11/the-new-intolerance-of-student-activism-at-yale /414810/

———. "The Princeton Faculty's Anti-Free-Speech Demands." *The Atlantic*, August 4, 2020. https://www.theatlantic.com/ideas/archive/2020/08 /what-princeton-professors-really-think-about-defining-racism /614911/

Gates, Henry Louis, Jr. "War of Words: Critical Race Theory and the First Amendment." Gates, Anthony P. Griffin, Donald E. Lively, Robert C. Post, William R. Rubenstein. Introd. Ira Glasser. *Speaking of Race, Speaking of Sex: Hate Speech, Civil Rights, and Civil Liberties.* New York UP, 1994. 17–57.

Ghomeshi, Jian. "Reflections from a Hashtag: My Path to Public Toxicity." *New York Review of Books*, October 11, 2018. https://www.nybooks.com /articles/2018/10/11/reflections-hashtag/

Gilley, Bruce. "The Case for Colonialism." *Third World Quarterly*, DOI: 10.1080/01436597.2017. 1369037. Retracted. Republished by the National Association of Scholars. *Academic Questions* 31.2 (2018). https:// www.nas.org/academic-questions/31/2/the_case_for_ colonialism

———. "Was It Good Fortune to Be Enslaved by the British Empire?" *National Association of Scholars*, September 30, 2019. https://www.nas.org/blogs /article/was-it-good-fortune-of-being-enslaved-by-the-british-empire

@BruceGilley3. "Astonishing act of totalitarianism by Princeton faculty, including a proposed committee for 'investigation and discipline of racist behaviors, incidents, research, and publication on the part of faculty.' Every signatory should be fired. Fight back Tigers!" *Twitter*, July 6, 2020, 7:12 pm. https://twitter.com/BruceGilley3/status/ 128027851055 3067520

———. "The Belgians should apologize to Congo for: * not colonizing the King's estates sooner * ending colonial rule despite mainstream Congolese opposition to independence * not arresting or killing Patrice Lumumba sooner And nothing else." *Twitter*, June 30, 2020, 11:07 pm. https://twitter.com/BruceGilley3/status/ 1278163382978240512

———. "If you are in an organization where BLM/Diversity Madness has taken hold, I offer here, based on my knowledge of Mao's politics, 'Three Strategies for Surviving the Great BLM Cultural Revolution.' Good luck!" *Twitter*, June 16, 2020, 6:08 pm. https://twitter.com/BruceGilley3 /status/1273059869424156672

Giorgis, Hannah. "A Deeply Provincial View of Free Speech." *The Atlantic*, July 13, 2020. https://www.theatlantic.com/culture/archive/2020/07 /harpers-letter-free-speech/614080/

Gluckman, Nell. "The Outrage Peddlers Are Here to Stay." *Chronicle of Higher Education*, November 17, 2020. https://www.chronicle.com/article/the-outrage-peddlers-are-here-to-stay

Goldberg, Michelle. "#CancelColbert and the Return of the Anti-Liberal Left." *The Nation*, April 2, 2014. https://www.thenation.com/article/archive/cancelcolbert-and-return-anti-liberal-left/

———. "Do Progressives Have a Free-Speech Problem?" *New York Times*, July 17, 2020. https://www.nytimes.com/2020/07/17/opinion/sunday/harpers-letter-free-speech.html

———. "This Professor Was Fired for Saying 'Fuck No' in Class." *The Nation*, July 2, 2015. https://www.thenation.com/article/archive/this-professor-was-fired-for-saying-fuck-no-in-class/

Gould, Stephen Jay. *The Mismeasure of Man*. Revised and expanded. W. W. Norton, 1996.

Griggs v. Duke Power Co. 401 U.S. 424 (1971).

Gross, Jenny. "Far-Right Groups Are Behind Most U.S. Terrorist Attack, Report Finds." *New York Times*, October 24, 2020. https://www.nytimes.com/2020/10/24/us/domestic-terrorist-groups.html

Guinier, Lani. *Lift Every Voice: Turning a Civil Rights Setback into a New Vision of Social Justice*. Simon and Schuster, 1998.

Guynn, Jessica. "Mark Zuckerberg Defends Not Banning Steve Bannon from Facebook for Beheading Comments." *USA Today*, November 17, 2020. https://www.usatoday.com/story/tech/2020/11/17/steve-bannon-fauci-wray-trump-facebook-zuckerberg-beheading/6331861002/

Hall, Colby. "'I Looked Into It': Steve Doocy Debunks Trump's Dominion Software Voter Fraud Conspiracy." *Mediaite*, November 13, 2020. https://www.mediaite.com/election-2020/i-looked-into-it-steve-doocy-debunks-sean-hannity-and-trumps-dominion-software-voter-fraud-conspiracy/

Hall, Evelyn Beatrice. *Friends of Voltaire*. Richard West, 1906.

Hanci, Fadil. "Hate Crimes Increase in the US since Trump's Election." *Politics Today*, July 22, 2019. https://politicstoday.org/hate-crimes-increase-in-the-us-since-trumps-election/

Hannah-Jones, Nikole. "Our Democracy's Founding Ideals Were False When They Were Written. Black Americans Have Fought to Make Them True."

The 1619 Project. *New York Times Magazine*, August 14, 2019. https://www
.nytimes.com/interactive/2019/08/14/magazine/black-history-american
-democracy.html

Harris, Leslie M. "I Helped Fact-Check the 1619 Project. The Times
Ignored Me." *Politico*, March 6, 2020. https://www.politico.com/news
/magazine/2020/03/06/1619-project-new-york-times-mistake
-122248

———and Karin Wulf. "The 1619 Project's Greatest Contribution." Letter to
the Editor. *Washington Post*, October 16, 2020. https://www.washington
post.com/opinions/letters-to-the-editor/the-1619-projects-greatest
-contribution/2020/10/16/5001b5dc-0e5d-11eb-b404-8d1e675ec701
_story.html

Hustace, Kip M. "Elevating the Discourse: An Interview with Robert C.
Post." *Boston Review*, March 1, 2012. http://bostonreview.net/robert
-post-democracy-expertise-academic-freedom-first-amendment

James, Mark S. "Feeling the Problem: Working through Diversity Work."
Transformations: The Journal of Inclusive Scholarship and Pedagogy 27.2
(2017): 217–28.

Jaschik, Scott. "AAUP vs. FIRE." *Inside Higher Ed*, July 9, 2021. https://www
.insidehighered. com/news/2021/07/09/aaup-university-oklahoma
-challenges-fire-statements-free-speech

———. "Cypress Suspends Adjunct over Her Comments on Police." *Inside
Higher Ed*, May 3, 2021. https://www.insidehighered.com/quicktakes
/2021/05/03/ cypress-suspends-adjunct-over-her-comments-police

———. "University Paid $504,000 to Get Rid of Professor." *Inside Higher Ed*,
July 6, 2020. https://www.insidehighered.com/quicktakes/2020/07/06
/university-paid-504000-get-rid-professor

JFK. Dir. Oliver Stone. Warner Brothers, 1991.

Johnson, Daryl. "I Warned of Right-Wing Violence in 2009. Republicans
Objected. I Was Right." *Washington Post*, August 21, 2017. https://www
.washingtonpost.com/news/ posteverything/wp/2017/08/21/i-warned
-of-right-wing-violence-in-2009-it-caused-an-uproar-i-was-right/

@SonofBaldwin (Robert Jones, Jr.) "We can disagree and still love each other
unless your disagreement is rooted in my oppression and denial of my

humanity and right to exist." *Twitter*, August 18, 2015, 10:19 am. https://
 twitter.com/SonofBaldwin/status/ 633644373423562753

Kang, Jay Caspian. "The Campaign to 'Cancel' Colbert." *New Yorker*,
 March 30, 2014. https://www.newyorker.com/news/news-desk/the
 -campaign-to-cancel-colbert

Kendi, Ibram X. "When Free Speech Becomes Unfree Speech." *Diverse: Issues
 in Higher Education*. October 20, 2015. https://diverseeducation.com
 /article/78479/

Kennedy, Randall L. "Racial Critiques of Legal Academia." *Harvard Law
 Review* 102 (1989): 1745–1819.

Klingenstein, Thomas D., and Ryan P. Williams. "America Is Not Racist." *The
 American Mind*, June 3, 2020. https://americanmind.org/salvo/america
 -is-not-racist/

Knapp, Steven, and Walter Benn Michaels. "Against Theory." *Critical Inquiry*
 8.4 (1982): 724–42.

Korn, Sandra Y. L. "The Doctrine of Academic Freedom." *Harvard Crimson*,
 February 18, 2014. https://www.thecrimson.com/column/the-red-line
 /article/2014/2/18/academic-freedom-justice/

Kors, Alan. "Cracking the Speech Code." *Reason*, July 1999. https://reason
 .com/1999/07/01/cracking-the-speech-code/

Ladner, Joyce. *The Death of White Sociology*. Black Classic Press, 1973.

Lawrence, Charles R., III. "The Id, the Ego, and Equal Protection: Reckoning with Unconscious Racism." In *Critical Race Theory: The Key Writings
 That Formed the Movement*. 235–56.

Lepore, Jill. "Foreword." *How Rights Went Wrong: Why Our Obsession with
 Rights Is Tearing America Apart*, by Jamal Greene. Mariner Books, 2021.

Li, David K. "Professor behind 'vile' racist and sexist tweets found dead."
 ABC News, July 24, 2020. https://www.nbcnews.com/news/us-news
 /professor-behind-vile-racist-sexist-tweets-found-dead-north-carolina
 -n1234801

Leonard, Thomas C. *Illiberal Reformers: Race, Eugenics, and American Economics
 in the Progressive Era*. Princeton UP, 2017.

"A Letter on Justice and Open Debate." *Harper's Magazine*, July 7, 2020.
 https://harpers.orga-letter-on-justice-and-open-debate/

@ConceptualJames (James Lindsay). "Critical Race Theory is literally a conspiracy theory that all of the liberal order, equality, rationalism, and the constitution are the conspiracy against non-white people in a hierarchical fashion." *Twitter*, November 10, 2020, 4:20 pm. https:// twitter.com/ConceptualJames/status/1326273589813915649

Lindsay, James. "Do Better than Critical Race Theory." *New Discourses*, June 1, 2020. https://newdiscourses.com/2020/06/do-better-than -critical-race-theory/

Lubet, Steven. "The Mess at Oberlin." *The Faculty Lounge*, August 4, 2016. https://www.thefacultylounge.org/2016/08/the-mess-at-oberlin .html

Maher, Bill. *Real Time with Bill Maher*. "Martyrs without a Cause." *YouTube*, January 22, 2016. https://www.youtube.com/watch?v=luhSVN5mg NY&t=146

Mangan, Katharine. "The U. of Iowa Keeps Losing Diversity Officers." *Chronicle of Higher Education*, October 29, 2019. https://www.chronicle .com/article/the-u-of-iowa-keeps losing-diversity-officers-the-turn over-has-raised-alarms/

Marchese, David. "In Conversation: Quincy Jones." *New York Magazine*, February 7, 2018.https://www.vulture.com/2018/02/quincy-jones-in -conversation.html

Marks, Jonathan. "Is Anti-Semitism a Firing Offense?" *Commentary*, November 27, 2016. https://www.commentarymagazine.com/jonathan-marks /is-anti-semitism-a-firing-offense/

Matsuda, Mari J. "Looking to the Bottom: Critical Race Theory and Reparations." In *Critical Race Theory: The Key Writings That Formed the Movement*, 63–79.

———, Charles R. Lawrence III, Richard Delgado, and Kimberlé Williams Crenshaw. *Words That Wound: Critical Race Theory, Assaultive Speech, and the First Amendment*. Routledge, 1993.

McInnis, Tatiana. "A Farewell Letter to DEI Work." *Inside Higher Ed*, August 20, 2020. https://www.insidehighered.com/views/2020/08/20 /diversity-equity-and-inclusion-offices-cant-be-effective-if-they-arent -empowered

McNair, Tia Brown, Estela Mara Bensimon, and Lindsey Malcom-Piqueux. *From Equity Talk to Equity Walk: Leading Change in Higher Education.* Jossey-Bass, 2020.

Mead, Lawrence. *Burdens of Freedom: Cultural Difference and American Power.* Encounter, 2019.

———. "Cultural Difference." *Society* 55 (2018): 482–87.

———. "Poverty and Culture." *Society* (2020). https://doi.org/10.1007/S12115-020-00496-1. Retracted.

Menand, Louis. "Illiberalisms." Review of Dinesh D'Souza, *Illiberal Education: The Politics of Race and Sex on Campus. New Yorker,* May 20, 1991: 101–07.

Mignolo, Walter D. "Epistemic Disobedience, Independent Thought and De-Colonial Freedom." *Theory, Culture, and Society* 26 (7–8) (2009): 1–23.

Miller, Adam. "The Pioneer Fund: Bankrolling the Professors of Hate." *Journal of Blacks in Higher Education* 6 (1994–95): 58–61.

Mills, Charles W. *Black Rights / White Wrongs: The Critique of Racial Liberalism.* Oxford UP, 2017.

Mishra, Pankaj. *Blind Fanatics: Liberals, Race, and Empire.* Farrar, Straus, and Giroux, 2019.

Moynihan, Daniel Patrick. *The Negro Family: The Case for National Action.* Office of Policy Planning and Research, United States Department of Labor, 1965.

Murawski, John. "The Deeply Pessimistic Intellectual Roots of Black Lives Matter, 'the 1619 Project,' and Much Else in Woke America." *RealClearInvestigations,* September 2, 2020. https://www.realclearinvestigations .com/articles/2020/09/02/the_deeply_pessimistic_intellectual_roots _of_black_lives_matter_the_1619_project_and_much_else_125033 .html#!

Neiman, Susan. *Learning from the Germans: Race and the Memory of Evil.* Farrar, Straus, and Giroux, 2019.

Nelson, Cary. "Steven Salaita's Scholarly Record and the Problem of His Appointment." *AAUP Journal of Academic Freedom* 6 (2015). https://www .aaup.org/JAF6/steven-salaitas-scholarly-record#.W-dRg3pKgdV

Niehans, Aly. "Why 'The Problem of Whiteness' Is an Essential Class at the University of Wisconsin." *University of Wisconsin Badger Herald,* January 18,

2017. https://badgerherald.com/opinion/2017/01/18/why-the
-problem-of-whiteness-is-an-essential-class-at-the-university-of
-wisconsin/

"Not John Deane or Doane." Comment on *Academe Blog* post by John K.
Wilson, "The Problem with Princeton's Racism Committee Proposal."
July 17, 2020. https://academeblog.org/ 2020/07/17/the-problem-with
-princetons-racism-committee-proposal/#comment-16770

Oliver, Revilo P. "Marxmanship in Dallas." https://www.revilo-oliver.com
/rpo/Marxmanship1.html. Originally published in *American Opinion* 7.2
(February 1964).

Open Letter from Stanford Faculty Regarding Dr. Scott Atlas. September 9,
2020. http://pids.org/wp-content/uploads/2020/10/open-letter-re
-scott-atlas-final-20-09-09.pdf

Patel, Vimal. "A Revolt at a Journal Puts Peer Review under the Micro-
scope." *Chronicle of Higher Education*, September 25, 2017. https://www
.chronicle.com/article/a-revolt-at-a-journal-puts-peer-review-under
-the-microscope

Patrice, Joe. "Amy Wax Relieved of Her 1L Teaching Duties after Bald-Faced
Lying about Black Students." *Above the Law*, March 13, 2018. https://
abovethelaw.com/2018/03/amy-wax-relieved-of-her-1l-teaching-duties
-after-bald-faced-lying-about-black-students/

Pilgrim, David. "Blacks, Picnics, and Lynchings." Ferris State University Jim
Crow Museum of Racist Memorabilia, January 2004. https://www
.ferris.edu/HTMLS/news/jimcrow/ question/2004/january.htm

Pluckrose, Helen, and James Lindsay. *Cynical Theories: How Activist Scholarship
Made Everything about Race, Gender, and Identity—and Why This Harms
Everybody.* Pitchstone, 2020.

Ponter, Evan. "Penn State Sorority Chi Omega under Investigation Due to
Racially Insensitive Image." *Onward State*, December 4, 2012. https://
onwardstate.com/2012/12/04/penn-state-sorority-chi-omega-under-in
vestigation-due-to-racially-insensitive-photograph-2/

Post, Robert. *Democracy, Academic Freedom, and Expertise: A First Amendment
Jurisprudence for the Modern State.* Yale UP, 2012.

Potter, Claire. "Natalie Zemon Davis 'Gets' Twitter, Supports Steven Salaita."
Chronicle of Higher Education, August 29, 2014. http://chronicle.com

/blognetwork/tenuredradical/2014/ 08/natalie-zemon-davis-gets-twitt
er-supports-steven-salaita/

Pozner, Lenny, and Veronique Pozner. "Sandy Hook Massacre
3rd Anniversary: Two Parents Target FAU Conspiracy Theorist."
South Florida Sun Sentinel, December 10, 2015. https://www.sun-sentinel
.com/opinion/commentary/sfl-on-sandy-hook-anniversary-two
-parents-target-fau-professor-who-taunts-family-victims-20151210
-story.html

Publius Decius Mus. "The Flight 93 Election." *Claremont Review of Books*,
September 5, 2016. https://claremontreviewofbooks.com/digital
/the-flight-93-election/

Reichman, Henry. "Amy Wax, Academic Freedom, 'Official' Positions, and
the 'Fitness' Standard." *Academe Blog*, July 29, 2019. https://academe
blog.org/2019/07/29/amy-wax-academic-freedom-official-positions
-and-the-fitness-standard/

———. Comment on *Academe Blog* post by John K. Wilson, "The Problem
with Princeton's Racism Committee Proposal." July 17, 2020. https://
academeblog.org/2020/ 07/17/the-problem-with-princetons-racism
-committee-proposal/#comment-16616

———. "Do Adjuncts Have Academic Freedom? Or Why Tenure Matters."
Academe, Fall 2020. https://www.aaup.org/article/doadjuncts-have-academ
ic-freedom-or-why-tenure-matters#.X_tntelKg6g

———. *The Future of Academic Freedom*. Johns Hopkins UP, 2019.

Repucci, Sarah. "Media Freedom: A Downward Spiral." *Freedom House*.
https://freedomhouse.org/report/freedom-and-media/2019/media
-freedom-downward-spiral

Richeson, Jennifer. "Americans Are Determined to Believe in Black Progress." *The Atlantic*, September 2020. https://www.theatlantic.com
/magazine/archive/2020/09/the-mythology-of-racial-progress
/614173/

Robbins, Rebecca D. "Campus Reacts to Inflammatory Flyers." *Harvard
Crimson*, November 30, 2012. https://www.thecrimson.com/article
/2012/11/30/final-club-invitation-door/

Rodriguez, Dylan. *White Reconstruction: Domestic Warfare and the Logics of
Genocide*. Fordham UP, 2020.

@realchrisrufo (Christopher Rufo). "Heading into the @WhiteHouse to
    celebrate our victory against critical race theory." *Twitter*, October 30, 2020,
    10:38 am. https://twitter.com/ realchrisrufo/status/1322186158735020032
———. "We have successfully frozen their brand—'critical race theory'—into
    the public conversation and are steadily driving up negative perceptions.
    We will eventually turn it toxic, as we put all of the various insanities
    under that brand category." *Twitter*, March 15, 2021, 3:14 PM. https://
    twitter.com/realchrisrufo/status/1371540368714428416
———. "The goal is to have the public read something crazy in the newspaper
    and immediately think 'critical race theory.' We have decodified the term
    and will recodify it to annex the entire range of cultural constructions that
    are unpopular with Americans." *Twitter*, March 15, 2021, 3:17 pm. https://
    twitter.com/realchrisrufo/status/ 1371541044592996352
Rufo, Christopher. *City Journal* Contributing Editor Webpage. https://www
    .city-journal.org/ contributor/christopher-f-rufo_1334
Rupert, Mark. "Teaching in the Time of Trump." 2019. https://www.academia
    .edu/42713086/Teaching_in_the_Time_of_Trump
Rutgers University. "Policy 60.1.12: Policy Prohibiting Harassment."
    http://oirap.rutgers.edu/msa/documents/60.1.12_000.pdf
Ruth, Jennifer. Comment on *Academe Blog* post by John K. Wilson, "The
    Problem with Princeton's Racism Committee Proposal." July 17, 2020.
    https://academeblog.org/2020/ 07/17/the-problem-with-princetons
    -racism-committee-proposal/#comment-16605
Saini, Angela. *Superior: The Return of Race Science*. Beacon, 2019.
Savidge, Nico. "Legislators Criticize UW-Madison Professor's Course,
    Tweets about Shooting of Officers." *Wisconsin State Journal*, December 21,
    2016. https://madison.com/wsj/news/ local/education/university
    /legislators-criticize-uw-madison-professor-s-course-on-race-tweets
    /article_b09c432a-6e83-5c96-8cbf-3599503f093c.html
Schackner, Bill. "Duquesne Fires Professor Whose Use of a Racial Slur in
    Class Reached Social Media." *Pittsburgh Post-Gazette*, October 7, 2020.
    https://www.post-gazette.com/news/education/2020/10/07/
    Duquesne-University-race-slur-academic-freedom-AAUP-Gary-Shank
    -FIRE-teaching-speech/stories/202010070141m

Schwartz, Matthew S. "FBI Says Soldier Vanessa Guillen Was Killed." *National Public Radio*, July 3, 2020. https://www.npr.org/2020/07/03/887167023/fbi-files-charges-in-vanessa-guillen-case

Schoeller, Betsy. Personal Statement. *UWM Report*, July 5, 2020. https://uwm.edu/news/personal-statement-by-betsy-schoeller-regarding-the-death-of-specialist-vanessa-guillen/

Scott, Joan Wallach. *Knowledge, Power, and Academic Freedom*. Columbia UP, 2019.

Seelye, Katharine Q. "Protestors Disrupt Speech by 'Bell Curve' Author at Vermont College." *New York Times*, March 3, 2017. https://www.nytimes.com/2017/03/03/us/middlebury-college-charles-murray-bell-curve-protest.html

Serwer, Adam. "The Fight over the 1619 Project Is Not about the Facts." *The Atlantic*, December 23, 2019. https://www.theatlantic.com/ideas/archive/2019/12/historians-clash-1619-project/604093/

Shephard, Alex. "Charles Murray Is Never Going Away." *The New Republic*, January 28, 2020. https://newrepublic.com/article/156330/charles-murray-never-going-away

Shibley, Robert. "U. of Illinois Totally Blows it on Salaita Defense." *TheFire.org*, August 22, 2014. https://www.thefire.org/u-illinois-totally-blows-salaita-defense/

Sitze, Adam. "Academic Unfreedom, Unacademic Freedom: Part One of Two." *Massachusetts Review* 58.4 (2017): 589–607.

Slobodian, Quinn. "The Globalization of the IQ Wars." *Jacobin*, April 24, 2018. https://www.jacobinmag.com/2018/04/race-iq-charles-murray-global-bell-curve

Smith, John David and J. Vincent Lowery, eds. *The Dunning School: Historians, Race, and the Meaning of Reconstruction*. UP of Kentucky, 2013.

South Florida Sun Sentinel Editorial Board, "Tenure Be Damned, Professor Tracy Embarrasses FAU." *South Florida Sun Sentinel*, December 17, 2015. https://www.sun-sentinel.com/opinion/editorials/fl-editorial-tracy-gs1218-20151217-story.html

@stevesalaita (Steven Salaita). "You may be too refined to say it, but I'm not: I wish all the fucking West Bank settlers would go missing." *Twitter*,

June 19, 2014, 9:59 pm. https://twitter.com/stevesalaita/status
/479805591401922561

Stephens, Bret. "The 1619 Chronicles." *New York Times*, October 9, 2020.
https://www.nytimes.com/2020/10/09/opinion/nyt-1619-project
-criticisms.html

Stern, Sol. "Think Tank in the Tank." *Democracy: A Journal of Ideas*, July 7, 2020.
https://democracyjournal.org/arguments/think-tank-in-the-tank/

Stovall, Tyler. *White Freedom: The Racial History of an Idea*. Princeton UP,
2021.

Strauss, Valerie. "'I have never ever ever seen a university statement like this.
My god.'" *Washington Post*, November 22, 2019. https://www.washington
post.com/education/2019/11/22/i-have-never-ever-ever-seen-university
-statement-like-this-my-god/

Strossen, Nadine. *Hate: Why We Should Resist It with Free Speech, Not Censorship*.
Oxford UP, 2018.

Sullivan, Andrew. "We All Live on Campus Now." *New York Magazine*,
February 9, 2018. https://nymag.com/intelligencer/2018/02/we-all-live
-on-campus-now.html

Taylor and Francis, "Withdrawal Notice." https://www.tandfonline.com/doi
/abs/10.1080/01436597.2017.1369037

Taylor, Sunaura. *Beasts of Burden: Animal and Disability Liberation*. New Press,
2017.

Telfair, Brittani. "You Are Not Entitled to 'Civility.'" *Daily Princetonian*,
October 21, 2020. https://www.dailyprincetonian.com/article/2020
/10/civil-discourse-entitlement-constitution-racism

Tiede, Hans-Jorge. "Extramural Speech, Academic Freedom, and the AAUP:
A Historical Account." In *Challenges to Academic Freedom*, ed. Joseph C.
Hermanowicz, 104–31. Johns Hopkins UP, 2021.

Toscano, Alberto. "The Long Shadow of Racial Fascism." *The Boston Review*,
Oct. 28, 2020.

Tomasulo, Frank P. Comment on *Academe Blog* post by John K. Wilson, "The
Problem with Princeton's Racism Committee Proposal." July 17, 2020.
https://academeblog.org/2020/ 07/17/the-problem-with-princetons
-racism-committee-proposal/#comment-16604

Torres, Ricardo. "Petition Started to Fire UWM Lecturer, Wisconsin Air Guard Colonel for Saying 'Sexual Harassment is the Price of Admission' to Military." *Milwaukee Sentinel Journal*, July 4, 2020. https://www.jsonline.com/story/news/local/milwaukee/2020/07/04/wisconsin-air-national-guard-uwm-lecturer-betsy-schoeller-blasted-gullen-post/5375491002/

Trump, Donald. "Remarks by President Trump at the White House Conference on American History." September 17, 2020. https://www.whitehouse.gov/briefings-statements/remarks-president-trump-white-house-conference-american-history/

US Department of Homeland Security's Office of Intelligence and Analysis, *Rightwing Extremism: Current Economic and Political Climate Fueling Resurgence in Radicalization and Recruitment*. 2009. https://fas.org/irp/eprint/rightwing.pdf

UWM-AAUP Statement on Dr. Betsy Schoeller's Comments about the Murder of Vanessa Guillen. July 6, 2020. https://web.archive.org/web/20200706235650/https://academeblog.org/2020/07/06/uwm-aaup-statement-on-dr-betsy-schoellers-comments-about-the-murder-of-vanessa-guillen/

Vaidhyanathan, Siva. *Antisocial Media: How Facebook Disconnects Us and Undermines Democracy*. Oxford U P, 2018.

Viren, Sarah. "The Accusations Were Lies. But Could We Prove It?" *New York Times*, March 18, 2020. https://www.nytimes.com/2020/03/18/magazine/title-ix-sexual-harassment-accusations.html

Vought, Russell, Director, Office of Management and Budget, White House. Memo of September 4, 2020. https://www.whitehouse.gov/wp-content/uploads/2020/09/M-20-34.pdf

Waldstreicher, David. "The Hidden Stakes of the 1619 Controversy." *Boston Review*, January 24, 2020. http://bostonreview.net/race-politics/david-waldstreicher-hidden-stakes-1619-controversy

Wax, Amy. "Here's What Amy Wax Really Said about Immigration." *The Federalist*, July 26, 2019. https://thefederalist.com/2019/07/26/heres-amy-wax-really-said-immigration/

———. "The University of Denial." *Wall Street Journal*, March 22, 2018. https://www.wsj.com/articles/the-university-of-denial-1521760098

Weissman, Jordan, "Facebook Kowtowed to Conservatives and Got Nothing in Return." *Slate*, December 12, 2020. https://slate.com/business/2020/12/facebook-conservatives-antitrust-trump-joel-kaplan.html

Whitford, Emma. "White Professor Accused of Antiwhite Racism." *Inside Higher Ed*, August 23, 2018. https://www.insidehighered.com/news/2018/08/23/professor-accused-antiwhite-racism-others-say-its-free-speech

Whittington, Keith E. "Academic Freedom, Even for Amy Wax." *Academe Blog*, July 28, 2019. https://academeblog.org/2019/07/28/academic-freedom-even-for-amy-wax/

Wilderson, Frank. *Red, White, and Black: Cinema and the Structure of U.S. Antagonisms.* Duke UP, 2010.

Williams, Joanna. *Academic Freedom in an Age of Conformity: Confronting the Fear of Knowledge.* Palgrave, 2016.

Williams, Johnny Eric. "The Academic Freedom Double Standard: 'Freedom' for Courtiers, Suppression for Critical Scholars." *AAUP Journal of Academic Freedom* 9 (2018). https://www.aaup.org/JAF9/academic-freedom-double-standard-%E2%80%9Cfreedom%E2%80%9D-courtiers-suppression-critical-scholars#.X-t8c-lKi3I

Wilson, John K. "Academic Freedom and Extramural Utterances: The Leo Koch and Steven Salaita Cases at the University of Illinois." *AAUP Journal of Academic Freedom* 6 (2015). https://www.aaup.org/JAF6/academic-freedom-and-extramural-utterances-leo-koch-and-steven-salaita-cases-university#.W-dRQ3pKgdX.

———. "The Problem with Princeton's Racism Committee Proposal." *Academe Blog*, July 17, 2020. https://academeblog.org/2020/07/17/the-problem-with-princetons-racism-committee-proposal/

Wood, Peter. "Pulitzer Board Must Revoke Nikole Hannah-Jones' Prize." *National Association of Scholars*, October 6, 2020. https://www.nas.org/blogs/article/pulitzer-board-must-revoke-nikole-hannah-jones-prize

———. "Sustainability: Higher Education's New Fundamentalism." *National Association of Scholars*, March 25, 2015. https://www.nas.org/blogs/article/sustainability_higher_educations_new_fundamentalism1

Wootson, Cleve R., Jr. "A Professor Wants to Teach 'The Problem of Whiteness.' A Lawmaker Calls the Class 'Garbage.'" *Washington Post*, December 28,

2016. https://www.washingtonpost.com/news/grade-point/wp/2016/12
/28/a-professor-wants-to-teach-the-problems-of-whiteness-a-lawmaker
-calls-the-class-garbage/?utm_term=. 925d56de0c8b

Wu, Tim. "Beyond First Amendment Lochnerism: A Political Process Approach." *Knight First Amendment Institute at Columbia University*, August 21, 2019. https://knightcolumbia. org/content/beyond-first-amendment-lo
chnerism-a-political-process-approach

INDEX

equity, 7–9, 18, 32–33, 43, 190. *See also* offices of diversity, equity, and inclusion (DEI)

ethnic/racial identities, 32

ethnic/racial stereotypes, 34–40, 36–37, 153, 231

ethnic slurs, 176, 176n2

ethnic studies, 9–10

eugenics, 15, 18, 19, 28–29, 109–10, 125–26, 146n9, 183, 224

evolution, 125, 144, 165, 224, 229

expertise, scholarly, 4, 69–72, 77–80; AAUP Committee A statement on, 70, 70n1; of academic freedom committee members, 8–9; extramural speech and, 5–6, 69–70, 73–74, 75–80, 200; risk-management approach, 80–89

extramural speech, 52, 66–126; AAUP provisions, 69–70, 71–72, 180n4; as academic freedom basis, 66–67; defined as intramural speech, 77; definition, 4, 69–70, 78; freedom of speech and, 13, 66–71; freedoms of research and teaching and, 67–68, 88–89, 93; institutional support, 67–68; Karega case, 99–101, 104, 105, 108, 227; Koch case, 72–75, 101; Oliver case, 100–104; protection by the state, 69, 88–89; Salaita case, 43–45, 52, 75–78; scholarly expertise and, 5–6, 69–70, 73–74, 75–80, 200; sexuality-related

speech, 72–75; Tracy case, 95–98, 99, 105, 108; white supremacy and, 5–6. *See also* Facebook; hate, racist, or offensive speech; social media; Twitter

faculty: as institutional representatives, 53–54, 69, 80, 95–96, 97; oversight of colleagues, 243–47; refusal to examine academic freedom, 7–8

faculty of color. *See* Black, Indigenous and Persons of Color (BIPOC) faculty

faculty review process, 105–6, 106n1, 240. *See also* academic freedom committees

faculty senates, 20, 61, 73, 212, 215–16, 229, 232, 241–48

Fagone, Jason, 112–13

Farrakhan, Louis, 99

fascism, 19, 185, 250, 250n15. *See also* Nazis/Nazism; neo-Nazis

Fauci, Anthony, 192

feminism, 142, 145

Ferguson, Niall, 115

Ferris State University, Jim Crow Museum of Racial Memorabilia, 63

filler words, 14, 61–63

Finkin, Matthew, 76, 78–83

fireable offenses, 40, 95–126; insubordination, 97, 98; white supremacy, 111–26

Pennsylvania State University, 20, 36, 37–38, 39–40, 63, 91n3, 186; Law School, 198n15

phlogiston, 28–29, 183

phrenology, 179, 182–83

Pierce, William Luther, 102

Pilgrim, David, 63–64

Pioneer Fund, 145–46, 146n9

Pipes, Daniel, 199

Pluckrose, Helen, 142

police violence, toward Black Americans, 18, 92–93, 145, 207. *See also* Floyd, George

political correctness, 39, 133, 134, 161, 174, 195

political left, 11, 84–85; anti-liberalism of, 18–19

political philosophy, 26–27, 31–32, 163–64

political polarization, 12, 238–39

political right, 11, 23, 84, 192; campaigns against liberal faculty, 20–21, 66; QAnon, 101–2; social media influence, 191–94, 192n10; weaponization of academic freedom, 29–30, 67

political science, 5, 19, 123–24, 229

Popper, Karl, 182

pornography, 133

Portland State University, 247–48; Office of Global Diversity and Inclusion, 215

Post, Robert, 70

poverty: public policy, 121, 122; racist theory, 114–22

Powell, Enoch, 199

Pozner, Lenny and Veronique, 96–98, 105

Princeton University, 8, 160, 163, 180–81; Faculty Letter, 137, 212–15, 223–24, 227; School of Public and International Affairs, 18, 124

professional fitness: determination, 14, 56, 69–70, 93–94, 100–101; standards for white academics, 205–6

professional fitness, lack of: academic freedom committee judgments, 227–28; as basis for dismissal, 66, 72, 75–80, 87; of editors, 86–88; Karega case, 104, 105, 108, 227; Koch case, 72–75; relation to extramural speech, 72–80; relation to scholarly expertise, 4; toleration, 227–28; Tracy case, 95–98, 99, 105, 108

promotion, 248; committees, 214–15; denial, 232–36

Proud Boys, 136

pseudoscientific theories: about COVID-19, 242–47. *See also* racist pseudoscience

public policy: based on controversial ideas, 242–43; influence of white supremacist views on, 202–3; on poverty, 121, 122

public shaming, 6–7, 84–85, 86–87

QAnon, 101–2, 200n16
queer theory, 142

Race and Ethnicity in Higher Education (American Council on Education), 32
"race realism," 111–13
racial contract, 28
racial equity, 32–33
racial hierarchy theory, 28–29, 123
racial humor: context, 46–47; satirical, 41, 45–46, 47; university administration response, 41–42, 50–53
racism: historical, 23, 224; impact *vs.* intent, 56–57, 61; institutional, 17–18, 21, 65, 90; as political tool, 230–31; poverty and, 114–22; public awareness, 23–24, 156; structural (South Africa), 209–11; structural (US), 129–30, 250; systemic, 23, 29–30, 125; "unconscious," 57n2; US history of, 23–24; white Americans' perception, 206–9; white studies and, 90–93
racist pseudoscience, 15, 28–29, 65, 113–14, 123, 125, 178–80, 183, 196, 250; absolutist exceptions, 184–85; *The Bell Curve*, 146n9, 151–56
racist speech. *See* hate, racist, or offensive speech
Rasmussen, Eric, 6–7
Rawls, John, 26–28, 124

Reagan, Ronald, 148–49
RealClearInvestigations, 142n6, 158–59
Reconstruction, 122–23, 141, 147–48, 172, 208
redface, 36, 39, 214–15
Reichman, Henry, 104–8, 177n3, 202–3, 214–15
religion: discrimination based on, 232–33; religious conservatives, 39, 136, 190–91, 230
Republican party, 90, 91–92, 130n2, 148, 228–29, 230–31
Repucci, Sarah, 250
research: racist, 214; review committees, 224
research, freedom of, 7, 67–68, 69, 76, 79, 80–81, 88–89, 93, 223–24
research fraud, 224
research integrity, 224
Richeson, Jennifer, 207–8
Rideau, Amelia, 61
risk-management approach, to academic freedom, 80–89
Robel, Lauren, 6
Rodriquez, Dylan, 28
Roth, Michael, 23
Rouse, Carolyn, 160
Rufo, Christopher, 139–40, 143–47, 165
Rupert, Mark, 229–32
Rutgers University, 50–53
Ruth, Jennifer, 20, 24–25, 214, 216–17, 247

Sajnani, Damon, 90–93, 145

Salaita, Steven, 20, 43–45, 52, 75–78, 103, 105–6

Sandy Hook massacre, 95–98, 109, 225

San Francisco State, 10

Sartarelli, Jose V., 235

satire: context, 45–46; of offensive speech, 41–58; on social media, 45–51

Schackner, Bill, 59

Schlafly, Phyllis, 103

Schoeller, Betsy, 47–51, 52, 53–56, 58, 65, 143

Scholars at Risk Global Congress, 67

Scott, Joan, 67–71, 70n1

Searle, John, 60

self-censorship, 39, 83, 89

self-determination, 18, 179–80

September 11, 2001, 82, 99, 109

Serwer, Adam, 166–67, 168–69

sexual discrimination complaints, 223n3

sexual harassment, 17, 47–48, 158; in the military, 47–51

sexuality, extramural speech about, 72–75

Shank, Greg, 59–61, 62, 65

shared governance, 8, 9, 13, 16–17, 55, 215–16, 223, 241–42. *See also* academic freedom committees

Shearer, Harry, 56

Shephard, Alex, 183n6

Shockley, William, 154n14

Shor, David, 85

Silverstein, Jake, 169

Singer, Peter, 180–81, 182n5

Sitze, Adam, 165, 209–11

1619 Project, 21, 165–73

Skokie, IL, neo-Nazis' march, 186–87

slavery, 1, 32–33, 118, 119, 125, 165, 166–67, 204, 205, 208; 1619 Project, 21, 165–73, 203; racist theories of, 3–4, 115–22, 163, 164, 179–80, 196

Snyder, Daniel, 46–47

social contract, 26–28, 70, 124

social justice, 26–27, 40

social media, 5, 13, 59, 66, 92, 158, 192n9, 225–26, 238–39; anti-democratic effects, 191–94, 192n9; appropriate restraint in, 43–46, 53–54; as decontextualization apparatus, 43–51, 58; lack of academic freedom protection on, 76–78; political influence on, 192–94, 192n10; Salaita case, 43–45, 75–80; satire on, 45–51; Schoeller case, 47–51, 52, 53–56; university administration's response, 41–42, 50–53

South Africa, 209–11

speech act theory, 60

speech codes, 61, 133–34, 175n1; AAUP statement on, 174–85

Spencer, Richard, 186